How to
Eradicate
Invasive
Plants

How to
Eradicate
Invasive
Plants

Teri Dunn Chace

TIMBER PRESS
PORTLAND — LONDON

Published in 2013 by Timber Press, Inc.

The Haseltine Building
133 S.W. Second Avenue, Suite 450
Portland, Oregon 97204-3527
timberpress.com

2 The Quadrant
135 Salusbury Road
London NW6 6RJ
timberpress.co.uk

Printed in China
Design by Laken Wright
Layout and composition by Ben Patterson

Library of Congress Cataloging-in-Publication Data

Dunn Chace, Teri.
  How to eradicate invasive plants / Teri Dunn Chace. — 1st ed.
    p. cm.
  Includes index.
  ISBN 978-1-60469-306-5
  1. Invasive plants—Control. 2. Noxious weeds—Control.
  3. Gardening. I.Title.
  SB613.5.D86 2013
  581.6'2—dc23   2012030761

A catalog record for this book is also available from the British Library.

Dedicated to
Jon (Barney) Kleist

Contents

"When we try to pick out anything by itself, we find it hitched to everything else in the Universe."

— JOHN MUIR
My First Summer in the Sierra, 1911

Introduction: Weedy Words

Earthlings, gardeners, fellow Americans: we have a problem. We have a weeds problem. They are everywhere. They have encroached on our roadsides, wetlands, salt marshes, lakesides and creeksides, and damp ditches. They have invaded our farmlands and orchards, fields and meadows. They want our golf courses and public parks, our back yards and front yards. They are already in our vacant lots, sidewalk cracks, property perimeters, and neglected and unwatched corners.

The lines we see or create between public land and private yard do not halt the spread of weeds. Some can clamber over a fence or wall or sneak into, or out of, a garden. Wind, water, birds, and more easily transport the seeds of some plants and the viable bits (that is, seedlings or root fragments) of others.

The common dandelion is a classic example. It pops up uninvited in front and back lawns, in city parks, in curb strips, in playing fields. Maybe when you were a kid, someone paid you a nickel per plush yellow flower to yank them out before they turned into white puffballs. Otherwise . . . poof! A slight breeze or the kick of a shoe, and those tiny seeds parachute all over town, setting the stage for an even bigger invasion next spring and summer.

Today, all manner of unsavory plants are increasingly in the news and on our radar, so to speak. Perhaps you've noticed that a crew of volunteers has been dispatched to a local wetland to undertake the hard work of digging up purple loosestrife rootstocks, which, once they've been in place for a while, are bulky as a buried tire and insidious as a tumor. Or, maybe you have observed in passing that the stands of Japanese knotweed on the outskirts of town are multiplying every year, sucking up water and nutrients and shoving aside all other plants. Kudzu has already engulfed and devoured much of the South. Cheatgrass, especially when it dries out in the hot summer sun, is blamed for giving devastating wildfires in the West entirely too much fuel. Freshwater boaters are warned with strategically placed, detailed signs to rinse off their hulls before and after putting into a lake or stream, lest they spread invasive, alien plants (and creatures). And so on and on.

Worldwide Weeds

Culturally, we live in a global village, thanks primarily to a dazzling array of technological advances in transportation and communication. Mixing it up, traveling and trading, importing and exporting, exploring and exchanging ideas and materials—all this is generally considered not only inevitable but also desirable. Awareness and diversity are good, indeed exciting and enhancing. We inhabit a web that binds us all together and seemingly shrinks the world.

Meanwhile, smaller, minority voices can also be heard, protesting that sometimes the local, the unique, the indigenous, is being threatened or lost. An American friend who traveled in Tanzania related that, in a remote bush village, she encountered a small boy wearing a tattered but recognizable John Lennon t-shirt: "Heaven knows where he got it or what its travels were," she reflected in her blog. "It was so jarring and incongruous. Was I glad or sad to see that shirt?"

A similar sensation may assail the informed gardener or botanist who spots a foreign plant in familiar ground. And what about the plant collector who imports and plants, say, a nifty exotic flowering akebia vine from Sichuan Province, China? Or the avid, adventurous gardener who snaps up a seedling of foreign origin at a specialized nursery or flower show, just because it looks to be beautiful, just for the challenge, or even simply because he or she values rare or cutting-edge plants? Even if the import is untested in this country?

Yes, gardeners—for a variety of aesthetic and practical reasons—have occasionally been credited or blamed with introducing a "problem plant" to American soil. The examples are legion. Will the aforementioned akebia, so lovely and tame *in situ*, turn out to be a monster here? Will importers and boosters of the rare, foreign, and exotic be praised or blamed in a few years or decades?

Not all introductions have been or are deliberate. In *Weeds: In Defense of Nature's Most Unloved Plants*, British nature writer Richard Mabey cites a variety of other vehicles on which plants have hitched a ride: in ballast,

A thicket of Japanese knotweed hovers on the sidelines, annually encroaching into a well manicured lawn.

in packing materials, in contaminated seed and feed, in fill soil, as well as in once-popular food crops and useful herbs that have gone rogue. Even on the smallest scale, most gardeners have, at one time or other, brought home a potted plant from the local nursery only to discover a stowaway tucked under the leaves, an unwelcome burdock or thistle.

Other plants have arrived with the best intentions, promoted as ideal for erosion control or low-maintenance landscaping. In Florida, the once-promising imported ornamental tree known as bishopwood has been rapidly wearing out its welcome by overtaking fragile native swampland communities. The agents? Native as well as introduced birds, which relish the seeds.

Occasionally an unsavory foreign relative of a native plant worms its way into and ultimately alters the gene pool, as is apparently the case with alders, to name but one example. All this brings to mind that pivotal moment in the sci-fi classic *The Andromeda Strain* when a scientist exclaims in panic, "There'll be a thousand mutations! It will spread everywhere! We'll never be rid of it!"

Agents of Movement and Dispersal of Invasives

packing material (hitchhikes in on)

contaminated hay or straw (hitchhikes in on)

ballast (stows away in)

seeds eaten by birds or animals (which then deposit them in a new location)

seeds attached to animal fur, human clothing or footwear (which then detach or fall off in a new location)

seeds or viable fragments embedded in topsoil, mulch, or fill

seeds or fruit that float on water (such as sea, river, stream, or lake) to a new location

plant explorers or foreign travelers that import

nursery and seed entrepreneurs that import

garden escapees

informal transfer (a gardener shares or sells "passalong plants")

planted for erosion control

bulk seed is "contaminated" (not pure)

potting soil (seeds germinate or fragments gain a foothold in nursery pots of desirable plants)

Invasives? Weeds?

Let us pause here for a moment and clarify. Weeds tend to be plants that are problems in human-made environments, such as dandelions in a lawn or pigweed in a cornfield. These plants are not so much an issue in natural areas, though, of course, some can be. Invasives are also considered weeds, but are additionally understood to be a threat to biodiversity and natural systems as a whole. Shrubby honeysuckles and Japanese knotweed, for example, overrun whatever vegetation they come across, thus altering in a negative way the local ecosystem.

The time may come in your yard when a weed is not merely an aesthetic threat, an inconvenience, or an annoyance. An invasion of bishop's goutweed, for instance, threatens your garden's diversity and overall health—and that is why you should care about controlling or eradicating it.

So, use the terms interchangeably if you like, or realize that it is a matter of degree, that a weed can easily become invasive. Each of the plants featured in this book is a problem somewhere; how great a problem, how much trouble and disruption it can cause, varies. In short, we are talking about a continuum.

A Small Yard

In *The Natural History of a Yard*, a book published in 1955, journalist and amateur naturalist Leonard Dubkin chronicled three years in the life of his postage-stamp property in North Chicago. He noted the squirrels, bugs, and birds, but he also observed the plants, especially grass and a beloved elm tree. He and his family planted and enjoyed a few flowers. Tiny mushrooms and sharp-spined thistles also came with the territory.

Reading his affectionate, observant account, you cannot help but recall yards you have known and loved, maybe a yard just as small. If you think diversity is not possible or practical in a little garden, think again. Dubkin mused that "to us this yard is a little cosmos, a little world unto itself." And you immediately anticipate his quaint but sincere conclusion: "To us it is sufficient . . . we find it as fruitful and as fascinating and as glorious as any we could wish for."

The larger truth here, in the context of uninvited little mushrooms and spiny thistles and other "bad plants," is that a garden is not truly separate from the world around it. In fact, it may be considered a microcosm.

Good Plants, Bad Plants

Let's face it; the cat is out of the bag. The heady, complex exchange of all sorts of plants, all over the world, is well underway and has been for quite some time. Alarms have been sounded before. It could be that only now some of these warnings, misgivings, and regrets are louder and more urgent because our home landscapes and civic green spaces are increasingly viewed as finite, limited, precious, vulnerable, or all of these. Appreciation for all things indigenous or native (sometimes belatedly) is also a factor.

And yet it is not always a simple matter of introduced plants being bad and native ones being good. The fact that the dreaded purple loosestrife forms large colonies over time actually delights beekeepers, for instance, who rave about the resulting delicious honey. And Erik Kiviat, a researcher in the estuaries of the upper Hudson River in New York State, found that local American gold-finches actually prefer to dine upon and nest among purple loose-strife stands that have invaded there. The birds evidently prefer purple loosestrife to the native cattails. Adaptation? Opportunity? Mystery? Tragedy? Net benefit to the ecosystem? Net loss? Let's just say, it's complicated.

But the subject at hand is gardening. Landscaping and raising food, including farming, takes thought and planning plus time and effort spent on care and maintenance. Planting seen as an act of stewardship ought to be at the heart of all this. Good plants can be welcomed and stay; bad plants must be controlled or eradicated.

You may have heard the famous Ralph Waldo Emerson quote to the effect that "a weed is a plant whose virtues have not yet been discovered." A pretty thought, Ralph, but you did not get out in the mud and pastures much, or live to see the times in which we now live. Some people might argue that a weed is a plant with no virtues.

What You Can Do

Consider getting involved on the local or state level by helping preserve or restore lands that are impacted by invasives—for the greater good, if not for the direct benefit of your own property. Organizations such as the Sierra Club and local Audubon Society chapters, for example, sometimes ask for volunteers and then train them. In some areas, determined volunteers have evicted clumps of purple loose-strife from their local wetlands with plenty of sharp shovels, picks, sweat, and camaraderie.

Food for Thought

Why do not more people seek out and enjoy wild edible plants? "The most obvious explanation is that in modern American society's high-tech rush toward affluence and convenience, we have left behind some of the simpler pleasures of earlier eras," declares Russ Cohen in *Wild Plants I Have Known . . . and Eaten*.

It is a reasonable point. We are a nation of couch potatoes. We buy our food swathed in plastic wrap in the grocery store. Knowledge of edible plants is being lost and forgotten. Perhaps also the plants are being lost and forgotten, due to habitat loss and the advancement of a society that does not value what wild nature has to offer.

Cohen's book restores some of that knowledge, at least in his geographical area in the Northeast. If you look, you can find his counterpart wherever you happen to live. Not all is lost. He waxes enthusiastic about and provides his recipes for all kinds of wild meals, from Stinging Nettle Soup to Black Locust Fritters to a green salad that includes dame's rocket. And yes, he is ahead of us here. Of the aforementioned dame's rocket, he remarked, "Don't worry about picking too many, as dame's rocket is an invasive species and the ecologists are glad to have your help in keeping it under control." Elsewhere in this intriguing, entertaining book, we find "Japanese Knotweed: If You Can't Beat It, Eat It," complete with a strawberry-knotweed pie recipe.

Cohen is correct. Certain "bad" plants are edible. It would probably take a lot of hungry people or creative chefs to make a dent in most unwanted plant populations, but you can always do your part in your own backyard. At the very least, giving it a try could change your perspective.

Kudzu Krafts

"Do something with it, use it up," said Georgia craftsperson Diane Hoots to a reporter from *National Geographic* magazine a few years ago. "But I don't suggest anybody plant it."

Artisans and entrepreneurs throughout the engulfed Southern states have come up with all sorts of uses and products for kudzu: paper, cards, posters, baskets, mats, dyes, soaps, sculptures, even small structures. It's not poisonous—though nobody will claim it's delicious, either—and has been incorporated into jellies, quiches, breads and other baked goods, even candy.

Nancy Basket of South Carolina is an accomplished basket-maker of Cherokee descent, but her first attempts at weaving with kudzu failed. She explains, "The plants knew we didn't respect them." She turned her attention to making paper out of the leaves and, once she mastered that, returned to basket-weaving with better success.

Whether or not you subscribe to Basket's sense that an unwanted plant needs to be respected first, it is easy to see that kudzu, no doubt along with numerous other "bad" plants, has its uses. If nothing else, all these rapidly growing invasives sequester carbon.

A little curiosity, a little understanding, a little creativity—might not these approaches suggest some uses for some of the plants we love to hate?

Describing the Problem

The database-heavy national website that identifies and monitors invasive species, invasive.org, is a work in progress. The site features a defining explanation of what a weed is in modern times, followed by five important facts about weeds. You can almost hear ponderous soundtrack music thudding in your gut as you read:

An invasive species is a nonnative species (including seeds, eggs, spores, or other propagules) whose introduction causes or is likely to cause economic harm, environmental harm, or harm to human health. The term *invasive* is used for the most aggressive species. These species grow and reproduce rapidly, causing major disturbance to the areas in which they are present. Things to know about invasive species:

- Invasive species, if left uncontrolled, can and will limit land use now and into the future.
- The longer we ignore the problem, the harder and more expensive the battle for control will become.
- Invasive species can decrease our ability to enjoy hunting, fishing, camping, hiking, boating, and other outdoor recreational activities.
- The United States suffers from $1.1 to 120 billion per year in economic losses due to exotic, invasive species.
- Approximately 42 percent of threatened or endangered species are at risk due to nonnative, invasive species.

Call these folks alarmists if you like, but this is genuinely sobering information. Studies and guidelines, protocols and laws, task forces and more databases abound in this field. Scores of scientists and students, sometimes working in concert with government agencies and/or private conservation organizations, such as local chapters of the Audubon Society and The Nature Conservancy, are devoted to identifying and addressing the problems caused by certain plants. So concerned are some of these people that control and eradication measures are underway even in the absence of complete inventories/censuses or detailed maps of affected areas. There is no time to lose, or the native vegetation of the Everglades will be lost, the West will have ever more catastrophic fire seasons, crops and grazing lands will be significantly reduced or ruined, and so on.

Medicinal Invasives

Quite a few invasive plants in the United States hail from Asia, where botanical medicine has been in place and respected for a long time, indeed for thousands of years in some cases. Thus appears another view: are we maligning and trying to kill off potentially useful, helpful, therapeutic plants?

The book *Invasive Plant Medicine* by the contemporary American herbalist and Chinese-medicine expert Timothy Lee Scott examines this interesting question.

> [T]he source of the ecological damage to this planet lies in our thinking . . . the problem is not lack of information about the planet and the impact of industrial society upon it. . . and truthfully, if you look at most of what humanity has known for many millennia, it never has been. The problem lies in the way we think, not what we think.

Fair enough. Scott's book is not for the casual reader, because of the level of technical information and detailed research. He includes chemical analyses, pharmacological actions, guidance on doses, and more. Many of the plants are familiar, though: tree-of-heaven, Oriental bittersweet, and bindweed. A small photograph of an emerging Japanese knotweed seedling prying apart a brick walkway is accompanied by a simple caption, "Just think—it grows everywhere for us."

Nor is the concern merely for human-centric activities. Habitat loss is a loss for the full spectrum of living creatures, from soil organisms to insects, reptiles to fishes, birds to mammals. If common as well as rare and endangered species succumb to the incoming wave of invasives, what are these creatures connected to that, domino-effect or weblike, is also threatened, forever altered, or wiped out? We may not fully understand or be able to predict all such connections and effects, but perhaps we can, as the Scots say, "ken" them.

So yes, it is serious.

Nonnative invasive species are also a problem for gardeners. We should not be part of the problem. We should not grow, harbor, or nurture bad or suspect plants, certainly. We should not seek out or buy such plants. We should question or abstain from patronizing nurseries and garden centers that sell them. We should obey applicable laws and heed common sense regarding moving such plants from place to place, including across state lines.

Of course, some plants are invasive in some settings and behave just fine in others. The sweet autumn clematis, for example, is decried as a "horrible pest, I cannot get rid of it!" in

Native vs. Introduced

As is so often the case in understanding the natural world, generalizations are hard to come by. Many, many weeds that are unwelcome in this country are nonnatives, alien imports, exotics, that is, introduced from elsewhere. But, not all. Three especially obnoxious North American natives are greenbriar, poison ivy, and poison oak. Ask anyone who contends with these in his or her yard.

And then there are the plants so commonplace that we are surprised to learn they were originally imports, which over time have become, as ecologists say, "naturalized."

Familiar examples include pampas grass in the West and Norway maple in the East. Meanwhile, countless well-behaved, valued garden plants were originally imports, everything from hellebores to most poppies, to mandevillas and jasmines, to daphnes and Japanese maples. The list is a long one.

Suffice to say that we should not be wed to assumptions, but instead, be wary and observant, holding plants accountable for their behavior rather than their origins or advertised growth habit. As the old cliché says, "Actions speak louder than words."

Georgia, while a gardener in the Pacific Northwest praises it as "lovely." It turns out that in a shorter growing season, this clematis does not have time to produce seed and thus does not romp through the landscape.

And many of those Asian imports we love to hate? Japanese hops, Japanese knotweed, tamarisk? They are not out of control in their native habitats, where they have developed in balance not only with other plants but also with bugs, birds, and all manner of other creatures that keep them in check.

By these reckonings, then, a weed is a plant not bad in any moral sense, but simply out of place. Far from home, or at least out of its aboriginal haunts. A new and different ecosystem and/ or climate, even if only subtly different, gives it the opportunity to spread or rampage unchecked. To become invasive. To displace or compromise the native plants or, for our purposes in this book, to outcompete or overrun desirable garden and landscape plants including lawn grass.

In contrast, what is a good, or desirable plant, anyway? Something pretty? How subjective. Something frail? Something dependent on the human hand to clear away unwanted competition in order to succeed? Something native? Something groomed? Something that needs us and our attention?

Successful Plants

Notice how we tend to cluck at an abandoned garden, pitying the overrun plants because no one is there to clear away the weeds, the bad plants, and let the good plants prosper once again. "Look at that poor weedy rose bush, all twiggy," we lament. "Oh my, the mint is out of control, the bachelor buttons have all gone to seed."

In such scenarios, the good plants are not bad, even if they have gone feral. They are swamped, and they are neglected. They need the human hand. You may remember from your childhood the story *The Secret Garden*, how the little girl carefully labored to remove the smothering layers of weeds to unveil and restore the originally planted flowers.

Just being a successful plant, incidentally, is not grounds for being called an invasive or a weed. While it is true that many plants tend to grow easily and often prosper in inhospitable or difficult conditions such as dry, gravely ground or muck, these abilities can be a virtue as easily as they can brand a plant a pest. You might want a whole embankment well-covered with lily-of-the-valley or ice plant, and appreciate your patch's gusto, tenacity, thick growth, and ease of maintenance. In other words, badness is in the eye of the beholder, or gardener in this case.

Consider for a moment, too, that prolific, successful growth has an odd way not just of being taken for granted, but also sometimes causing our civilized selves to recoil. In her Pulitzer Prize–winning book *Pilgrim at Tinker Creek*, Annie Dillard mused,

Invasives can gain a foothold before we notice, like this deceptively frail-looking bindweed snaking its way into a Japanese maple.

I don't know what it is about fecundity that so appalls. I suppose it is the teeming evidence that birth and growth, which we value, are ubiquitous and blind, that life itself is astonishingly cheap, that nature is as careless as it is beautiful.

Uninvited dandelions take over a back yard.

Ponder that, the next time you watch dandelion fluff drift over your yard. Or, consider the thousands of seeds emitted by one pampas grass plant or poplar tree. There is outrageous excess and much waste.

Nature hedges bets in other ways, too. Wily weeds may use more than one means to reproduce, such as seeds and suckers, concurrently or at different times. Seeds and root or rhizome fragments may lie dormant for long periods until germination conditions are right. Root systems or seeds may be allelopathic, that is, harm or thwart adjacent, competing plants chemically. In this way, species manage to survive and persist. As a high-school horticulture teacher of mine memorably declared, "Plants want to live." This includes the denizens of the overrun garden and especially the weeds.

And so, for our purposes here, perhaps the best possible definition of a weed is simply a successful and unwelcome plant—a backyard invader. Arguably, gardening is by turns a quixotic, frustrating, satisfying, and yes, important human activity. No matter the size of our patches, we aim to tend and nurture their health and beauty. The badness or goodness of any given plant, then, may be measured by whether it contributes to the health and beauty of the entire picture in our yard and neighborhood. It should be a citizen, not a thug.

How to Use This Book

If you have suspected thug plants invading your landscape, the pages ahead will help you take an effective two-pronged approach. Chances are you can "get them gone," especially if you intervene early, but you need to be well-armed with knowledge before acting.

First, find out the name of the thug plant. What is it called? The plant profiles in this book provide information and diagnostic photographs that should help you make a firm identification, at least for the most commonly seen thugs and problem plants. Study the images and the descriptions. Get to know the culprit better.

After that, decide upon a plan of attack. All the plant profiles have brief references to control and eradication measures, from less toxic options to chemical warfare. These tactics are also described and discussed in more detail in chapter 2, which you can thumb back to as you consider your options.

You can always get more information on the internet or by consulting a good local landscaper, nursery, lawn service, or Cooperative Extension office. If you choose to deploy an herbicide, be sure to read all the fine-print cautions that describe the safest methods of application and protect you, valued plants, your pets, and your garden soil. Chemicals can create more problems or do unwanted harm and should never be used inadvisably or improperly. Try alternatives first.

Finally, realize that an unwanted plant romping through your garden is quite likely not an isolated problem. Assuming you did not plant it yourself, it came from somewhere, whether a nearby wild or uncultivated area, or via some bird or creature, or some other unintentional source. Look around (especially upwind of your property), talk to others, and be alert. You do not garden in a vacuum. Can and should something be done about an interloper or the areas in your vicinity where it is growing? If yes, alert and/or educate your neighbors and community.

1

Know Thy Enemy

There are plants we do not want in our gardens, and then there are plants we really, really do not want in our gardens, namely, ones that were not invited or that wear out their welcome. Merely digging up and tossing these on the compost pile or worse, giving them away, is not going to work. These interlopers must be evicted and destroyed. But first, know thy enemy.

Whenever you encounter an unfamiliar plant in your home landscape, be suspicious, but do not jump to conclusions. Zero in on the plant's name, and information and insight will follow. Knowledge is power.

How Invasives Invade

The transit of plants from yard to yard, yard to field and farm, state to state, region to region, and the reverse, not to mention globetrotters, is nothing new. Sometimes the transfer is deliberate; sometimes it is accidental. The agents of movement and dispersal are many.

Stopping the flow of invasive plants is, at best, a challenge. Under optimal conditions in a new location—that is, with sufficient space, light, water, and necessary nutrients—an imported or traveling plant will surely grow, prosper, and spread further. As we all know, things can get out of hand if such an incursion is unchecked by alert people and is further compounded when the plant lacks natural enemies or controls, such as competing plants, the threat of nibbling insects or other hungry creatures, or mitigating environmental factors. Open space alone, especially recently cleared or disturbed land, is frequently all an opportunistic plant needs.

Kudzu and loosestrife are among the top invasive plants in the United States. Both illustrate the unintended consequences of promoting a plant before its behavior is fully understood.

Weed Prevention for Gardeners

Since it generally is easier to prevent a problem than to solve one, you might want to consider ways to keep weeds from infiltrating your property rather than wait until an infestation occurs and then look for ways to eliminate it. Yes, weeds are resourceful and have seemingly unlimited ways of moving from place to place, but you can do something about them long before you learn the name of the enemy weed.

Here are nine ways to keep out invaders in the first place. Most of these are a matter of being vigilant. Weeds are opportunists, but can be slowed down or thwarted by a sharp eye and quick, appropriate action.

1. PATROL YOUR YARD Walk around your yard regularly and keep your eyes open and your nose to the ground. Evict suspicious seedlings the moment you see them.

You May Have an Invasive Plant in Your Yard If . . .

You do not recognize it, did not plant it, or can clearly see it coming across your property line.

It appears in your yard after a neighboring property fills with weeds due to neglect, construction, re-grading, logging, or other disturbance.

It overruns your flowerbeds or vegetable patch, especially engulfing new, young plants trying to become established.

It grows rampantly, exhibiting "explosive growth."

It is not fussy about location or growing conditions.

It has stems and/or tendrils that quickly grasp and cover a fence, hedge, wall, tree, or other garden plants.

It resists control. When you tear it out, it returns quickly.

When you pull it up, you find a surprisingly extensive handful of questing roots or runners.

It produces an abundance of flowers and fruit, and therefore seed.

You notice it popping up all over the yard.

When you cut it back, it responds like Medusa in the Greek legend by generating an alarming number of fresh new stems.

There is more of it each year.

When you spray it, it grows back anyway.

Someone visiting your yard recognizes it and recoils in horror.

A neighbor complains that the plant has moved into their yard.

You spot it growing somewhere else, such as in parkland, a neighbor's yard, or along a roadside, and learn that it is a problem plant.

Loosestrife on the Loose

There once was a popular clump-forming perennial that bore purplish flower spikes in late summer. Purple loosestrife (*Lythrum salicaria*) it was called, and everyone agreed that it was a handsome plant.

Like all attractive plants, it gained fans and boosters. It also began to establish itself in wetlands and along streambanks and riverbeds, which allowed intrepid outdoorsy people to admire its beauty. It colonized ditches along the Massachusetts and Maine Turnpikes, an appealing sight even when motorists cruised past it at 55+ miles per hour. And painters and photographers sprouted in its pretty wake, turning out colorful images showcasing its profuse growth.

Gardeners and landscapers liked this plant because it brought vivid color to an otherwise slow time of year, when many other perennials were finished blooming and flagging in the hot dog days of August. It was also valued for growing well in damp ground, which is not always easy to landscape, and this propensity, if the soil was consistently moist, also made it an endearingly low-care plant.

In the late 1980s and early 1990s, horticulturists took notice and capitalized on variations. Soon nurseries began touting cultivars. Among these were richly hued 'Dropmore Purple', bright carmine 'Morden's Gleam' and pale, rosy pink 'Morden's Pink'. One nursery hailed its beauty in its catalog but saw fit to add, "Please do not plant near wetlands: loosestrife flourishes in wet areas and can displace native plant species."

In retrospect, all the warning signs were there. Gardeners began to get suspicious, then proactive. Nurseries tried claiming that the cultivars were actually derived from the apparently less aggressive relative *Lythrum virgatum*. Some botanists warned that cultivated plants were cross-pollinating with wild ones, while others countered that the cultivated varieties were sterile. In the end, the hue and cry was too loud, and all the purple loosestrife variants were maligned and banned and soon disappeared from the market. Arguably, it was too late, for purple loosestrife, regardless of genetic makeup or origins, was swamping wild wet areas. Indeed, two decades later, infestations continue to present a challenge from New England to the Columbia River Gorge in the Pacific Northwest.

Pine straw is a popular mulch in the South, but this bale comes with a very aggressive hitchhiker, Japanese climbing fern.

2. MIND THE BORDERS Abutting properties, whether a vacant lot, conservation land, or a nongardening neighbor, can bring unwanted, rampantly spreading plants to your yard. Look over the fence or past your property line, particularly at areas upwind from you. Talk to neighbors, where possible, and implore them to control any invasive plant(s). If they do not know what to do, review the options with them, make suggestions, or even offer to do the work for them (see the next chapter for many ideas). If that is not practical, create a barrier with a fence (sunk deeply into the ground) or a trench (filled with gravel, or bare) or a buffer zone (paving, paving stones, gravel, even mulch). The goal is to halt and thwart the invader's advance onto your property.

3. COVER OPEN GROUND Few plants relish open ground as much as opportunistic weeds. Birds, squirrels, and other animals may deposit seeds deliberately or accidentally, seeds may blow in on a breeze or wander in via water (runoff), or dormant seeds and plant bits may awaken once the ground is cleared or stirred up. If you clear an area in your yard, do not just rake it over and leave it, not even for a day or two. Cover it with the mulch of your choice or a tarp until you are ready to plant it.

4. MULCH, MULCH, MULCH Nothing prevents weed growth better than a cloak of mulch. Mulch blocks light, air, and even moisture from getting through and nurturing seeds and seedlings that you do not want. Whether it is a vegetable patch or a flowerbed, mulch all open or bare spots around and between your desired plants. Over time, of course, the plants will grow and spread out and cover over the spaces with shading foliage, further preventing weeds. Keep an eye on things and replenish the mulch until they do, and maybe even beyond, because tenacious weeds might get a foothold and grow unnoticed until they burst upward or shove aside your garden plants.

5. AVOID TILLING THE SOIL Experienced gardening authors from Lee Reich (*Weedless Gardening*, 2001) to Edward Faulkner (*Plowman's Folly*, 1943) remind us that digging up, traditional plowing,

Sad but True: How the "Miracle Vine" Went Awry

Once upon a time, there was a Japanese vine called kudzu. So proud were the Japanese of this handsome plant with its big furry leaves and trailing, sweetly scented purple flowers that they introduced it to the American public by featuring it in their garden exhibit at the Centennial Exhibition in Philadelphia in 1876. Clearly a warmer-climate plant, it soon gained easy popularity in the American South as a quick and attractive natural screen, ideal for shading porches, gazebos, and arbors. Nurseries sold it; gardeners shared it.

Kudzu turned out to be a versatile plant, which furthered its spread. It made good forage and hay for pigs and goats. Touted by the U.S. Soil Conservation Service, it was planted widely during the Depression years for erosion control, particularly on red-clay farms where the land had been devastated by over-cultivation of tobacco and cotton crops. In the 1940s, the government actually paid farmers $8 an acre to plant it. In addition, the CCC (Civilian Conservation Corps) planted millions of seedlings along roads and other disturbed sites. Kudzu clubs were formed to distribute and promote "the miracle vine." Thus encouraged, kudzu grabbed ahold of the South, and its thuglike personality began to emerge.

Unchecked by any natural enemies, insect or animal, and abetted by easy growing conditions and a friendly climate, kudzu encroached everywhere—on cultivated fields, roadsides, embankments, forests, parks, orchards, and gardens. It engulfed poles, fences, abandoned homesteads and vehicles, and mounted barns, houses, and other buildings. It became "the vine that ate the South."

rototilling, and generally disrupting the soil can be counterproductive. Weeds may regenerate from chopped-up bits of plants, while dormant weed seeds are delivered to the light and oxygen they need to germinate and flourish.

A main benefit of turning over the soil is to aerate it, but if it was not highly compacted in the first place, maybe you should rethink the practice. Your garden might be better off, and you will not work as hard, if you instead undertake soil improvement one new planting hole at a time. Coupled with diligent mulching between the new plants, this tack may surprise and delight you by dramatically reducing your weed population. Moreover, interlopers will not find openings.

6. INSPECT NEWCOMERS When you bring home a potted or balled-and-burlapped plant from the nursery or garden center, look it over carefully before or immediately after planting it in its new home. Tiny pesky seedlings might be lurking. Check back often as the new plant establishes itself. Sometimes unwanted seeds that

hitchhiked in via the soil mix do not germinate immediately but manifest themselves after a week or more.

7. EXAMINE AMENDMENTS Unwanted seeds and viable plant parts can sneak into your yard via a topsoil or loam delivery, farm and other mulches, cheap soil mixes, manure, and compost, as well as hay or straw. Designate a staging area for such deliveries and leave the new material there for a week or more before using. This will give you an opportunity to yank out any interlopers. Sifting the material through a screen or even your fingers as you add it to your garden may catch seedling invaders, but often not seeds. After you have used the new stuff, keep a wary eye on the spot where you put it and act immediately if you spot weeds growing there. You might have to pay more for quality, uncontaminated amendments. You should also spread the word to other gardeners when you find a bad source and especially when you find a good source.

8. KNOW WHAT YOU PLANT It is a good idea to add only plants whose identities you know to your yard and garden. Gift plants, free plants, sale plants, impulse purchases, incorrectly labeled plants, plants dug up by the roadside or taken from some wild setting—any of these might be trouble. Learn not only a newcomer's name but also details about its appearance and habits.

9. BE A SAVVY SHOPPER Only buy plants you know or know of, and avoid those with a reputation for rampant, aggressive growth. If you think you see a "bad plant" for sale, speak to the seller. Make sure you have correctly guessed its name and bad nature, and if so, be bold and request that they not sell or grow it. Only patronize nurseries that sell healthy, correctly identified, garden-appropriate plants.

//

Invasive Plants Protocol

DO

Get a correct identification for any suspect plants in your yard or garden, particularly ones you do not recognize or know you did not introduce.

Keep a watchful, suspicious eye on seedlings and sprouts in your yard.

Either remove flowers, seedheads, and/or fruits and berries before they ripen, or remove the plant altogether.

Learn about the native plants of your area and add ones you like to your yard and garden. These tend to be in balance with your regional climate/weather as well as local insects and creatures—and thus tend not to spread aggressively.

Find appropriate substitutes. If you wish to find "good plants" whose appearance or other qualities are similar to the "bad plants" you are giving up or avoiding, do some research. A local or state native plant society, where available, is an excellent resource.

Educate yourself about nursery-bought plants. Some are native; some are not. Not all exotics present problems.

Look out for stowaways and hitchhikers. Unwanted plants can enter your property in potted plants from nurseries (local or mail order), as seeds or tiny seedlings lodged under or next to the plant you purchased.

Beware of tainted mulch, soil mixes, and top-soil. When you buy these items and bring them home, or have a load delivered, you may inadvertently be introducing seeds or viable plant bits to your yard. Look over the load carefully beforehand, if possible, and extract and properly dispose of suspect seedlings. Once the new dirt or mulch is in place, however, unwanted plants can pop up—so be vigilant.

Keep your tools and equipment clean and especially, require the same of any hired lawn or yard contractors. This includes riding mowers, rototillers, shovels, hoes, rakes, and more.

Talk with your local nursery and other area gardeners about troublesome plants. Learn about, exchange information on, and advocate for plants that are not weedy or invasive.

Speak up if you spot an invasive plant, especially one that is getting out of control, in a neighbor's yard or garden, a local park or other public space.

DON'T

Don't purchase invasive and weedy plants. Don't patronize nurseries that sell them—and tell them why.

Don't use plant or wildflower mixes from far-off places (for example, a Mountain Meadow mix in a lowland backyard). Read the label and don't plant or sow a blend that includes ingredients you don't know or have questions about. Often these include not only seeds of nonnative plants but aggressive filler annuals and grasses.

Don't dig up plants in the wild and move them into your yard and garden.

Don't share suspect plants with other gardeners—don't give them away, don't trade them, don't sell them.

Don't let these plants stray from your property's boundaries.

Don't discard seedheads, fruits, roots, plant parts or entire plants in your compost pile or "back forty." Do not dump them in a wooded or wild area, or toss them anywhere they might germinate or grow. Instead, dispose of them in your municipal trash.

How Weeds Reproduce

Any botanist can tell you that all plants are resourceful, and certainly, the plant world is full of fascinating examples of the ways in which plants survive, thrive, and protect themselves. The plants we do not like or come to fear and loathe, the ones we call weeds and invasives, are the cleverest, most adaptable, most resilient ones of all, at least in certain settings.

In general, and this is sure to strike you as you thumb through the plant profiles in this book, these plants will do anything and everything to live and multiply. Often they reproduce by more than one means, such as by seed in sunny settings and by runners in shady settings, or by runners in spring and summer and by seed in autumn. In fact, "a plant reproducing by more than one means" is a fair definition of many an invasive plant or weed.

Understanding how the problem plant in your garden reproduces is crucial. It may suggest a vulnerability or Achilles' heel. It gives you a point, or points, of attack. If, for example, the plant is an annual that produces many seeds, you will want to get rid of those seeds before they ripen to arrest the plant's further spread. If the plant spreads via runners, you know you will have to extract their entire lengths. If the plant develops a big, wandering root system, plan to dig down and get it out; get it all out if possible. Additionally or alternatively, you may be able to starve this root system by chopping back the topgrowth repeatedly, valiantly, and tirelessly.

If you choose to use an herbicide, it too must be matched to the plant and its reproductive strategy or strategies. Pre-emergent herbicides target seeds. Systemics enter the leaves or can be painted on a cut stem or trunk; in either application, the herbicide is conducted down into the roots, ultimately killing the entire plant.

Thick-growing ivy can, and will, smother anything in its path. Eradication begins with tracing the vine back to its roots, not just to the nodes that have rooted along the way.

More Suspect Behaviors

Plants that enter an ecosystem or your garden and outcompete or elbow aside the original residents do so in myriad ways. Watching for these behaviors is important, as they may be signs of trouble. That is, they may be signs that you need to take up arms.

EARLY AND LATE LEAFING OUT Some unwanted plants leaf out earlier in spring or persist longer into fall or winter than the natives, which gives them a competitive advantage. They might also grow faster, taller, and broader. This behavior gives them a physical advantage, so that they can literally run over or shade out the natives and garden favorites.

PROLIFIC FRUITING Plants with fruits or berries, and therefore seeds, that are dispersed efficiently and readily often turn into a problem. For example, wind-dispersed seeds may be lightweight or have "parachute" features to help them move, and bird-dispensed seeds will be tasty and nutritious. If these fruits are also produced abundantly, it is only a matter of time before the species spreads far and wide. In other words, more seeds mean more seedlings.

EASY MIXING Plants that, for whatever reason inherent in their unique biology, are able to hybridize or cross-pollinate with existing natives, are also damaging. They alter, and thus some would say, sully the gene pool, perhaps permanently, and not always for the better. Familiar examples include mulberry trees and spartina grass, but there are more, and this remains an area of study for botanists. Gardeners should just keep a sharp lookout for invading plants that elude exact identification—a hybrid could be the explanation.

TENDENCY TO REVERT In horticulture, nurseries and plant breeders are always looking for new plants they consider desirable and marketable. These may be imports with as-yet-unknown habits, or they may be natural variations.

Shrubs and groundcovers with new leaf colors or variegated leaves often fall into the second category. The new plant may be well-behaved, but after some time in your garden, it may "revert" to the appearance and habits of its less-desirable parents. Or, it might produce viable seeds and thus seedlings that revert back to the appearance and habits of its less-desirable parents. In general, plants of all-green foliage are more robust, and thus often more aggressive, than their variants.

Sports and chance seedlings are two kinds of plants that result from natural variation. The variation may be either accidental or engineered in a test field or tissue-culture lab.

PRODUCING ALLELOPATHIC CHEMICALS In this intriguing phenomenon, a plant is able to defend itself and its immediate, staked-out territory by chemical means. The roots exude a detrimental biochemical into the soil, something that prevents the germination and/or growth of adjacent, competing plants. Or, the defensive chemicals are lodged in the leaves and flowers, and the litter at the base of the plant becomes not merely physically but chemically inhibiting to other plants.

Perhaps the most famous example is the black walnut tree, which exudes a chemical called "juglone" into the soil around the tree. This chemical kills off many plants, including lawn grasses, that might otherwise grow under the tree.

Plenty of examples are found in the invasive-plant world, notably eucalyptus, tree-of-heaven, garlic mustard, and nutsedge. Note that these are also pungent plants; sometimes, strong scent can be an indicator that allelopathic chemicals are present.

//

Identification Tips

Whether you are setting out to identify a pretty spring wildflower or to pin down an obnoxious garden invader, plant identification is not a mysterious process. Certain features can give away the identity quickly, and certainly, a cluster solves the puzzle best. Be observant of the following features as you study the profiles in this book and/or seek confirmation from other sources:

HABIT Is the plant a sprawler or a climber? Herbaceous or woody? Does the plant grow from a single stem or does it have multiple stems? Does the plant produce suckers? Does it form a colony? Are there aboveground runners, perhaps rooting at the nodes? What can you tell about the root system?

LEAVES Are the leaves arranged opposite each other along the stem or do they alternate? What is their shape: heart-shaped, lance-shaped, lobed, dissected, or something else? Note the color. Is it variegated? Does it change with the seasons? Are the leaves smooth or hairy, glossy or not? Are the margins serrated, scalloped or otherwise marked?

FLOWERS AND SEEDHEADS When plants are closely related, oftentimes the blossoms or seedheads will immediately narrow things down, not just to the genus, but also to the very species. Observe color. Count petals, pistils, stamens. Note size and/or width of flowers and seeds. Try to work with a plant that is fully mature or open, rather than one that is just unfurling or starting to flag or fade away. Note bloom time and duration.

FRUITS AND BERRIES Fruits and berries give away a plant's identity quickly, too, particularly when they are fresh and ripe. Note whether they are carried individually or in clusters. Do they hang along stems or are they only at the ends of the stem? What size and color are they? Cut open a fruit or berry to see the density and color of the flesh and to look at the seeds. By observing the fruits on the plant, you might even be able to determine which animals or birds like to eat them.

HABITAT This basic piece of information sometimes makes or breaks plant identification. If you find a plant growing in a dry spot but in researching it learn that it grows in wetlands, you might

To prevent its spread, cut back Queen Anne's lace before it goes to seed; to get rid of an infestation, dig up the plants by the roots.

have to start over. Ditto if you find a plant prospering in shade when your research says that it is a sun-lover. Likewise, if a plant grows in chalky (alkaline) soil, but the literature shows that it prefers acidic soil, you might have to go back to the drawing board to identify the plant correctly. That said, realize that many weeds and invasives are resilient and can show up in unexpected places or tolerate a broad range of growing conditions.

RELATIVES Does the unidentified plant resemble a plant you already know? Does it look vaguely familiar or related? For instance, while it is no beauty in terms of blossoms or bush, it is easy to see that the multiflora rose is a rose. Ox-eye daisy is obviously a daisy. And so on.

Overall, close observation of any suspect interloper should provide clues that lead to correct identification. Two hundred plant profiles appear in the pages ahead, which cover just about any nasty customer you might encounter in the United States. Further confirmation from other sources—printed, internet, helpful or knowledgeable person—is worthwhile if you do not feel certain. Through the process of narrowing down its identity, you will gain useful information about the plant. Know thy enemy, and then move on to combat.

2

Combat Thy Enemy

Although it may be a weedy world out there, it is important to look for ways to create healthy and sustainable ecosystems in our landscapes. Gardeners, especially, strive to preserve their own domains or Edens while simultaneously sustaining the plants and creatures that keep them healthy. The question becomes, how can we do this and control weeds?

You might be surprised at the number of options you have. If the low-impact approaches described here fail, then proceed to the stronger arsenal that follows. The many tactics in this chapter expand on the brief recommendations that appear with each plant profile elsewhere in this book. The tactics have worked for other gardeners and proven effective in some situations and regions. You might deploy one, or a combination, as you battle the problem plants in your garden. Overall, success comes when you take action as follows:

Intervene early. An established patch or invasion growing for some time is simply harder to stop or eradicate. Offending seedlings and sprouts, once correctly identified, on the other hand, can be attacked more easily. A watchful eye on every corner of your garden and surrounding environs is always wise.

Time it well. Some plants are more vulnerable in early spring when new growth emerges. Others are most effectively battled in late summer or fall when they are trying to send food and moisture reserves down to their root systems in preparation for next year's continued growth and expansion. You need to determine when the best time to act is.

Concentrate your efforts. Draw battle lines, literally if need be, by roping or blocking off an affected area. Protect desirable and harmless plants in the vicinity. Create a buffer zone if need be. Do not treat any more real estate than necessary.

Persist. One treatment rarely suffices for the more tenacious weeds and invasives. Be thorough, be consistent, keep trying, and give it time.

Also, realize that, while you might wish to eradicate completely the offending weed, you may have to settle for merely controlling it or keeping it at bay. Perhaps the plant finds it easy to return (your surrounding environs are overrun with it, for instance), because you waited too long to start battling it, or because you find yourself unwilling to spend the time, money, and resources to completely vanquish it. Or, you may find yourself unwilling to deploy an herbicide. As organic gardeners say, "some for me, some for nature"—maybe you can tolerate and manage a minor presence without going so far as to indiscriminately blast your little piece of ground.

This brings to mind a memorable article that ran in *Discover Magazine* years ago, entitled "Why I No Longer Regard Plants as Salad that's Not Dead." The author, James Gorman, described his epic struggle against Japanese knotweed or, as he called it, Japanese bamboo. "Before I knew about its qualities," he recounted, "I chopped and mowed a plot to a grisly stubble one day. In two weeks, the bamboo was chin high and laughing." Outraged, he then considers "flying over my yard at dawn in a fleet of gunships, blaring Wagner, and scorching the earth with lethal herbicides"! All joking aside, there are daunting plants and daunting situations.

"Two wrongs don't make a right" applies to weed warfare. Your yard and surroundings should not suffer harm in the process. Please, think this through and proceed with care and respect—for your enemy as well as for the environment.

///

Less-Toxic Controls

The following is a menu of options that should be low-impact if used correctly. Again, combos of these, or using one in one season, and another at a different time of year, might be worth trying. Granted, some of these practices are labor-intensive, but if they work for you and allow you to avoid herbicides, consider them worthwhile.

HAND-PULLING OR DIGGING UP If the infestation is not large and well-established, and assuming you have the time and energy, this remains the easiest way to evict unwanted plants from your yard and garden. Work after a soaking rain, or after watering, when the soil is soft and the root systems are so much easier to get out of the ground.

Use a trowel, weeding fork, dandelion fork, shovel or hoe, or whatever tool works best for you and the situation. Make sure it is sharp.

Bring along a box, tub, wheelbarrow, or tarp, and toss the discards into it as you go. This minimizes the chances of spreading viable plant parts or seeds around, makes cleanup easier—and gives you a gratifying sense of accomplishment as the pile grows.

CHOPPING DOWN Lopping off a plant while it is growing and photosynthesizing deprives it of needed sustenance. Thus, the lower you cut and the more leaves you get rid of, the better. Note that new, succulent growth is often easier to chop than dry, wiry stems and branches. Use a sharp tool so the work goes quickly and efficiently—such as a scythe or machete, loppers, clippers, or a string trimmer/weed whacker. Then gather or rake up the leavings and dispose of them properly. In addition, be prepared to repeat this process more than once.

Timing matters. Cutting down plants that are about to or have already gone to seed, while doable, is often doomed because you end up letting loose the seeds. Cutting plants early in the season, while doable and usually worthwhile, may result in the plant regenerating because its root system is robust and in full swing; in this case, you will have to return and repeat.

MOWING Larger areas and lower-growing plants may be attacked with a lawn or riding mower. Make sure the tool's blades are quite sharp, and be prepared to repeat as needed. This limits spread,

Combating Lawn Weeds

Here is a surprisingly simple way to keep sun-loving weeds at bay in the lawn. Do not mow low. Allow your grass to grow a bit taller—between 2½ to even 4 inches or so—experiment. Then keep your lawn healthy and dense with watering and good care. This has the desirable affect of shading out many pest plants, including but not limited to dastardly crabgrass.

When you do mow, remove no more than a third of the total height of your grass at any one time. If the result is still too high, wait two days and mow again.

and eventually you may starve the pest plants' root systems.

There are two schools of thought on what to do with what you have mowed down. Leave it in place, and it can mat down and suppress regeneration. Rake it up and cart it away, and you (theoretically) prevent tenacious viable seeds or fragments from gaining new purchase and starting to grow. What you do pretty much depends on the plant, the timing of your mowing, and the extent of the problem.

Mowing will not work if you have bad timing, that is, if you inadvertently release seeds, or mow after the plant has already released ripe seeds. It will not work if your pest plant regenerates easily from a robust, extensive, and/or creeping root system or from root fragments.

Overplanting after a thorough and properly timed mowing, or nourishing (adding water, organic matter, fertilizer, even aeration) existing desirable plants afterwards will discourage a return. The desirable plants will monopolize the available resources and/or shade out weedy seedlings that manage to emerge.

DEADHEADING This term simply means removing individual flowers or flowerheads before they mature and form and ripen seed. This can reduce the spread of a plant or help you manage a grouping or small patch, but it will not kill the plant, of course. Instead, the plant's response will be to continue generating more new growth, including more flowers—particularly in the heart of the growing season. Deadheading at season's end tends to have the effect of inspiring the plant to shut down for the year.

CUTTING OFF SEEDHEADS This tack prevents a weed that reproduces via seed from propagating new generations. If you cut off the seedhead of an annual, that could very well be the end of it; it will not return next year. If you cut off the seedhead of a perennial weed, or remove seedpods from a shrub or tree, you halt only that mode of reproduction. If that plant is capable of spreading vegetatively, that is, via roots and runners, only part of your battle is won.

Cutting off the fruit of carrotwood before seeds ripen may offer some measure of controlling this fast-growing evergreen tree that threatens Florida's mangroves.

As for timing, obviously it is key that you act before the seeds ripen and can disperse or be eaten or carried off by birds and other wildlife. Dispose of unwanted seeds and pods properly.

SMOTHERING Small, or even large, patches of unwanted plants might be prevented from growing and eventually killed if you cover them over so thoroughly that they cannot breach the cover. The earlier in the growing season you act, of course, the better, so you are not trying to bury tall, actively growing plants.

Some materials that have proven effective are plastic (including but not limited to black plastic, old shower curtains, tarps), bricks, straw, weed-free mulch, untreated bark, old newspapers or flattened cardboard boxes, planks or old doors or tabletops, heavy canvas sheets, old carpets or carpet remnants, gravel or stones.

Be generous with depth. Pour or layer on more than you think you might need so the plants simply run out of steam in a vain effort to reach light and air. For instance, if you use old newspapers, spread them four or five pages thick, at least.

Securing or anchoring down your cover is also crucial. You do not want it to be dislodged by anything or anyone. The most effective smothering projects involve using one or more materials, such as straw topped with a tarp.

Then, be patient. Leave the cover in place for an entire season, over the winter, well into the following year, whatever it takes (you can peek). Tack it down again if a corner comes loose and replenish materials that blow or wash away. Removing the covering too soon and witnessing a resurgence is not what you want.

One final word about this method: when the time comes to remove the covering, do not leave the now-bare area exposed. If the remains of the dead plants can be removed and or dug up and discarded, do so. If they can be plowed or rototilled under, do so, but make sure they are dead; some weeds regenerate from chopped-up root bits and you do not want to aid and abet. Then, undertake soil improvement as necessary, such as digging in organic matter or improving drainage in the area. Last but not least, overplant with something that grows well and quickly—a nice plant, that is. If you have no immediate landscaping plans, plant a cover crop.

STARVING Leaves are food factories; deprive a plant of its food factory and it starves. Yes, you can kill an unwanted plant by diminishing or taking away its ability to photosynthesize and grow. Smothering, described above, is one way. Other ways include depriving it of needed light and the correct moisture—by shading the area (perhaps with a strategically placed upended box, trash can, or picnic table, or by planting overhanging shrubs or trees adjacent to it), or changing the drainage so its soil dries out or floods.

Repeatedly cutting back a plant also may eventually discourage and kill a root system. Even clipping, stripping, or plucking off leaves repeatedly can do the trick. Your goal is to thwart the plant from getting whatever it needs to grow and prosper.

SOLARIZING Essentially this is a "cook until dead" tack. You cut down, pull up, and bag all plant parts in clear- or black-plastic refuse bags. Use heavy-duty ones (contractor grade) and make sure no stems poke through. When full, cinch up and seal the top tightly, and set the bag in a sunny spot (right on black pavement, such as a corner of the driveway, is best). Leave it there for a couple of weeks. The contents will broil and then rot. Then send away with your municipal trash collection or, if you dare, compost (see below).

Another variation on solarization is the *in-situ* method, or covering an infested area with plastic. You can do this anytime during

Black vs. Clear Plastic

When using plastic to control, smother, or cook unwanted plants, consider the pros and cons of color. Black plastic is the most readily available and often cheapest. It prevents light from reaching the soil surface, thwarting growth. It also absorbs sunlight, heating up the soil below, raising the cooking temperature, so to speak.

Clear plastic tends to encourage even higher soil temperatures below it, but it allows light through, and living plants, especially really tenacious ones, may actually grow thanks to the warmth and trapped moisture.

For a bit more money, you can buy so-called biodegradable or recyclable bags, sheets, or rolls. Some are starch-based and said to break down safely, but others are still made of petroleum-based materials, so buyer beware.

the growing season, though obviously high summer works fastest due to higher temperatures and sunnier days. Prepare the area first. Cut down and cart off as much of the offending plants as you can. Then, break up the soil to a depth of 6 to 8 inches, which loosens compaction and brings weed seeds to the surface; a few passes with a tiller should do the trick. Lastly, on the day you plan to cover the area, dampen the ground. Research has shown that seeds (and pathogens, for that matter) lurking in dry soil are less affected by solarization's induced high temperatures.

Lay clear plastic sheets over the problem area, pull the edges tight, and anchor them securely. Some people create a trench around the perimeter. Clear plastic allows sunlight through and the result is that the soil below gets very hot—up to 140°F on the surface and nearly as hot below. If you leave this cover in place for several weeks, two months, or even a whole season, most or all viable weed seeds below will be cooked until dead. Even crabgrass.

Yes, beneficial microorganisms in the soil are also likely to be killed during the heating process, but they do rebound. Earthworms evidently just retreat to lower, cooler soil levels (interesting factoid—the common earthworm is a nonnative species).

BOILING WATER Yes, dousing a single or few nasty weeds with boiling water, or dumping panloads on a bigger patch, has been tried and been successful. Obviously because water is so heavy, you are not going to be able to boil a big cauldron and dump it on a big patch. Therefore, this is most useful as a spot-treatment weed-killer, such as when pest plants invade cracks in a walkway or a driveway, or maybe a terrace.

Boiling water kills plants by scalding. It works best on annual weeds; perennial ones will also succumb, but only after repeated doses. A few tips to maximize its effects: first, cut the plant off at ground level, at the crown. When you boil the water, take it out to the plant ASAP, as it will start cooling the moment you remove it from the flame. Pour the water on from only a couple of inches above, to avoid splashing. Do not forget to protect yourself by using an oven mitt to handle the kettle or pan and by wearing shoes, not sandals, and long pants; you do not want to scald your own skin.

When you pour the water on the plant, aim with care. The roots of nearby desirable plants might be cooked, too. If this is a concern, create a little trench or hole around the targeted plant so the boiling water is channeled right where you want it.

The only other concern you might have is that the hot water may also kill beneficial microorganisms in the soil. Not to worry—they are resilient and will rebound.

CORN GLUTEN This is not actually a weed killer; it is a weed thwarter. It inhibits seed germination and thus is most effective with weeds that reproduce primarily by seed, that is, annual weeds (including crabgrass). As such, it is considered a pre-emergent herbicide.

Scatter it around where pesky annual weeds grow in the hopes of clearing an infested area before replanting. Timing is critical. Corn gluten works best when broadcast a month or more before annual weeds are slated to germinate. In colder climates, this means late winter or early spring; in milder climates, try late fall. The recommended rate for corn gluten is 20 pounds per 1000 square feet. Moisture will activate it, although drenching, as from zealous watering-in or lots of rain, will simply wash it away.

A nice side effect of corn gluten, by the way, is that it slowly releases nitrogen into the soil over several months.

For best results, repeat the treatment annually for three or so years. You may only kill half a population in any given season, but consider such results preferable to treating the area with a chemical pre-emergent.

PROPANE TORCHES AND FLAME WEEDERS Despite the risk of causing an unintentional blaze in your yard or neighborhood, this method has its fans. Homeowners or landscapers who deal with chronic weed issues along a driveway, within or edging walkways, or on bluestone- or pebble-covered patios and terraces like torching. It kills topgrowth, of course, but can also scorch the life out of roots and any shed seeds in the vicinity. One caveat is that torches should never be used on poison oak, poison ivy, or other plants with high oil content.

To torch a plant, wave the flame over the plant briefly. The plant does not need to be vaporized or literally burnt; the intense heat will destroy the cells and the effects will be obvious quickly. Rake away the burnt debris afterwards and enjoy the clean look. You will have to watch for regrowth and return if necessary. This is especially true of tenacious perennials like dandelions.

As for timing, this method is most effective in summertime, when hot days cause weeds to be stressed anyway. On the other hand, it is safer to torch shortly after a rain or watering, when things are damp and the project is less chancy.

The tool in question is a portable, smaller-size propane torch, typically a 1-pound tank (between 10K and 20K BTUs). An extension of up to 3 feet long is very helpful, so you can work standing up straight and thus keep a good eye on your work while sparing your back. The torch should have a heat shield to help you avoid burning adjacent vegetation. Also, get one with a push-button ignition, which is safer because it allows you more control. A rolling-tank model with more BTUs might be in order if you have a larger infested area to kill.

Obviously, safety is paramount. Wear heavy shoes, not sandals. Keep the hose (pre-primed) or a bucket of water with you as you work so you can immediately douse any unintended flare-ups. Never use a torch on a windy day, and be extra-cautious during dry weather. Avoid working around mulch or close to anything flammable. This includes wooden structures and fences as well as shrubs, hedges, or evergreen trees whose interiors are brushy and dry.

CONTAIN AND CAGE You might be able to live in a state of truce with an aggressive invader that you still find worthwhile, useful, or aesthetically pleasing if you can confine it and prevent its spread. Establishing realistic boundaries can be done. Barriers should be made of stern stuff and sunk deep into the ground so questing roots cannot sneak under. Likewise, barriers should rise up high and sturdily enough so probing stems and tendrils cannot mount them, get over them and away.

What kind of stern stuff? It depends on the situation, of course, but among the materials that others have used successfully are corrugated metal, PVC and other durable, weather-resilient plastics, thick boards, bricks, chain-link fencing, poured concrete, and even recycled or repurposed items like old doors or windows. Alternatively, a trench several inches to a foot deep around the growing area, kept clear and empty or filled in with gravel or stones, might be sufficient.

Physical barriers alone will not contain some plants. You will have to supplement the imprisonment with frequent, judicious pruning and the removal of seeds, pods, or fruit before they ripen.

CONTROLLED BACKYARD BURNS This technique is not to be confused with the burning of brush and leaves that some municipalities allow, especially in autumn or after there is snow on the ground—that is just a way to get rid of a pile of debris (see Disposal below). *Controlled burn* refers to deliberately setting fire to a prescribed area that is overgrown with live, objectionable plants.

First, this option is not for everybody. These fires are not safe in close quarters or when done incorrectly, and thus may not be allowed in your town. So, please, check first and abide by the rules. You might need a permit, to notify neighbors and your local fire department, to confine the blaze in certain ways, and/or to keep it small and low-intensity. Or, you may be required to hire a qualified, certified "burn boss" and stand by while the entire operation is conducted like a military maneuver.

Look into this method if your invasives are exotic trees and shrubs, or if you have a substantial area infested with unwanted and aggressive plants.

Chemical Controls

Once you have exhausted the nontoxic methods of control and your pest persists, it may be time to consider chemical controls. These options run the gamut from relatively safe to potentially risky to yourself and animals including pets and beneficial insects, not to mention the environment itself (soil, water, air). Try these only when all else fails, or when an area cannot feasibly be treated with other measures, for instance, because it is too large or because the plant is toxic, like poison oak or ivy. And always, *always follow the labels.*

Do *not* treat a plant or infested area with a product that is not labeled for it. Do *not* overdo. As with aspirin, more is decidedly not better and can harm much more than you meant to. Plus, there are legal limits as to how much herbicide can be released per acre.

Also, remember that just because a product is organic or touted as natural does not automatically make it safe for humans or pets. Probably such items leave less of a footprint on the environment, but they are still toxic—they still kill something. In short, use herbicides thoughtfully and sparingly.

You will see the terms *pre-emergent* and *post-emergent* in any discussion of weeds, including lawn weeds. You will also see them on the labels of various chemical treatments.

A **pre-emergent** herbicide is applied to the soil surface to prevent weed seeds from germinating. In cooler climates, it is best applied to ground that is beginning to warm up; in milder climates, late summer or early fall is better, depending on moisture and temperature. Products that offer to weed and feed simultaneously tend to contain a pre-emergent. They are often effective on crabgrass and annual weeds such as chickweed and henbit. Caution: do not use a pre-emergent on a lawn if you are planning to seed or reseed it.

A **post-emergent** herbicide attacks actively growing weeds, controlling or killing them. Proper timing is critical—heed the guidelines on the product label. Post-emergents may be classified as either contact or systemic. Contact herbicides affect only the part of the plant on which they are applied. Systemic herbicides enter a plant through its leaves or stems and then travel to the roots before killing the plant in its entirety.

After you spray or treat unwanted plants with a systemic herbicide, please be patient. Most plants should start to look sick within a week or two, but some may take several weeks; the label on the chemical will advise you of what to expect. Do not waste

Herbicide Application Safety Tips

Protect your skin and body. Wear a hat, gloves, goggle, long pants, a long-sleeved shirt, and closed-toe, heavy shoes. Rinse off or launder afterwards as warranted.

Read the label on the container thoroughly before using it, paying particular attention to recommended mode(s) of application, concentrations to be used, safety precautions, and disposal requirements.

Protect desirable plants during treatment. For individual plants, smaller plants, or smaller groupings of garden plants, upend a trashcan, cardboard box, or jug over them, or toss a towel, tarp, or old blanket over them. For entire beds or larger plantings, put a tarp or old blanket over the area and secure the edges with rocks or bricks.

Do not spray on a windy or breezy day.

Avoid spraying when plants are wet or damp, which will dilute effectiveness.

For isolated plants, you may be able to treat with a cut and drip method, which specifically targets individual plants, thus limiting potential damage to nearby desirable plants. Follow directions on the label.

Use the nozzle-adjustment feature on your sprayer to tailor it to the job at hand (from broad spray to direct stream—the direct stream feature is best, of course, if you are trying to avoid hitting nearby desirable plants).

Store unused products in their original labeled container(s), and any applicator(s), in a cool, dry, secure place out of reach of children and pets.

Dispose of containers and any unused herbicide safely and legally. This information should be on the label. Also, check whether your municipality has a "toxic waste day."

effort, money, or product by spraying a plant more than once. Sick plants cannot absorb systemics through their leaf surfaces or move the toxin(s) down to their roots.

Finally, if you need more information about chemical controls, check websites for more complete information. Those of the Cooperative Extension Service and research universities are particularly useful.

The following is not a comprehensive list, as new and improved products enter the market from time to time or have highly specialized uses. The EPA adds or bans uses of previously approved chemicals. You absolutely must read and heed the label. It is the law.

VINEGAR Vinegar (also called acetic acid) is sometimes touted as a weedkiller. Technically, it constitutes a contact herbicide, that is, it is able to kill only what it touches, namely, exposed plant parts such as foliage or stems. It works best on younger plants with relatively frail or undeveloped root systems—sprouts and seedlings

Homemade Weedkiller Recipe

Although the ingredients are common household products, they are indeed toxic to plants—all plants are vulnerable, not just the weeds or invasives you are battling. So deploy with care, using either a hand sprayer or a brush to apply to individual plants if overspray is a concern.

In a large plastic jug, combine:

1 gallon of white vinegar (5 percent acidity)
1 cup table salt
1 tablespoon dishwashing liquid

Mix well by shaking. Label. Store extra out of reach of children and pets.

included—because once the top growth is killed, there's nothing left to support those roots and thus the entire plant dies off. The acid in vinegar breaks down and dries out cell membranes, causing the plant to collapse, dead.

That said, be advised that regular household-use vinegar is not highly concentrated, and thus may not be effective against its intended target. Nor does boiling it down work, alas. This is true whether you use white, cider, balsamic, red wine, or any other kind of vinegar; while, granted, each has a different natural acidity, all are diluted with water to the 5-percent acidity point, table strength, before they are bottled and sold in the grocery store.

Highly concentrated, horticultural-grade vinegars, wherein the natural acidity is manipulated to reach 20 percent, are registered with the EPA for use as herbicides. If your local garden center does not carry these products and cannot order them for you, take your search online.

Your best bet is to hit unwanted plants with a blast or a brush of vinegar soon after they emerge. Work on a sunny day—this seems to be more effective. The plants may resprout and so you may have to repeat. Mature plants and established patches are simply more resistant and harder to kill.

Vinegar is not toxic and breaks down easily in water, but profligate use could lower soil pH in a confined area. Take care to protect desirable garden plants; vinegar does not play favorites. In addition, you should avoid using vinegar of any kind near a concrete patio or walkway, as it can damage or disfigure these as it interacts with any limestone content. Take care not to get vinegar on your skin or in your eyes, especially higher concentrations. If you do accidentally get vinegar on your skin, flush liberally with water.

One last note: Reportedly, thistles are particularly vulnerable to vinegar—maybe news you can use?

PLANT-BASED OILS So-called organic herbicides whose active ingredient is citrus oil, cinnamon oil, clove oil, or similar plant products are available in some outlets or online (Avenger® is a widely available example). These kill or injure broad-leaved weeds on contact, down to the roots, so repeated treatments are usually necessary for persistent pests. The acid content in these sprays strips leaves of their protective waxy cuticle, drying them out past the point of no return. As ever, be careful to protect plants you want to keep, as such concoctions are nonselective, meaning that they kill anything they touch. Follow the directions provided on the label.

SOAP-BASED HERBICIDES Soap-based herbicides such as Weed Aside can be effective for spot control. They coat leaves and stems with a soapy film that suffocates the plant, causing death by dehydration. Although they operate a bit like insecticidal soap, they are not the same thing—soap-based herbicides are processed differently. Spritz on your target plant on a hot, dry, sunny summer day.

These work best on annual weeds. Perennial weeds with extensive root systems or robust taproots will require repeated applications along with the use of other methods, such as Smothering described on page 42.

BLEACH Chlorine bleach, the kind sold as a household disinfectant, is strong enough to use in weed combat, but it is toxic, and must be used with care. Put it in a spray bottle and spot-treat pest plants. Wear gloves and/or wash your hands well with soapy water afterwards. If spray accidentally gets on a desirable plant, rinse it off.

Bleach will kill annual weeds easily and perennial weeds with repeated treatments. The smell and the harmful chemicals usually take two days or more to dissipate.

Be forewarned that bleach used too heavy-handedly or too often in the same spot can raise soil pH, making it inhospitable to any plant growth, including the plants you want. It can also kill beetles and other soil-dwelling insects.

Never mix bleach with other cleaning products, and do not mix it with vinegar. If you want to extend the amount, add only water.

SALT You may recall from World History class that once Rome conquered Carthage, the victors dumped salt on the fields of their enemy, killing the crops and making the land inhospitable for plant growth for some time to come. Nasty indeed. Moreover, if you live in an area with snowy winters, you also know that rock salt and related ice-melt products kill plants.

Salt kills by desiccating a plant. Water dilutes its effects, but watch where runoff goes—anything downstream may be killed just for being in the way. So, this is not a remedy to use in rainy seasons or where sprinklers run.

Instead, try a pinch or small handful of salt at the base of objectionable plants. Or, mix one part salt with two parts water, heat it to boiling until the salt is thoroughly dissolved, and pour it on the targeted plant. Either way, create an informal basin around the base if confining salt's effects is important.

Flush the area with water after a few days, once you are sure the weeds are dead. Do not use salt in arid climates, where the salt will accumulate.

GLYPHOSATE Glyphosate (brand names include Roundup, Rodeo, Kleen-up, Pronto, Kleeraway Grass & Weed Killer, Buccaneer, Razor Pro, Genesis Extra, Aqua Neat, and Aquamaster) remains the most widely recommended and widely used broad-spectrum herbicide in the United States. Its availability and popularity continue even though concerns have been raised about its environmental friendliness and safety. Its effectiveness, when deployed carefully, according to label directions, is rarely impugned.

Glyphosate itself is not a poison. It works by interfering with a plant's ability to manufacture key amino acids, thus thwarting protein production. This interference, essentially, makes it impossible for the plant to photosynthesize and go on living. Surfactants are included in consumer formulations to penetrate the waxy coating on leaves, as is water.

This herbicide is systemic. Plants take glyphosate in through their leaves and other green plant tissue and translocate it down to their root system. In this way, an entire plant is killed, not just the aboveground parts. This is the reason glyphosate is a popular weapon against deeply rooted plants, more mature plants with established root systems, and plants with taproots. It is also the reason gardeners reach for glyphosate when a pest plant they thought they had killed regenerates. This often happens with, for example, Bermuda grass, when gardeners actually only kill the topgrowth and, after a pause, the plant marshals its underground resources and sends up fresh new topgrowth.

Let us spend a few moments on the safety concerns and bad press associated with glyphosate. Unlike, say, the highly toxic and now illegal DDT, glyphosate in lower concentrations has relatively low toxicity, degrades quickly, and is fat-insoluble (lipophobic). On the other hand, a number of scientific papers have sounded the alarm about glyphosate's role in birth defects—yes, in mammals—and suggested it may also be carcinogenic, particularly in highly

The Glove-in-Glove Method

Gardeners and homeowners wishing to use a strong chemical herbicide, but not wishing to use a paintbrush and wanting to avoid overspray, may consider this controversial method.

Basically, you put on a long, heavy rubber glove, tugging it up high on your arm and taping it securely in place so nothing can get under it. Next, you put a shorter, cheap cotton glove over it. Then you dip your hand into a bucket of herbicide. Wring out the excess, and then carefully wipe down the pest plants you want to kill. Work slowly and carefully to avoid dripping on yourself, your clothing or body, the ground, and nearby desirable plants. When finished, dispose of everything safely and wash off your skin well with hot, soapy water.

Why is this controversial? Because you will not find this method expressly described or blessed on the label. As pointed out above, herbicide labels in this country are the law.

Is it illegal? Not expressly. If an application method is not prohibited on a label, you could reason that it is permissible. The glove-in-glove method is risky, particularly if your gloves are not sufficient protection for your arm and hand or if you are sloppy or have an accidental spill, splash, or exposure.

concentrated doses the likes of which homeowners will never encounter. All of these charges the manufacturers are quick to deny or counter. Reports issued by Earth Open Source, a nonprofit study collaborative based in the United Kingdom which received international attention back in the summer of 2011, maintained that an "urgent," worldwide review, with more research and better, more consistent regulation, is needed.

Additionally, these herbicides have been shown decisively to be lethal for amphibians in certain formulations. The surfactant, or adjuvant, used in Roundup is the toxin polyoxyethyleneamine (POEA); it is illegal to use Roundup near water. Rodeo and other glyphosate-based products specifically labeled for use on wet sites lack this additive.

Finally, some research has found that the salts in glyphosate-based herbicide spray persist in the soil, transferred by the roots of dying weeds. The victims here are more than the roots and include the soil food web. The residue allegedly harms soil microorganisms and other underground residents.

Will you ever use these herbicides in doses high enough to place you, your family, or your neighbors at risk? Or, are these problems a far greater concern in high-concentration agricultural spraying settings? The answers to these questions are not conclusive, but in the face of reasonable doubt from the above-mentioned

Restricted Use Herbicide

When you see this designation, stop! It means that use is limited to people who are "licensed applicators," possibly also helpers under their supervision. That could be a landscape or lawn-service contractor, or a government employee. Such people are trained in safe application, and limitations may apply (they may not be allowed to use the product on certain plants or in certain settings or situations). In any event, the designation means YOU cannot legally buy and use the product.

The reason? Certain products (Picloram is an example), while effective, are dangerous—to humans and wildlife (mammals, reptiles and amphibians, birds, insects), and improper use poses a risk to soil, groundwater or waterways, and nontarget plants including garden plants and food crops.

Consult such an expert if you are willing to use such a product on invasive plants on your property. They can advise you on whether its use is warranted and safe, and do the work for you (for a price, of course) if you agree to go ahead.

You are likely to observe that the licensed applicators protect themselves—they don heavy clothing, rubber boots, rubber gloves, and/or a facemask. When application is complete, they may cordon off the treated area and will leave a sign warning you and your neighbors that a toxic chemical has been used. You agree to stay away from the area, keep neighbors, pets, and children out, and leave the sign in place for as long as they recommend.

Earth Open Source summary and other studies, many gardeners eschew the use of these products. Others, including many Master Gardeners and those who look after conservation land trusts, feel that the benefits of glyphosate-based herbicides outweigh the risks and that, as chemical herbicides go, these are the safest—the least of many evils.

Should you choose to use this herbicide, mitigate environmental harm by painting on, rather than spraying, which is more diffuse and less targeted. In some cases, you may have to use a higher concentration for stem painting to be effective. Yes, use a small paintbrush—and then, for heaven's sake, wrap it up, and store it safely away alongside the remaining unused product, and never use it for any other purpose. If you spray, review the safety information on page 49.

TRICLOPYR Triclopyr (brand names include Garlon, Bonide's Stump Out and Vine Killer, Brush-B-Gon, Access, Turflon, Access, Crossbow, ET, PathFinder II, Redeem, and Remedy) is the active ingredient in another powerful chemical herbicide,

Eradicating this Japanese dodder will likely involve killing the host plant as well.

generally deployed on serious weed infestations and especially tenacious foes such as poison ivy, poison oak, and kudzu. It targets broadleaf, herbaceous plants and some woody plants; it has little effect on grasses, which is why it is useful for ridding lawns of broadleaf weeds.

Triclopyr is a synthetic auxin or auxin mimic—auxin is a plant-growth hormone. It works by causing plant growth to "go haywire" and become uncontrolled, leading to cell destruction and plant death.

The formulation commonly sold to homeowners is 8.8 percent. It comes in a little bottle with a built-in applicator (like the kind found on shoe polish) that allows you to "paint" it directly on the stumps or stems of the offending plants. As always, follow the label directions very carefully, and protect yourself and any nearby desirable plants. Best results come when it is used on a cool, windless day.

This is a systemic herbicide, that is to say, once applied, the toxins are conveyed throughout the plant, killing both topgrowth and the root system. It is labeled for use on pesky vines, broadleaf weeds, brush, and stumps. It is not appropriate for use on unwanted grasses. If the unwanted plants are many and well established, be prepared to repeat.

As with glyphosate-based ones, these herbicides are controversial; please review the discussion above. Evidently, triclopyr breaks down in sunlight and water, but at varying rates according to the formulation and its other ingredients (including salts). It can leach into the soil and linger in unremoved dead plants. The ester-based formulations are toxic to fish and aquatic invertebrates.

IMAZAPYR Imazapyr (brand names include Arsenal, Habitat, Chopper, and Stalker) is another broad-spectrum herbicide, most often used to combat larger pest plants, that is, invasive shrubs and trees. It can control other herbaceous plants, however, including grasses and water and wetland species. Relatively speaking, it is slow acting.

It is a "weak acid" herbicide, and works by thwarting the synthesis of branched-chain amino acids within its target plant. The pH in the environment in which it is deployed affects its persistence and mobility. (Also, research has shown that certain legumes are able to resist or reject its actions.) It breaks down in sunlight but is slow to degrade in soil, a caution if you have desirable plants nearby the treated area or wish to landscape the area after the battle is done.

Again, consult the label and use only on approved plants and in the manner prescribed. Try less-toxic controls first—this is a product most often used in larger areas by farmers and land managers, and its deployment should not be the first choice for ordinary homeowners and suburban properties.

2,4-D 2,4-Dichlorophenoxyacetic acid (brand names include Weed B Gon, Weed Pro, PAR III, Trillion, Tri-Kil, Killex, Weedaway Premium 3-Way XP Turf Herbicide) is a popular weapon against broadleaf weeds, particularly in lawns. This chemical works like some of the others described above. That is, it is a synthetic auxin and its effect on plants is to cause abnormal, uncontrolled growth followed by death.

It acts on dicots (most weeds) and not monocots (grasses, grains, corn crops) and thus has been used extensively on farms, and defenders tout it as one of the most trusted and effective tools for modern agriculture. Evidently, soil microbes break it down quickly in soil, limiting but not decisively preventing any harm it may cause to groundwater, waterways, wildlife, pets, and humans.

Yes, it was a component of Agent Orange, which has been implicated in miscarriages, birth defects, various cancers and other health problems. Some countries are restricting or banning its use (notably Sweden, Norway, and Denmark), but it is still on the market in the United States and elsewhere and manufacturers vociferously defend it as "safe when used as directed." So tread carefully when this product is recommended. Educate yourself; explore less controversial, safer alternatives.

Protecting Desirable Plants

In any war, the generals will tell you that "collateral damage" is difficult to avoid. In the war on weeds, there are steps you can take to protect and preserve the garden plants you want to keep. Should you lose some, however, hopefully they are replaceable—just make sure the area is safe and suitable for replanting first.

If the objectionable plants are a groundcover under desirable shrubs, trees, roses, or perennials: Hand-pull, mow, or hoe, ideally while the pest plants are still small/just sprouted and ground is damp. Mulch to smother. (It may be possible to deploy a pre-emergent herbicide, but not a post-emergent.)

If the objectionable plants have invaded or intertwined with desirable ones (bad groundcover mixing with good groundcover, bad vine on a tree or within a shrub): Cut back the bad plant as low as you can. Then dig up the root system, or smother, or spot-treat the cut stems or trunks with an herbicide.

If the objectionable plants are nearby or adjacent to desirable ones: Temporarily protect the good plants with boxes, paper bags, upended pots, jugs, or baskets. Then wade in and chop back the problem plants; dig them up or spot-treat what is left of them with an herbicide. One caveat is that in some cases there can be root transference of systemic herbicides, so it pays to be careful or to avoid this approach if possible.

Natural Enemies, or "Biological Controls"

Another weapon in the battle against unwanted and exotic pest plants is any natural enemy. These would be things may have kept them in check in their place of origin and are lacking in the place where the plants now spread rampantly. It may be an insect that feeds or breeds on the plant. It may be a pathogen, that is a disease, a harmful virus, which keeps the population in check back home. It could even be a bird or animal that considers the plant an important food source or habitat component (or a goat—some goats will eat anything).

A Cautionary Tale: Australian Rabbits

In case you missed it when it hit the newswires, or were not in school when biology and ecology teachers regaled their classrooms with what happened in Australia, here is a recap. It is a cautionary tale regarding invasive species.

Once upon a time, in 1859 to be precise, a wealthy British man relocated to Australia. Because he loved hunting, and especially rabbit-hunting, he looked to set it up on his new estate. Alas, there were no rabbits to be found. So, he sent for some from England. The records show that a helpful nephew filled the order for over a dozen bunnies, an assortment that included the unfortunate choice of a particularly resilient domestic type.

Time passed and the domestic-type bunnies, especially, multiplied . . . and escaped. And multiplied throughout the land.

Hunting them for food, pelts, and even just to try to reduce the burgeoning rabbit populations made no significant dents. You see, the rabbits had no natural predators and the setting was amenable.

Among the responses of an increasingly panicked populace were the importation of predators (they did not multiply enough to match their prey), a big fence (not long enough, not high enough, not impermeable), diseases (which for a time were also thought to fatally infect humans, fanning the fires of hysteria), and poison. Farmers even ran dagger-teethed machinery over infested fields, destroying rabbit tunnels (warrens) and—yes—chopping up live bunnies. Not a pretty picture.

Ultimately, in 1950, a virus was released that eventually cut back the rabbit population from 600 million to a mere 100 million. Surviving bunnies, as you might guess, were resistant. So even today, bunnies are not gone from Australia, but their numbers have never again gotten sky-high.

The moral of this awful story is that tampering begets tampering, and the whole thing can get messy and out of control. This is something to bear in mind as American scientists look to deploy predatory bugs or creatures (from the plants' native haunts perhaps) or debilitating diseases on our invasive-plant problems.

Where certain pest plants proliferate and spot treatments or less-toxic tactics are not practical controls, biological controls are sometimes considered. Scotch broom, *Cytisus scoparius*, for instance, has been fought with the Scotch broom seed beetle (*Bruchidius villosus*), the Scotch broom seed weevil (*Apion fuscirostre*), and the Scotch broom twig miner moth (*Leucoptera spartifoliella*). Black-margined loosestrife beetles (*Galerucella calmariensis*), called "mortal enemies" of purple loosestrife, have been released into overrun wetlands. Results of such endeavors are sometimes heartening, sometimes mixed, sometimes slow. Understanding how many insects to deploy, and when, and how, is not simple, as you might imagine.

In addition, it goes without saying that tampering with any ecosystem is inherently tricky business. Few places are "virgin" or "native" anymore in terms of plants or animals, and change—both "natural" and manmade—is part of the picture as well. Land managers who look to biological controls are well aware of these challenges as they look to combat, restore, and heal a damaged or compromised system.

In any event, biological controls are really the domain of larger-scale plant invasions. They simply are not practical on the level of the typical half-acre or quarter-acre yard where most of us live and garden—it is hard to imagine any pest-plant infestation large enough to warrant this kind of intervention. This is not to say that gardeners never "tamper." Think of the organic gardeners who order and release cartons of lacewings and ladybugs into their yards in hopes of controlling pest insects—with mixed results. Sometimes the beneficial creatures "fly away home."

//

Disposal

Dead, nearly dead, yanked up, or poisoned plant parts present a disposal challenge for the home gardener. Please bear in mind that you do not want the refuse to regenerate somehow in your yard or wherever it is hauled off to. Otherwise, the infestation might return or pop up elsewhere—not good.

OUT WITH THE TRASH Dump or rake all debris into a municipal trash bag. Stuff tightly and chop up or shred as needed. Then, seal or cinch tightly. Some places allow heavy-duty plastic bags, others require biodegradable tall paper "leaf bags" designated and sold for organic waste. Either way, if possible, do not haul to the curb immediately. Instead, leave the bags in an out-of-the-way place for several weeks, safely sealed up, to allow the contents to dry out and perhaps even cook down a bit.

They are safe to discard when the contents are completely dead and rotted or dehydrated. The bags may also be less heavy after such a waiting period, which makes getting them to the curb or roadside, or into a truck, a bit easier. There may be a weight limit, such as 50 pounds, so bear that in mind as well.

Some municipalities compost yard waste; others incinerate such debris. Do not mix in other items, therefore, especially non-biodegradable trash. Some places charge to haul your bags away or to accept such materials at a transfer station. Therefore, it behooves you to dry out and condense the materials, and to use the right type of bag.

COMPOST Here is a method that fails or is never even considered. Disposing pest plants in a compost pile simply helps them find a fertile growing substrate, utterly defeating the purpose, not to mention rendering your compost unusable when plant parts root or weed seeds germinate. Nevertheless, it can be done.

One option is if you have used another (nontoxic) method that you are certain has killed the torn-up plants, you can add them to a hot, "active" compost pile along with the things you usually add and wait for them to break down along with everything else.

Another option is to create a separate compost pile. For the contents to break down, it cannot be "weeds only"—you will need to do the same layering you employ in a regular compost pile. Intersperse the layers of weeds with "brown" or carbon-rich materials such as straw.

The Sin Bin

A local community garden has a "sin bin" near the communal shed. It is a large barrel only half-filled with water, and members are encouraged to deposit pulled weeds within. The pest plants drown and rot, smelling ripe in the process. Eventually the contents break down and, later, dry out. The remains, now considerably reduced in bulk, are buried.

Warning: Composting weeds and invasives that have or might have ripe seeds is never a good idea. Some can germinate quickly, others can bide their time, managing to remain viable even when lodged in inhospitable conditions. A hot compost-pile temperature of 135°F to 150°F for about six to eight weeks is the minimum needed to kill most weed seeds, and that, of course, is not easily attained or sustained, even when you cover the pile.

BURY Another way to dispose of unwanted pest plants and their pieces is to dig a hole and bury them. Such a pit is best located in an out-of-the-way spot in the yard where it will not be tampered with and nobody will be tempted to plant over it.

Yes, a pit. A shallow grave will not do. To be extra-cautious, dig down at least 3 feet. Use a large plastic trash bag or those biodegradable autumn-leaf bags to line the hole, then pitch the leavings inside that and when full, seal it closed and cover over the pit with a board, flagstones, or old tires. This weights it down and marks the spot. Over time, the debris will rot and break down, losing volume, at which point you could add another load.

BURN Where safe and legal (get a permit if required), you can get rid of a significant pile of weeds or brush from invasive trees and shrubs, including root systems, by burning. (Larger pieces are best chopped up into smaller pieces, if possible.) Make a bonfire and burn until everything is completely incinerated, then make sure to douse the embers thoroughly. Stomp on them, douse them thoroughly, dump dirt or sand on the site.

This method is fast and thorough. Just pick an appropriate and safe spot and be very careful. Basic safety tips include: do it away from buildings and overhanging vegetation; do it away from anything flammable (an open area of dirt or sand is best); keep the blaze small; keep several buckets of water and/or a primed hose close at hand; do not use anything flammable to kick off the fire (such as barbeque starter or gas), though a bit of shredded newspaper as kindling is permissible.

Not all plants should be burned, however. Never burn poison ivy or poison oak, which release volatile oils that are harmful if breathed.

BANISH Some yards have a "back forty" or uncultivated area to the back of the property or behind a garage. If you have no particular plans for this area and will not be creating an eyesore visible from, or smell-able from, your house, garden, or the street, you could make a debris pile and leave it there. Assuming the stalks, branches, and yanked-out root systems are *no longer alive*, such a pile will slump and break down over time. Maybe a long time.

A precaution you might take is to spread the area first with an old tarp, plastic, or base of sand or gravel, then dump the refuse. When you transport material to the pile, drag it atop a tarp or in a large wheelbarrow to avoid any chance of spilling on the way over there.

Mercenary Territory: Hiring Help in Removing Unwanted Plants

If you have waited too long and a plant has spread or invaded a big or difficult-to-work-in area, or if the eradication project is daunting to you in any way, do not give up and do not delay. Hire help. Possible types of helpers include a lawn service, a landscape contractor, or even just some strong repairperson with heavy-duty tools. Ask for references at your local garden center or nursery or contact your nearest Cooperative Extension agent for advice and leads.

Call and describe the problem. Does the contractor sound confident and knowledgeable? Do they have references you can check, or similar projects you can view? Do they have or need some sort of insurance for this work?

Discuss timing. Should the contractor come in early spring when the plants are just emerging? Should they act in mid- or late summer before a plant forms fruits, berries, or seeds? How long will the project take? Do they anticipate more than one visit?

Have the contractor over to view and walk around the afflicted area. Confirm the plant's identity and the scope of the project.

Get a signed contract and estimate.

If chemical herbicides will be deployed, discuss their risks to people (them, you and your family, your neighbors), pets, insects/birds/bees, the soil, and the water table. Again, the contractor should sound knowledgeable and confident. He or she should also be certified to use such products.

Decide on a safe and legal plan for disposing of the removed and dead plant materials.

Discuss what to do should the plant manage to return. Some of these plants are very tenacious and the contractor justifiably may be unable to guarantee 100 percent success.

3
Water and Bog Plants

Water-loving plants can be both beauties and beasts. Gardeners who work to landscape naturally damp areas of their yard or to install a full-blown, self-contained (enclosed) water-garden display sometimes contend with invasive plants. Certain plants suited for such projects are aggressive spreaders simply by never being denied their most basic need: ample moisture. They tend to bloom, and expand, with gusto.

Once the show is in place, or established over several years, such displays become low-maintenance in the sense that you will not have to do more planting or fuss with extra fertilizing. Instead, you will find yourself tearing out excess plants. Add those unwanted plants and bits to a hot, active compost pile or bag them up and send them away with your municipal trash collection. Do not be careless or sloppy with these discards, lest they invade neighboring properties or public waterways or ponds.

A final caution: if any of these plants are problematic for you, undertake eradication by herbicide with care. Some products are expressly labeled "not for use near water."

Butomus umbellatus

Flowering rush

A slender, erect rushlike plant growing 2 to 3 feet tall. Leaves emerge with a purplish tinge but mature green, developing sharp edges and narrowing to a point. Umbels of red-centered, rosy pink flowers appear on their own stalks amid the foliage in mid- through late summer.

PROBLEM

Flowering rush can become aggressive in damp ground. It most likely will be killed in areas where the average winter low temperature is -20°F.

REPRODUCTION

Seeds, if they fall in hospitable ground such as damp ground or mud. Also via spreading rhizomes.

ORIGIN

Native to Europe and Asia, probably imported as an ornamental.

NOTES

Is a pretty, late-blooming "marginal" for home water gardens and damp borders, but best confined to a container. The starchy rhizome is edible and, when dried and powdered like flour, has been used in baking in northern Eurasia.

NONINVASIVE ALTERNATIVES

Some semidwarf or dwarf hybrid cannas offer the same or a better splash of late-summer color in a home water or bog garden.

LESS-TOXIC CONTROLS

Pull out unwanted plants while they are still young. Can be successfully confined to a pot.

CHEMICAL CONTROLS

None recommended as spraying with herbicides in areas of standing or running water is risky to ecosystems and the water table.

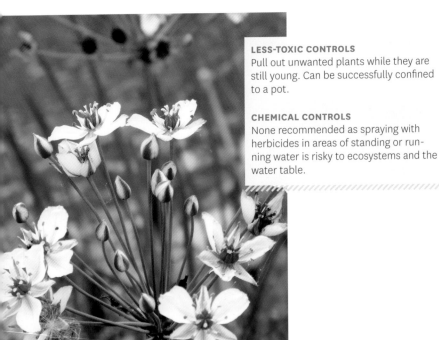

Cabomba caroliniana

Fanwort, Carolina fanwort, Green cabomba, Fish grass, Washington grass

This spreading, floating plant has been known to grow 2 inches per day. It has lacy-textured foliage that whorls into fans, reddish brown to bright green, mostly submerged but with some stems floating on the water surface. In summer, it produces plentiful tiny white flowers less than ½ inch in diameter.

PROBLEM
In standing or slow-running water, escaped plants, including those from home water gardens or aquariums, multiply quickly.

REPRODUCTION
Although it produces seed, the plant mainly reproduces quite easily and prolifically via stem and root bits.

ORIGIN
Hails from South America's Amazon River basin area.

NOTES
Home water gardeners notice that their fish like to spawn among the leaves of this plant (even as they nibble on it a bit), and when the fry appear, they can hide under its shelter.

NONINVASIVE ALTERNATIVES
Water-garden suppliers might be able to recommend other similar attractive floating plants for home displays in your area.

LESS-TOXIC CONTROLS
Scoop excessive plants out of unwanted water and discard far from water. If practical, drain or divert water away from the problem area.

CHEMICAL CONTROLS
None recommended.

Caltha palustris

Marsh marigold, Kingcup, Cowslip

This sunny-flowered buttercup relative does well in sunny to partly shady spots with moist, rich ground. The prolific blooms really brighten up springtime with their exuberant display. Each flower is 1 to 1½ inches across and has between 5 and 9 sepals (petal-like parts). A mounding habit 12 to 18 inches high by 9 to 12 inches wide and fleshy, heart-shaped, glossy leaves make for a handsome profile. The plants go dormant as summer advances, when soil begins to try out.

PROBLEM

Given opportunity and time, marsh marigold will dominate a damp-soil area and spread to the exclusion of other plants.

REPRODUCTION

Via underground runners. Can generate new plants from root pieces.

ORIGIN

Native to North America, Europe, and northern Asia.

NOTES

Reportedly deer-resistant, as the leaves are not palatable and in large quantities are poisonous. That said, reportedly Native Americans made a cough medicine from the leaves by boiling them repeatedly to remove toxins and then sweetening with maple syrup. The stems are hollow and grooved along one side. Fig buttercup (*Ficaria verna*), a wet-loving wild plant that resembles marsh marigold, has smaller flowers with up to a dozen petals. It, too, can spread widely and crowd out other plants in the same habitat.

NONINVASIVE ALTERNATIVES

Double-flowered cultivars may be found in the water-gardening trade under various names including 'Flore Pleno', 'Multiplex', and 'Monstrosa'; these are allegedly not as vigorous as the species, which also goes by the synonym 'Multiplex'.

LESS-TOXIC CONTROLS

Excess runners may be pinched or cut back, which controls spread as well as inspiring more blooms.

CHEMICAL CONTROLS

None recommended.

Colocasia esculenta

Elephant ears, Elephant's ear, Taro, Dasheen

This dramatic plant has big, heart-shaped leaves up to 3 feet across that may be marked with purple or cranberry red or have contrasting margins or veins. Tropical in origin and therefore cold-sensitive, it can be treated like a houseplant (in cooler climates, keep it indoors over the winter months). Mature size varies with the cultivar and growing conditions, but is generally between 2 and 6 feet tall and about half as wide.

REPRODUCTION
Grows from a starchy tuber/corm. Can generate new plants from pieces.

ORIGIN
Hails from Southeast Asia.

NOTES
The tuber has been called "the potato of the tropics." All plant parts are toxic when raw, however, due to the presence of calcium oxalate crystals, which can lead to kidney stones. Seek good advice on handling, cooking, and recipes before ingesting. A garden cultivar called 'Black Magic' is very popular because of its striking dark purple (nearly black) leaves; 'Illustris' has gorgeous blue-black leaves with thick green veining, and stays about 3 feet tall.

LESS-TOXIC CONTROLS
Yank out and dispose of unwanted plants, taking care to get the entire root system. To be on the safe side, gardeners should always grow these plants in large pots, not directly in the ground.

CHEMICAL CONTROLS
None recommended.

PROBLEM
In milder climates, elephant ears can escape and take over streamsides and other damp areas, crowding and shading out native vegetation.

NONINVASIVE ALTERNATIVES
There is no real substitute for this plant; if you must have it or one of its cultivars, and don't want the plant to be invasive, grow it in a pot and yank out and dispose of any unwanted seedlings. Remember, cold winters outdoors will kill elephant ears.

Egeria densa

Waterweed, Brazilian waterweed, Brazilian elodea, Anacharis

Synonym *Anacharis densa*

This is one of a class of water-garden and aquarium plants some nurseries call "submerged grasses." It is not much to look at, just whorls of small, rough-textured leaves on long, trailing stems, but it has an important role to play: it produces oxygen underwater by day, helping to keep your water garden and fish healthy. Stems can easily reach 6 feet long. The whorled leaves are ½ to 1 inch long and no more than ¼ inch wide.

PROBLEM

Escaped waterweed thrives in shallow waterways, where it forms dense mats, crowding out native vegetation and affecting boat traffic, water intakes, and fish migration.

REPRODUCTION

Readily spreads vegetatively. Stem and rhizome fragments root easily. Seeds are rare, as are flowers, because male and female plants seldom occur in the same location.

ORIGIN

South America, particularly Brazil.

NOTES

Popular in home aquariums. Evidently, it secretes antibiotic substances that help prevent blue-green algae, though it is equally capable of outcompeting algae by sheer biomass.

NONINVASIVE ALTERNATIVES

None. If you choose to add this plant to your home water garden—provided it is legally for sale in your state—be careful that it never escapes its allotted boundaries.

LESS-TOXIC CONTROLS

Grow plants in pots lowered into place in your display, rather than letting them freely root in the muck at the bottom. Yank out unwanted and excess plants and discard them on a compost pile or dig them into your garden soil as extra organic matter.

CHEMICAL CONTROLS

None recommended for home gardeners.

Eichhornia crassipes

Water hyacinth

This plant's glossy green leaves and spikes of lovely lavender or purple, occasionally white, flowers have been likened to "floating orchids." They look undeniably pretty among waterlilies of compatible hues and contribute to water-surface coverage, important in a home water garden where you want to minimize algae. The spongy stems are inflated, enabling the plants to float, while feathery roots trail below. Individual plants are between 6 and 12 inches high and wide.

PROBLEM
Unchecked in the right wet environment, this plant becomes a rampant pest that is difficult to eradicate. Many states, particularly in milder climates, have banned its propagation and sale.

REPRODUCTION
Offsets are produced on runners—rapidly and prolifically.

ORIGIN
Subtropical and tropical America.

NOTES
The roots take nutrients out of pond water so efficiently that some municipalities have used this plant to assist in removing pollutants at water-treatment facilities.

NONINVASIVE ALTERNATIVES
Numerous other floating plants are suitable for home water gardens. Check with your local water-garden nursery for those that are allowed/not banned in your state. If you just want purple blooms in your display, consider one of the beautiful, moisture-loving cultivated varieties of Japanese iris.

LESS-TOXIC CONTROLS
Yank out and safely discard unwanted plants in a hot compost pile, dig into your garden soil as organic matter, or seal in your household garbage.

CHEMICAL CONTROLS
None recommended.

Houttuynia cordata 'Chameleon'

Chameleon plant

This rambling groundcover is suitable for part-sun and shady spots and is valued for its heart-shaped green leaves, which are liberally splashed with cream to yellow and pink to red, no two alike. Flowers, if they appear, are only about ½ to 1 inch across and consist of a prominent little white spike and small white bracts ("petals"). Mature plants are 6 to 12 inches tall, with a spreading habit.

PROBLEM

This plant loves moist soil and greedily spreads far and wide in such a setting. It can also grow rampantly in average, fertile soil.

REPRODUCTION

Via runners that can root at nodes.

ORIGIN

Native to Japan, Korea, and Southeast Asia.

NOTES

This plant can grow submerged in several inches of water, which makes it a charming candidate for a "kettle garden" or other potted display, solo or as part of a larger water garden. In addition to the ubiquitous 'Chameleon', some nurseries offer 'Tricolor', 'Variegata', and 'Court Jester', but these all look very much the same.

NONINVASIVE ALTERNATIVES

Pulmonaria species and cultivars also do well in moist semi- to full shade, have handsome dappled and speckled foliage, and are much better-behaved.

LESS-TOXIC CONTROLS

Yank out and discard unwanted plants. Alternatively, work to change the problem area by letting in more sun (remove overhanging plants or branches) and draining or diverting away moisture (drier ground tends to slow it down).

CHEMICAL CONTROLS

A pesky patch could be eradicated with glyphosate, but only as a last resort and if there are no desired plants in range of the chemical.

Iris pseudacorus

Yellow flag iris

This moisture-loving iris has characteristic, handsome straplike foliage in clumps 3 feet tall and 2 to 3 feet wide. Plentiful bright yellow blooms of around 4 to 5 inches across start in spring and continue on and off through the summer months. Produces oblong, 2-inch seedpods.

PROBLEM
In damp to outright wet ground, this iris spreads aggressively, forming ever-larger and imposing clumps as well as self-sowing, to the exclusion of other plants.

REPRODUCTION
Seeds sow easily in damp soil. Rhizome pieces may also generate new plants. Established plants increase their rhizomes and topgrowth with each passing year.

ORIGIN
A European import that escaped from gardens. Also native to western Asia and North Africa.

NOTES
Pollinated by bees and long-tongued flies. Glycosides in the foliage render the plants unappealing to deer and other nibbling wildlife. Because the plants are able to take up metals from wastewater, they have been used for sewage treatment.

NONINVASIVE ALTERNATIVES
Native *Iris* species are worth considering, especially blue flag (*I. virginica*). You might also look into some yellow cultivated varieties that may or may not have this plant in their background. Two examples are 'Golden Queen' and 'Roy Davidson', neither of which produces viable seed.

LESS-TOXIC CONTROLS
Yank out by rhizomes and roots, and/or try to drain or dry out the afflicted area. Larger patches can be cut back or mowed down, the earlier in the season the better.

CHEMICAL CONTROLS
The leaves of actively growing plants can be sprayed or wiped with glyphosate.

Lysimachia nummularia

Creeping Jenny, Creeping Jennie, Moneywort

The coin-shaped, dark green leaves are small and float on a water garden's surface, wending their way among blooming waterlilies and forming a skirt at the base of vertical growers. When their numerous, little yellow, cup-shaped (¾ inch) flowers appear in early summer, rising a bit above the leaves, the scene sparkles. This plant is also sometimes grown as groundcover. Only 1 or 2 inches high, it spreads to 3 feet.

NOTES
Because of its trailing habit, it is a fine choice for containers, window-boxes, and hanging baskets, provided it is given enough moisture. It has also been suggested as a lawn substitute in partially shady yards, as it can tolerate less sun and some foot traffic.

NONINVASIVE ALTERNATIVES
A yellow-leaved cultivar called 'Aurea' is less vigorous than the species.

LESS-TOXIC CONTROLS
In a water garden, yank out and safely dispose of unwanted plants. To rein in an out-of-control groundcover, do not just tear out and discard unwanted stems; take steps to drain or dry out the growing area.

PROBLEM
Creeping Jenny can become too aggressive and thick in a water garden as well as in moist or boggy sites in a yard.

REPRODUCTION
Via seeds, roots, and stem and stem pieces.

ORIGIN
Native to Europe.

CHEMICAL CONTROLS
Glyphosate, deployed with care during the growing season, will kill an unwanted patch.

Myriophyllum aquaticum

Parrot's feather

Bright green, unbranched stems are lined with delicate-looking feathery whorls of leaves, each leaf up to 3 inches in diameter. This vigorous plant pokes its head out and even trails over a display's edges or a container's rim, depending on how you grow it. The stems are 6 to 24 inches long, with a spreading habit. Male and female plants are separate. The female flowers are tiny and yellow.

PROBLEM
The fast, vigorous growth creates a dense mat on the surface of some water displays, crowding out other aquatic plants.

REPRODUCTION
By stem and rhizome fragments. Male plants are rarely seen, so seed is seldom produced.

ORIGIN
Hails from South America, the Amazon River basin.

NOTES
Underwater leaves are lighter green and softer; once the plant breaches the surface, leaves are darker and stiffer. Parrot's feather is now banned in many states. If by chance it is legal in your state, exercise caution. Related plants *Myriophyllum heterophyllum* (two-leaf or variable water milfoil) and *M. spicatum* (water milfoil) are just as exuberant and also banned in some areas—the same warnings apply.

NONINVASIVE ALTERNATIVES
A related plant, *Myriophyllum proserpinacoides*, is reputed to be more compact and manageable—if you can find a nursery or aquarium specialist that sells it.

LESS-TOXIC CONTROLS
Yank out unwanted and excess plants and discard them on a compost pile or dig them into your garden soil as extra organic matter.

CHEMICAL CONTROLS
None recommended for home gardeners. Triclopyr, 2,4-D, and glyphosate have been deployed on large, problematic wild populations, with mixed results.

Pistia stratiotes

Water lettuce, Water cabbage, Nile cabbage

The handsome, textured leaves of this floating water plant are soft, velvety, and shed droplets of water when splashed. Individual rosettes can attain 8 inches across and 4 inches high. Long, dangling roots trail underneath, tiny green flowers above. Can be sensitive to too much direct sunlight, yellowing or developing burnt-brown edges; the solution is to grow it in partial or part-day sun.

PROBLEM

Over time, water lettuce forms dense colonies that can clog a home water garden and, if escaped into a river, pond, or wetland, jam up an area to the exclusion of native plants.

REPRODUCTION

Although it may bloom and set seed, its main mode is vegetative, with individual rosettes producing offsets.

ORIGIN

Widely dispersed throughout tropical and subtropical waterways, but thought to have originated in North Africa.

NOTES

Banned in many states. However, it has some fans; treatment plants value it for its ability to clear polluted water, and home water gardeners appreciate the way it outcompetes algae in their displays.

NONINVASIVE ALTERNATIVES

Water-garden suppliers can recommend other similar attractive floating plants for home displays, among them water snowflake (*Nymphoides indica*) and water clover (*Marsilea mutica*), but you have to keep an eye on these

LESS-TOXIC CONTROLS

Rip out and safely discard unwanted plants.

CHEMICAL CONTROLS

The state of Florida, where it has become a real thug in some rivers and lakes, has deployed aquatic herbicides, but these are not recommended, nor indeed warranted, for home use.

/////////////////////////////////////

ones, too, making sure they never escape into wild or man-made/municipal waterways.

4

Annuals, Biennials, and Tropical Perennials

The technical definition of an annual is a plant that germinates from seed, bears flowers, then produces a new generation of seeds, all in one season. In other words, it moves quickly and although an individual plant has a short lifespan, it leaves behind offspring.

Anyone who has ever dealt with annual weeds knows this story all too well. The key to stopping or at least slowing down the spread of annual weeds is, of course, to thwart this cycle. Prevent seeds from germinating in the first place. One way to do this is to encourage inhospitable conditions by blocking sunlight, drying out the area, baking plants under a tarp or smothering them with mulch. Another tack is to mow or hoe down recently germinated plants while they are still quite small. If you knock off their first leaves, the roots will not survive.

Do not make the mistake of thinking winter's cold will kill off these annual pests. If your climate is mild, some annual weeds may deploy their "tender perennial" habits. Or, resilient seeds may sleep quietly under the snow and ice, waiting for warmer days to return so they can burst forth a new generation. Or, if a biennial, the first-year rosette will hang on and send up blooms the coming spring, with the aim of creating future generations before dying back. Future survival is always the name of this game.

Ambrosia artemisiifolia

Ragweed

A coarse and unmemorable-looking plant between 1 and 5 feet high, ragweed has hairy, branching stems, highly dissected "ragged" leaves about 4 inches long at the largest, and greenish flowerheads in clusters near the top. Technically these flowers are male; the female ones are inconspicuously tucked into small clusters at the leaf axils. The plant blooms from midsummer to midautumn, dispersing a bounty of yellow pollen. Cooler weather turns the stems and leaves reddish. The plant develops a fibrous root system.

PROBLEM
This wind-pollinated plant is the major culprit in hay fever, not the far showier goldenrod (*Solidago*), which blooms at the same time. If not arrested, a patch of ragweed will overtake any available open areas, including ones with poor soil.

REPRODUCTION
Seeds, which remain viable in the soil for several years.

ORIGIN
North America.

NOTES
Insects are not drawn to the drab flowers, which is why wind-pollination is its means of dispersal. Interestingly, the oil-rich seeds stay on the plants over the winter and are a food source for songbirds and upland game birds. The caterpillars of several moths also like ragweed and will dine on the leaves, stems, and seeds. Research has shown that ragweed has allelopathic properties that inhibit the growth and development of neighboring plants.

NONINVASIVE ALTERNATIVES
None.

LESS-TOXIC CONTROLS
Tear out young plants when spotted in early spring. Mow down larger patches before they can go to seed.

CHEMICAL CONTROLS
Glyphosate is effective.

Anagallis arvensis

Scarlet pimpernel, Red pimpernel

A sprawling, low-branching plant whose slender stems are lined with unstalked, ovate (egg-shaped), opposite, tiny leaves ¼ to 1¼ inches across. In summer they are joined by cute little ¼-inch starlike flowers, which adorn stalks that line the stems. These are usually orange to red (scarlet), but are sometimes white or even blue. Close inspection reveals they are five-lobed and have fringed edges. These open each morning and close in late afternoon. Plants get no taller than 4 to 12 inches.

LESS-TOXIC CONTROLS

Do not let the flowers go to seed. Tug out the plants as soon as you spot them and keep after them throughout the growing season, by hand or with a sharp hoe. If they have invaded a larger area, try smothering them.

CHEMICAL CONTROLS

None recommended.

PROBLEM

Though small, this weed can become a force to be reckoned with, spreading quickly in sandy and well-drained soil, including flowerbeds, open spots, and roadsides.

REPRODUCTION

Seeds.

ORIGIN

Introduced from Europe and Asia.

NOTES

In England, this wee weed has gained the nickname "poor man's weatherglass" because it closes its flowers when the weather becomes overcast or rain is threatening. The leaves contain a sap that is irritating to some people and can cause a rash.

NONINVASIVE ALTERNATIVES

An appealing and tough groundcover, *Portulaca* is an annual that also sports orange or red flowers. Its flowers are larger and the foliage is thinner.

Anthemis cotula

Mayweed, Wild chamomile, Stinking chamomile, Dog fennel

This low-growing, mound-forming plant has long, finely dissected fernlike leaves and small, ¾- to 1-inch white daisy flowers for most or all of the summer. It prefers full sun and well-drained soil, where it grows between 1 and 2 feet tall, with a thick, sprawling growth habit.

LESS-TOXIC CONTROLS

Hand-weeding or hoeing, best under-taken when plants are still small in early spring. Prevent this weed's establish-ment or return to a lawn by encouraging thick, healthy grass.

CHEMICAL CONTROLS

Glyphosate is effective in some settings but not recommended for use in lawns as you risk also killing the grass; use a broadleaf herbicide in a lawn if you must.

PROBLEM

A rampant grower and spreader, espe-cially in open or waste places, may-weed can insinuate itself into a lawn and is hard to eradicate.

REPRODUCTION

Seeds.

ORIGIN

Introduced from Europe.

NOTES

Although this plant resembles chamo-mile (*Chamaemelum nobile*), it has an unpleasant, acrid smell and the sap in the foliage causes blisters or skin rashes for some people. Related plants include pineapple weed (*Chamomilla suaveolens* or *Matricaria matricarioi-des*) and lesser swinecress (*Coronopus didymus*). The flowers are hermaph-roditic (have both male and female organs) and are self-pollinated and pollinated by flies and beetles.

NONINVASIVE ALTERNATIVES

Try true chamomile (*Chamaemelum nobile*) or feverfew (*Chrysanthemum parthenium*).

Arctium lappa

Burdock

This is a coarse, dramatic, big plant studded from midsummer onwards with lots of prickly pink to lavender flowerheads, each about ¾ inch across and wrapped in overlapping green bracts. The strong stalks support large basal leaves up to 20 inches long and progressively smaller leaves as they alternate up the stalk. The foliage is green on top and woolly below. The plant grows between 6 and 8 feet tall and forms a long, thick taproot.

PROBLEM
An aggressive colonizer of open spaces, burdock self-sows vigorously and forms dense colonies that exclude other plants.

REPRODUCTION
Via seeds often dispersed when the prickly heads (burrs) hitch a ride on animal fur or human clothing. The burrs are often dubbed "Nature's Velcro." The bracts enclosing the burrs end with curved hooks, which are attached to sheaths. The seeds are inside these sheaths. When the hooks are yanked in an attempt to dislodge, the sheaths open and release the many seeds.

ORIGIN
Europe and Asia.

NOTES
Butterflies and birds are attracted to the flowers. All plant parts have been employed throughout history for various medicinal and culinary uses. Medicinal uses include everything from treating acne and dandruff to relieving insect bites. The plant, especially the thick root, is rich in inulin, a form of edible starch, and the stalks are prepared like asparagus.

LESS-TOXIC CONTROLS
Preventing seed formation is key. Mow or cut down plants before the flowers ripen and go to seed. It may also be possible to dig out smaller plants by the roots.

CHEMICAL CONTROLS
Glyphosate and other herbicides will kill this plant.

NONINVASIVE ALTERNATIVES
Celeriac (*Apium graveolens* var. *rapaceum*) is an edible alternative. Purple-flowered globe thistle (*Echinops ritro*) is an ornamental alternative.

Artemisia annua

Sweet Annie, Mugwort

A bushy, graceful, almost fernlike herb reaching 1½ to 9 feet tall. Lance-shaped, toothed leaves are softly pungent when crushed. The inconspicuous greenish yellow flowerheads are only ¹⁄₁₆ inch in diameter and appear in late summer and fall.

PROBLEM

This weed takes over and thrives in neglected areas of poor, well-drained soil, including vacant lots and roadsides.

REPRODUCTION

Plentiful seeds are dropped when the flowers fade in late summer or early fall; since the flowers are so small and inconspicuous, this moment is easy to miss.

ORIGIN

Native to Europe as well as China, Russia, India, Korea, and Japan.

NOTES

Artemisinin, derived from both leaves and flowers, has been shown to kill malarial parasites and has been used in prevention and treatment.

NONINVASIVE ALTERNATIVES

Those who value gray- or silver-leaved plants in their flowerbeds or bouquets should instead plant dusty miller (*Senecio cineraria*) or one of the cultivated artemisias (*Artemisia ludoviciana* 'Silver King' is a fine choice).

LESS-TOXIC CONTROLS

Dig it up while it is still small, in spring; get all the roots. Do not let the plant go to seed in late summer. (Cut stems for bouquets.) For large infestations, mow in mid- to late summer.

CHEMICAL CONTROLS

Spray in late summer, before the flowers go to seed, with glyphosate.

Centaurea calcitrapa

Purple star thistle, Red star thistle

This thistle looks like the nasty weed that it is. It arises from a rosette of deeply lobed or divided leaves up to 10 inches long; higher leaves are smaller, not lobed, and may clasp the stems. New growth is covered in cobwebby hairs. Sharp spines occur on the rosette's middle as well as on and around the flower bracts and seedheads that follow. The reddish to pink flowerheads top the stiff stems from midsummer into fall. Plants are 1 to 4 feet tall and wide and develop deep taproots.

LESS-TOXIC CONTROLS
Pull out entire plants, making sure to get the taproot; the younger the plant, the easier this is. Mowing only encourages regrowth. Do not let plants go to seed. Once plants are removed, overplant the area so it cannot return.

CHEMICAL CONTROLS
Herbicides containing dicamba or 2,4-D have proven effective, particularly when used early in the growing season while the plants are still small.

PROBLEM
Purple star thistle takes over dry, open areas in mild climates.

REPRODUCTION
Seeds. In milder climates, this annual occasionally can be biennial or even a short-lived perennial.

ORIGIN
Asia, in the area between the Black and Caspian Seas. Evidently, it hitch-hiked into California in the late 1800s in seeds or hay.

NOTES
The species name refers to an ancient spiky weapon, the caltrop. When the plant invades rangelands, livestock avoid it not only because of the spikes but also because of its bitter taste.

NONINVASIVE ALTERNATIVES
The pretty, long-blooming, perennial cornflower, *Centaurea montana,* is not aggressive.

Centaurea cyanus

Bachelor's button, Cornflower

This easygoing, casual-looking plant is not particular about soil or water. Its most popular use is as an ingredient in a wildflower mix. It comes in various shades of blue and purple as well as pink and white. The little flowers, up to 2 inches across, tolerate autumn frost; the petals are slow to shatter and usually just fade away. Mature plants are 1 to 3 feet high and 4 to 8 inches wide.

LESS-TOXIC CONTROLS
Pull, cut, or mow a patch in late summer or early fall, as blooms begin to flag but before they go to seed.

CHEMICAL CONTROLS
None recommended.

PROBLEM
Escaped from cultivation, this plant self-sows rather too enthusiastically in sunny spots, including empty lots and waste places, fields, meadows, and roadsides. It is especially troublesome in parts of the Pacific Northwest.

REPRODUCTION
Seeds.

ORIGIN
Europe. Introduced as a garden plant.

NOTES
Its ability to hold its bloom color and petals well, and its wiry stems, make it a favorite for bouquets. Wreath makers and dried-flower arrangers also like these flowers.

NONINVASIVE ALTERNATIVES
Try its cousin, perennial cornflower (*Centaurea montana*), which is a more substantial plant and has larger blooms. Another nice, well-mannered source of blue flowers is the various (perennial) garden campanulas, such as the mound-forming *Campanula carpatica* 'Blue Clips' or the taller *C. persicifolia* 'Telham Beauty'.

Centaurea diffusa
Diffuse knapweed, White knapweed, Tumble knapweed

A wiry-stemmed, branching wildflower 1 to 4 feet tall. The numerous flowers are white to pink with spine-tipped bracts; they bleach out as they age. Leaves are deeply cleft.

ORIGIN
Native to Asia Minor, the Balkans, Ukraine, and southern Russia.

NOTES
A study at the University of Massachusetts Amherst showed that phytotoxins in the plant actually facilitated its nutrient uptake, particularly iron, which is otherwise in short supply in the dryish, alkaline soils this plant tends to colonize.

PROBLEM
A fast and aggressive colonizer, this knapweed has been a problem in farmlands, where it reduces yields and mixes with good crops, particularly alfalfa, and in ranches, where it decreases grazing areas and can damage the mouths and digestive tracts of livestock. When present in rural and suburban sites, it is hard to eradicate due to the numbers and persistence of seeds.

REPRODUCTION
Via seeds numbering 18,000 per plant and dispersed mainly by wind but also by animals or water. Can also regenerate from root fragments.

NONINVASIVE ALTERNATIVES
There really are no "nice knapweeds," but if you like the profile and color range, try the harmless annual globe amaranth (*Gomphrena globosa*).

LESS-TOXIC CONTROLS
Never let these plants go to seed. Dig them out or mow them down as early in the season as possible. Some people have used controlled burns. Whatever method you use, be advised that you must then fill the area with other plants to discourage a resurgence.

CHEMICAL CONTROLS
Spray before the plants go to seed with 2,4-D, dicamba, or glyphosate.

Euphorbia maculata

Spotted spurge, Eye-bright, Nodding spurge, Stubble spurge, Slobber-weed, Prostrate spurge

Synonym *Chamaesyce maculata*
A fast-growing, sprawling, mat-forming plant with tiny leaves on long, reddish stems. Tiny white flowers appear in midsummer. Plant reaches 16 inches in diameter. Prefers full sun and tolerates many soils.

PROBLEM
Spotted spurge is able to insinuate itself into flower gardens and sunny yards as well as cracks in patios, sidewalks, and rock walls; it is an expert at invading bark mulch. It also multiplies in dry, gravelly soil as found in meadows, pastures, empty lots, and roadsides. The plant is dispersed from Massachusetts south to Florida, and west to North Dakota and south to Mexico.

REPRODUCTION
Produces many seeds.

ORIGIN
North America.

NOTES
Because this plant grows so fast and produces tons of seeds quickly, act early and often to rein it in. Yes, like its nonweedy, better-looking euphorbia relatives, the stems do bleed a milky sap when snapped.

NONINVASIVE ALTERNATIVES
Creeping thyme (*Thymus serpyllum*) is a much better-behaved, sprawling plant for walkways and walls, with the added benefits of purple flowers and pleasant fragrance.

LESS-TOXIC CONTROLS
In spring, tear out or hoe down emerging seedlings. Yank out established plants at any time; fortunately, the trailing stems do not root along their nodes like some other weeds. In late summer, yank out or mow plants down before they go to seed. Dispose of unwanted plants properly; do not add them to a compost pile, which will not be hot enough to kill any seeds.

CHEMICAL CONTROLS
None recommended.

Impatiens glandulifera

Jewelweed, Himalayan balsam, Policeman's helmet

A larger, more sprawling plant than the common orange-flowered jewel-weed. Sports the signature succulent stems (sometimes red-tinged), lance-shaped leaves, and plump, pointy-ended seedpods that explode when ripe and brushed against or pinched. It has been cultivated in Europe for its pretty pink flowers, which appear in mid- to late summer and are about 1 inch tall and half as wide on plants between 3 and 6 feet tall.

PROBLEM
This jewelweed is an aggressive spreader, particularly in damp settings, and can wear out its welcome in a garden and escape into the wild.

REPRODUCTION
The flowers produce lots of nectar, attract many pollinators, and thus a bounty of ripe seedpods, which can disperse their seeds up to 20 feet away.

ORIGIN
Native to the Himalayas.

NOTES
Already out of favor in Europe due to its rampant ways. In England, some local wildlife trusts organize "balsam bashing" events to help control its spread. Pods, seeds, stems, and young leaves are all safe to eat and may be included in salads or stir-fries.

NONINVASIVE ALTERNATIVES
The native jewelweed, *Impatiens capensis*, may be less invasive in some settings. A pink-flowered perennial wildflower, obedient plant (*Physostegia virginiana*), is a nice way to fill up a damp-soil area with similar color.

LESS-TOXIC CONTROLS
Yank the plants out while they are still flowering and before seedpods can form. Flood the growing area, which seems to stifle germination.

CHEMICAL CONTROLS
None recommended.

Lamium amplexicaule

Henbit, Dead nettle

Henbit has square stems and pink to purplish flowers in bloom for the spring and repeating in the summer months. The leaves are rounded and scalloped; those lower on the stem are stalked, while upper ones half-clasp the stem. Thrives in cool, moist spots. Some plants sprawl and reach only about 2 inches high; others are more erect and grow 4 to 12 inches.

PROBLEM
Henbit likes rich garden and field soils, and spreads rapidly during the cooler days of spring and fall.

REPRODUCTION
Seedpods are small nutlets laden with tiny granular seeds. Note that in mild climates it may bloom in winter and go to seed by spring; elsewhere, it is one of the earliest weeds to flower in spring.

ORIGIN
Introduced from Europe and western Asia.

NOTES
Where common, henbit is an important nectar and pollen plant for honeybees, helping to start the spring buildup.

NONINVASIVE ALTERNATIVES
Cousins such as the cultivars of spotted henbit (*Lamium maculatum*) give you a good groundcover, are perennial, and are much more handsome.

LESS-TOXIC CONTROLS
Yank out young plants before they can go to seed. Larger populations may be controlled with hoeing or tilling under, again, while the plants are still small. If henbit is invading your lawn, sow more grass seed or patch bare spots to get denser growth and thus crowd it out.

CHEMICAL CONTROLS
A selective postemergent herbicide can be deployed; use it when henbit is actively growing but not yet gone to seed and follow application and interval directions with care.

Lantana camara

Lantana, Ham-and-eggs, Spanish flag

The distinctive flowers are actually flower clusters, usually about 1 inch across, in cheery shades of pink, yellow, white, and/or orange, emerging from the leaf axils. They are followed by small seed-filled berries. The leaves are rough-textured, oval and teethed, and appear along the square stems in pairs. Sometimes the stems have small prickles. Shrubby growth typically reaches between 6 to 8 feet high and wide.

PROBLEM
Not only do the plants grow vigorously and densely, but also their stems release allelochemicals into the soil that discourage other plants. In addition, the plants hybridize with wild populations, altering their gene pool.

REPRODUCTION
Shoots root easily, and birds spread the seed, which is not poisonous to them.

ORIGIN
Imported from Central and South America, where it is a perennial ornamental shrub. In North America, winters tend to kill the plants, rendering them annuals.

NOTES
Butterflies and bees are drawn to the flowers. Snapped stems or bruised leaves emit a strong, sharp smell, which is unpleasant to many noses. The foliage is harmful or even poisonous to pets and livestock. Lantana is a major problem in Hawaii, where the mild climate gives it free rein.

LESS-TOXIC CONTROLS
Yank or dig out unwanted plants while they are still small; protect your hands with gloves.

CHEMICAL CONTROLS
Treat actively growing plants with glyphosate.

NONINVASIVE ALTERNATIVES
Newer hybrids are said to be sterile, notably 'Dallas Red', 'Irene', 'Miss Huff', 'Mozelle', and 'New Gold'.

Melilotus albus

Sweet clover, White sweet clover, Honey clover

This common, lanky weed has a misleadingly delicate look, with slender, wispy, tapering clusters of tiny white flowers; some spikes are as much as 8 inches long. The leaves, as is so characteristic of the pea family, consist of three-part pinnately divided leaflets; close inspection reveals that they have toothed edges. The plant, when bruised or crushed, radiates a fresh, appealing aroma of new-mown hay. It is between 3 and 8 feet tall and develops an extensive, long taproot.

PROBLEM

A fast and successful colonizer, this plant can fill in open areas, roadsides, and fields to the exclusion of other plants.

REPRODUCTION

Seeds, which float and thus can be water-dispersed.

ORIGIN

Introduced from Eurasia.

NOTES

Dried clippings, with or without flower spikes, gain a strong, more vanillalike scent, and thus they have been used in perfumes and sachets as well as in cooking. Poultices made from fresh bits have been used for centuries to ease topical inflammations. The nectar is popular with bees and thus this plant is prized by beekeepers. Along with its close relative, yellow sweet clover (*Melilotus officinalis*), this plant has been put to use in pastures as a forage crop as well as to enrich the soil with nitrogen.

NONINVASIVE ALTERNATIVES

For nonweedy white spires, try Culver's root (*Veronicastrum virginicum*), white wild indigo (*Baptisia leucantha*), or even white lupine (*Lupinus albus*).

LESS-TOXIC CONTROLS

Yank out or hoe out scattered plants. Large patches may be repeatedly mowed down before they can go to seed, the remains dug into the soil, and then the area overplanted.

CHEMICAL CONTROLS

None recommended.

Mirabilis jalapa

Four-o-clock, Marvel of Peru

Sports colorful, distinctive trumpet-shaped 2-inch flowers with five lobes ("petals") in a flared, flattened configuration. Individual flowers open in late afternoon and die by the following morning, hence the common name four-o-clock. Colors range from red and magenta to pink, yellow, and white, with markings of more than one color on individual blooms and with flowers of different colors on the same plant. The flowers waft a light, sweet scent. Plant habit is low and bushy, about 2 feet high and wide, with ovate leaves.

PROBLEM

Plants self-sow enthusiastically, and soon you have many more than you bargained for.

REPRODUCTION

Via black, ⅜-inch-long, oblong, and ridged seeds.

ORIGIN

Native to Mexico. Introduced to the United States as an ornamental during the 1800s.

NOTES

Popular with hummingbirds and moths. "Mirabilis" means "wonderful," though not everyone would agree. Seeds and other plant parts are toxic. Technically a tender perennial in semitropical areas; dies back in most North American winters and thus is considered an annual.

NONINVASIVE ALTERNATIVES

Nasturtiums (*Tropaeolum* spp.) are just as colorful and do not become pests.

LESS-TOXIC CONTROLS

Pinch off flowers just as they start to fade (or pick bouquets) so there is no chance they can go to seed. Pick out volunteer seedlings early, while they are still small, as it is harder to dig out the tuberous roots of established plants.

CHEMICAL CONTROLS

None recommended.

Onopordum acanthium

Scotch thistle, Cotton thistle

This robust biennial thistle begins by forming a large, spiny-leaved rosette. The entire second-year plant is whitish with cottony down. Flowerheads are lavender or dark pink, with cottony sepal-like bracts below that end in sharp, spreading yellow spines. The stem and woolly leaves are also armed with sharp spines. The plant is 2 to 4 feet high and half as wide, and forms a deep taproot.

PROBLEM

It spreads rapidly and forms dense stands. It is difficult to eradicate due not only to its prickly nature, but also to its prolific seed production and deep, drought-resistant roots.

REPRODUCTION

Seeds, which are dispersed by wind, water, animals, and humans. Research suggests that seeds remain viable for up to 20 years. However, they need light to germinate, so only develop when close to the soil surface.

ORIGIN

From Europe and western Asia. Introduced as an ornamental plant.

NOTES

This thistle is the national emblem of Scotland. Evidently, invading Vikings cried out in pain as they bushwhacked through stands of thistle, thus alerting the Scots they were trying to surprise and allowing them to fight back. The flowerheads were eaten like artichokes.

NONINVASIVE ALTERNATIVES

Friendly, noninvasive, drought-tolerant purple flowers abound, notably gayfeather (*Liatris spicata*). Alternatively, if you want a tough, dramatic plant that is also edible, grow your own artichokes (*Cynara cardunculus* Scolymus Group).

LESS-TOXIC CONTROLS

Never let this plant go to seed. Dig out rosettes as soon as you spot them. Mow down established stands well before the flowers can go to seed.

CHEMICAL CONTROLS

Many herbicides are effective, but be sure to treat at the rosette stage—late fall or early spring.

Stellaria media

Chickweed, Starweed

A straggly, sprawling, branching plant adorned with tiny white starlike flowers in the axils of the upper leaves. The little leaves are oval, stalked, and succulent. Stems can reach up to 2 feet long; plants may stay as low as 2 to 4 inches and rise up to around 15 inches. They grow fastest in cool, damp conditions.

PROBLEM
Its amazing vigor and tenacity allow it to spread far and wide in sunny lawns and gardens. Unlike many other weeds, it loves fertile soil.

REPRODUCTION
By seeds as well as by creeping stems that root at the nodes.

ORIGIN
Introduced from Europe.

NOTES
Has enjoyed a modest reputation in its native Europe over the centuries as a medicinal plant, particularly for a soothing ointment made from steeping the leaves, though a simple poultice of fresh leaves applied to infections or abscesses reportedly also provides relief.

NONINVASIVE ALTERNATIVES
If you are seeking a medicinal herb that is useful for soothing cuts and abrasions, try aloe or comfrey (*Symphytum officinale*).

LESS-TOXIC CONTROLS
Luckily, this pest is shallow-rooted. Diligent hand-weeding, starting early in the season before flowers, and consequently seeds, can form, can control it. Smothering it with mulch may also work. In new lawns, rake it down and mow low, then encourage thick grass growth, which will eventually outcompete chickweed.

CHEMICAL CONTROLS
An herbicide assault on this plant is not recommended in home gardens because of the risk to the desirable plants or lawn grasses that share the same area. If a large, open spot is infested, maybe.

Tradescantia fluminensis and *T. zebrina*

Wandering Jew

The dark green and light green stripes are easily recognized in *Tradescantia zebrina*; in other species, the foliage is plain green or has cream stripes; leaf undersides may be purple. Trailing stems bear three-petaled flowers at their ends; these may be white or purple. Black seed capsules may follow them. An unfettered plant can reach 2 to 3 feet long and wide.

PROBLEM

An easy and handsome houseplant for some, it may also be grown outdoors in mild climates as a groundcover—which is where it can become a pest, particularly if it escapes into wild or uncultivated corners, lots, or areas and starts crowding out native or desirable vegetation.

REPRODUCTION

Trailing stems root at the nodes. Seeds also produce new generations.

ORIGIN

Native to the tropical forests of Brazil or Mexico, depending on the species. Behaves as a perennial in those climates and as a houseplant. Introduced to North America as a houseplant.

NOTES

In some people, handling the plants causes an irritating skin rash. Roots easily from cuttings.

NONINVASIVE ALTERNATIVES

For a weed-excluding groundcover, landscape thickly with a better-behaved plant such as mondo grass (*Ophiopogon japonicus*) or liriope (*Liriope* spp.).

LESS-TOXIC CONTROLS

Yank or rake out unwanted plants. In larger infestations, mow the area low and then cover with a thick mulch or plastic sheeting to smother the remains.

CHEMICAL CONTROLS

In severe infestations, cut-down plants can be killed with an herbicide containing triclopyr.

5

Herbaceous Perennials

A wag once described a perennial as "a plant that, had it lived, would've bloomed again." In the wide world of perennial weeds, you cannot only bet it will live, but be assured that it will bloom again. These characters are truly tenacious and include groundcovers-from-hell as well as nasty things that grow from bulbs, corms, or rhizomes.

Part of the reason for the continued success of perennials is that many of them have more than one strategy for survival. Deep roots resist drought and seek nourishment far below; if you do not or cannot extract them, the plant will be able to regenerate. Flowers produce seeds that fall nearby or travel by wind, water, or host (animal, bird, human) to new homes. Creeping roots generate new plants along their lengths ("creeping stolons, rooting at nodes") or to poke up somewhere nearby. Others simply add to their bulk with each passing season—a bigger root system, more stalks and flowers above. Quite a few perennial weeds use more than one method to keep going year after year.

Faced with this arsenal, the home gardener has every right to feel daunted. The enemy is wily, adaptable, and resourceful. However, as any general will tell you, knowledge is power. Find a vulnerability and attack, and the career of herbaceous perennials/weeds in your yard can end.

Achillea millefolium

Yarrow, Milfoil

A clump-forming perennial plant 3 to 4 feet tall and about half as wide. Ferny, olive-green, lightly fragrant foliage is topped in summer with plentiful flat blooms up to 5 inches across, usually white or a shade of yellow or pink.

PROBLEM
Yarrow thrives in well-drained soil and spreads easily over the years. It can become rampant in open, disturbed-soil or meadow areas if not watched and arrested.

REPRODUCTION
Seeds are dispersed in the fall as the flowerheads dry out. Also spreads by rootstocks/creeping runners.

ORIGIN
Europe and Asia.

NOTES
Attractive to bees and butterflies; deer-resistant. The genus name refers to the Greek warrior Achilles, who allegedly brought the plant with his army to the battle against Troy. Long used as a styptic (to stop bleeding from cuts and wounds). Additionally, a tea made from the leaves has been used to treat everything from the common cold to baldness.

NONINVASIVE ALTERNATIVES
Cultivated varieties are better behaved and appropriate in low-maintenance, rock, and wildflower gardens and are also nice in bouquets, fresh or dried. Recommended: 'Coronation Gold', 'Moonshine', and 'Paprika'.

LESS-TOXIC CONTROLS
Yank out unwanted plants by the roots while still young. Or, cut back or mow down plants and patches before the seeds mature.

CHEMICAL CONTROLS
Attack large, out-of-control infestations with glyphosate.

Aegopodium podagraria
Bishop's weed, Goutweed, Herb Gerard

One to 2 feet tall, the plant has a spreading, thick growth habit, with serrated leaves borne in leaflets. The foliage is plain green in the species; in the commonly grown variegated form 'Variegata', leaves tend to be lighter green and edged with creamy white. The plentiful white, flat-topped flowers, which resemble those of (relatives) Queen Anne's lace (*Daucus carota*) and angelica, rise above the foliage in early summer. Will grow almost anywhere, including dry shade.

PROBLEM
With a little soil fertility and moisture, it pops up everywhere and repeatedly, earning its nickname "the groundcover from hell." Worst in Northeast and upper Midwest.

REPRODUCTION
Seeds and underground runners.

ORIGIN
Europe and northern Asia. Brought to the United States in the mid-1800s as an ornamental herb.

NOTES
Called "bishop's weed" because it is found near ecclesiastical ruins. Evidently valued by the monks of the Middle Ages, who cultivated it particularly for treating gout, thus the other common name. Can be suitable as a groundcover in difficult, shady locations where its dominance is not a problem.

NONINVASIVE ALTERNATIVES
A good variegated groundcover for shade that is not as aggressive as bishop's weed would be ribbongrass (*Phalaris arundinacea* 'Picta'); for plain green leaves, try pachysandra.

LESS-TOXIC CONTROLS
In smaller patches, repeatedly yank out or whack back unwanted growth. If practical, also remove flowers before they go to seed. Digging up plants only works if you manage to get all the trailing roots/rhizome bits. For larger areas, try slashing or mowing followed by a heavy mulch or laying down black plastic; maintain this barrier for months, or longer.

CHEMICAL CONTROLS
Spray with glyphosate.

Alliaria petiolata

Garlic mustard

Often a biennial, it starts out as a low-growing rosette of kidney-shaped, scallop-edged leaves. The following year, flowering stalks emerge, with smaller, heart-shaped leaves alternating along their length and topped with small white flower clusters; individual flowers are about ¼ inch and four-petaled. Slender seedpods follow, 1 to 2½ inches long, laden with tiny black seeds. Crushed leaves smell pungently of garlic. Rosettes are about 6 inches across; the flower stalks reach 3 feet.

PROBLEM
Because it leafs out early, it can overtake or outcompete garden plants. It is a fast, aggressive grower that forms dense colonies.

REPRODUCTION
Seeds (up to 6000 per plant), which are dispersed in late summer and fall and remain viable up to five years.

ORIGIN
Native to Europe, Asia, northwestern Africa. Introduced to North America from Europe in the early 1800s.

NOTES
It is not related to garlic or onions, but instead is a member of the mustard family and high in vitamins A and C. Valued for its leaves, which remain green over the winter months, it was used as a soup ingredient and an early-spring salad green. Herbalists traditionally used it as a digestive aid and as a treatment for ulcers. Milk from cows that eat this plant tastes garlicky.

NONINVASIVE ALTERNATIVES
None.

LESS-TOXIC CONTROLS
Yank out unwanted plants by their roots and discard safely; do not compost. Never let the plants flower and go to seed.

CHEMICAL CONTROLS
Mow in early spring or late fall, then spray with glyphosate.

Allium vineale
Wild garlic, Wild onion, Crow garlic, Field garlic

Aboveground, the plant is unremarkable, with slender, hollow leaves, the lower half covered with sheathing leaf-bases. Flowers consist of small pink or white umbels. Belowground, the small first-year bulbs, which are 1 inch in diameter, are soft, becoming hard over the course of their first winter and then germinating the following year or beyond. Entire plant smells strongly of garlic or onions. Tolerates a wide range of soils, from dry to soggy. Reaches 1 to 3 feet tall.

PROBLEM
Wild garlic is an aggressive grower and spreader.

REPRODUCTION
By bulbs and aerial bulblets. Seed is rarely produced, especially when the plants are growing in colder climates.

ORIGIN
Europe, western Asia, and North Africa.

NOTES
Farmers especially dislike this plant, as its strong scent taints beef as well as milk and eggs. Additionally, wheat and other small grains gain a garlic-like odor and/or flavor due to the presence of aerial bulblets at the time of harvest. While edible for humans, the bulbs have an unpleasant skunky aftertaste.

NONINVASIVE ALTERNATIVES
Grow and enjoy real garlic, or related plants such as spring onions, scallions, chives, and shallots.

LESS-TOXIC CONTROLS
Dig up and discard the entire plant, including bulb or bulbs, the earlier the better. Mow down larger patches in late fall and again the following spring to starve the bulbs, which absorb nutrients from the foliage.

CHEMICAL CONTROLS
None recommended. Herbicides do not cling well to the vertical, smooth, waxy leaves and are therefore not very effective.

Buddleia davidii and cultivars
Butterfly bush

Although this plant grows to shrub size, it is actually a perennial in the Northeast, upper Midwest, and much of the Pacific Northwest. In other words, it dies to the ground in cold winters and revives the following spring. Since it flowers on new growth, gardeners in mild climates would be well-advised to cut their plants back late every fall anyway. The canes are rather succulent and pliable and the plant's profile becomes full and arching. Leaves are gray-green or blue-green. Fragrant flowers appear in early summer as 4- to 10-inch clusters ("cymes"), usually in a shade of purple. Mature plant size is between 5 and 8 feet tall.

PROBLEM
Some nurseries bill this plant as "durable," but for those gardeners who find it too exuberant, it is a pest. Seedlings can pop up all over a yard or gain a foothold in sidewalk cracks, empty lots, and roadsides. Unlike hybrids of many plants, hybrids of this plant have been shown to produce viable seeds.

REPRODUCTION
Prolifically via winged seeds, up to 3 million per plant. Nurseries use cuttings, which root easily.

ORIGIN
Originally from China or Russia. Introduced into cultivation in Europe around 1890.

NOTES
Butterflies and bees relish the flowers.

NONINVASIVE ALTERNATIVES
The same color range and profile/size can be had from lilacs (*Syringa* spp.) in colder climates and from bushy ceanothus plants in milder climates.

LESS-TOXIC CONTROLS
Yank out unwanted seedlings and keep after them. Dig out larger unwanted plants. Do not let plants go to seed; cut off the flowers—harvest bouquets.

CHEMICAL CONTROLS
Should not be necessary, and none are recommended.

Carduus nutans

Musk thistle, Nodding thistle, Nodding plumeless thistle

Distinguished from other nasty, weedy purple-flowered thistles by a nodding flowerhead (at maturity) and strongly reflexed bracts. The flowerhead can be up to 3 inches across, though is typically somewhat smaller, and the leaves may be 1 foot long. The entire plant is spiny, especially the leaves, which also sport a distinctive white midvein. Prefers dry, gravely soils. Plant height varies between 1 and 3 feet, though 8-foot-tall plants have been spotted.

PROBLEM

It forms dense stands that crowd out other, more desirable plants. On farms and agricultural fields, animals avoid it and eat plants around it, which only allows it to spread opportunistically even further.

REPRODUCTION

Via seeds. By some estimates, a single plant can generate 11,000 seeds. These are dispersed by birds, small animals, farm animals, wind, and water, and can remain viable for up to 10 years.

ORIGIN

Introduced from Europe, probably inadvertently in ballast water. Also hails from western Asia and North Africa.

NOTES

Often a biennial, making a rosette the first year and blooming the second. Appears to release chemicals into the soil that inhibit other plants.

NONINVASIVE ALTERNATIVES

For easygoing perennial purple flowers that do not cause trouble, consider coneflower (*Echinacea* spp.).

LESS-TOXIC CONTROLS

Cut off rosettes at ground level with a sharp hoe. For patches, mow down as early in the season as possible. Do not let it go to seed.

CHEMICAL CONTROLS

Spraying with glyphosate, in late summer, is effective.

Carpobrotus edulis

Ice plant, Hottentot fig, Highway iceplant

Synonym *Mesembryanthemum edulis*

This is the classic groundcovering ice plant seen at beaches, in parking lots, and blanketing embankments, particularly in California and Oregon. The chunky leaves, borne on trailing stems, are succulent and triangular in cross-section, and help established plants survive periods of drought. Flowers vary from rose to pale yellow, are 2½ to 6 inches in diameter, and are pollinated by bees and beetles. Fleshy (edible) fruit, shaped like a spinning top, follow. Mature plants are up to 5 or 6 inches tall and broadly spreading.

PROBLEM

In mild-climate areas of the West, Florida, and the Gulf Coast, it grows rampantly to form large mats, outcompeting other desirable plants.

REPRODUCTION

The fruits are full of seeds that germinate easily. In addition, the plant roots at nodes, and root and stem bits can regenerate.

ORIGIN

Originally from South Africa.

NOTES

Under the right conditions, a stem can grow up to 3 feet per year.

NONINVASIVE ALTERNATIVES

A close relative, sea fig (*Carpobrotus chilensis*), is smaller and less aggressive; however, given a chance, the two hybridize readily, confusing the issue. Sea fig flowers are smaller and bright pink/purple. Alternatively, the handsome rose verbena (*Verbena canadensis*) is also a drought-tolerant groundcover with colorful flowers and is much easier to control.

LESS-TOXIC CONTROLS

Yank out individual plants by hand. You may surprised by how extensive a single plant turns out to be. In larger areas, try mowing them down but follow up by also extracting remaining plant bits and/or laying down a suppressing mulch.

CHEMICAL CONTROLS

Spray with glyphosate.

Centaurea solstitialis

Yellow star thistle

This bushy plant has multiple rigid stems that extend in all directions from the base and may be as much as 6 feet high and wide. Foliage is gray-green, flowers are about 1 inch in diameter, bright yellow, and protected with long, sharp spines, and the tough taproot can extend up to 3 feet or more underground.

PROBLEM
In North America, it lacks natural enemies, including various insects, and thus has spread its nasty ways far and wide, particularly in the mild-climate areas of the West.

REPRODUCTION
Seeds. In one season, a single plant can produce 150,000 seeds; these may remain viable in the soil for several years.

ORIGIN
Came from Eurasia and mild-climate areas of the Mediterranean. Seed is thought to have first arrived in California during the gold rush years as a contaminant in alfalfa.

NOTES
It is toxic to horses, but goats will eat the spiny flowers and all.

NONINVASIVE ALTERNATIVES
There are no nice thistles. If you seek bright yellow flowers, look to any number of domesticated cousins of this obnoxious plant, from sunflowers to coreopsis.

LESS-TOXIC CONTROLS
Never let a plant go to seed. Cut off the flowerheads as they form. Dig out individual plants, aiming to get the entire taproot. Larger patches can be chopped or mowed down, again, before the heads mature, then smothered under a mulch or black plastic.

CHEMICAL CONTROLS
Treatments such as picloram, a restricted-use herbicide, and 2,4-D have been used in agricultural fields but are not advised for home-garden use.

Centaurea stoebe
subsp. *micranthos*

Spotted knapweed

Synonym(s) *Centaurea maculosa, C. biebersteinii*
A sparse-looking but tenacious thistle relative with an erect, branching habit
of wiry stems with plenty of pink or purple 1-inch flowers in late summer. When
these dry out and seeds begin to develop, you can observe black-tipped bracts.
Rosette leaves are deeply lobed. This weed likes dry well-drained areas, including hillsides, roadsides, vacant lots, and fields. It may be biennial or it may be a
short-lived perennial. An individual rosette reaches 8 inches across; flowering
stalks grow 3 or even 4 feet tall.

PROBLEM
In wild places and rangeland, it crowds
out native plants. In gardens, if not
arrested, it elbows out desirable plants.

REPRODUCTION
While there is some expansion from
individual rosettes, this plant mainly
relies on its prodigious seed production—up to 1000 per plant. Seeds survive up to eight years.

ORIGIN
Native to Europe and western Asia. Seed
probably arrived in North America in
contaminated alfalfa seed or in ballast.

NOTES
Catechin, an allelopathic chemical
found in this species, was thought to
have a toxic effect on adjacent plants,
but a USDA study debunked this and
found instead that the chemical actually cleansed toxicities and restored
the balance of microbial life in the
adjacent soil.

NONINVASIVE ALTERNATIVES
Grow cultivated centaurea relatives
such as perennial cornflower
(*Centaurea montana*).

LESS-TOXIC CONTROLS
Yank out or dig out individual plants. Wear
gloves to protect your hands from the allelopathic chemical. Larger patches can be
mowed down early in the season or sub-
jected to controlled burns.

CHEMICAL CONTROLS
None recommended.

Cerastium tomentosum

Snow-in-summer, Mouse-ear chickweed

A low-growing, mounding plant with grayish, velvety leaves up to 1 inch long. The cute white flowers, individually about ½ to 1 inch across, are borne in clusters in late spring and early summer. Over time, the plant forms a dense, groundcovering carpet between 6 and 19 inches tall.

PROBLEM

The aggressive, creeping habit allows plants to go where they are not wanted, especially in fertile soil. They can exceed flowerbed boundaries, invade the lawn, or encroach on pathways. Large plantings tend to develop unattractive dead patches here and there. Snow-in-summer is not a good choice for tidy gardeners or small spaces.

REPRODUCTION

Self-sows prolifically. Also spreads by runners.

ORIGIN

Native to the alpine regions of Europe and western Asia.

NOTES

This plant prefers well-drained soil and the leaves will turn black and rot in soggy ground; high heat and humidity also damage it, especially as the summer wears on. After blooming, to maintain a neat look, plants should be clipped hard or mowed to 2 inches tall. Beware: this plant is popular with ants, and therefore anthills, probably because of the shelter it provides. It is also very cold tolerant.

NONINVASIVE ALTERNATIVES

Cultivated varieties are less aggressive and have a more compact growth habit; 'Yo Yo' is the most common one.

LESS-TOXIC CONTROLS

Yank or dig out unwanted plants early and often. Pluck faded flowers by the handfuls to prevent self-sowing. Create barriers in your garden to confine its spread, sinking them into the ground at least 6 inches deep; use bricks, plastic edging, or stones.

CHEMICAL CONTROLS

None recommended.

Cichorium intybus

Chicory

The jaunty blue summertime flowers actually open for only a few hours a day. Eventually, they fade to white. An erect, branching plant between 2 and 5 feet tall with sparse, jagged leaves up to 1 foot long, chicory has a long, divided taproot.

PROBLEM

It grows quickly and aggressively in sunny, well-drained spots, though it does not tend to invade regular garden spaces, preferring instead to colonize the outskirts. If you do not get out the entire taproot, the plant just grows back.

REPRODUCTION

Seeds and roots.

ORIGIN

Native to Europe. Imported to the United States as a culinary and medicinal plant (Thomas Jefferson sought it out). Evidently, it has been in cultivation for thousands of years, including in ancient Arabia and Egypt.

LESS-TOXIC CONTROLS

Dig out plants with a dandelion fork or shovel; this is easiest when the ground is saturated.

CHEMICAL CONTROLS

None recommended.

NOTES

Perhaps because it has widely naturalized, or perhaps because it is not an especially attractive plant, its varied and valuable uses in food and medicine seem to have been forgotten. The roots, if given garden conditions that carrots like, produce a robust edible crop. Dried (brown), ground roots are a coffee substitute or supplement and have been used as a diuretic and laxative. Young leaves may be eaten fresh or cooked in salads and stir-fries, or made into a poultice to dress swellings and abrasions.

NONINVASIVE ALTERNATIVES

If you like easygoing blue flowers, try a tall campanula such as *Campanula lactiflora* or balloon flower (*Platycodon grandiflorus*). For edible greens, try closely related endive or radicchio.

Cirsium arvense

Canada thistle

This dreaded burly thistle has a tall, erect stem that becomes branched and arrays clusters of smallish flowerheads ½ to 1 inch in diameter, usually rose-purple. Technically, there are separate male and female plants, but patches contain plenty of both. Leaves, smaller as they alternate up the stem, are prickly and lobed. A mature plant is between 1½ and 5 feet tall.

PROBLEM

Canada thistle is an aggressive spreader with deep roots, difficult to eradicate. Yards near or downwind of an infested lot or farmland are vulnerable. Beware of spilling birdseed that contains this or other thistle seeds; supposedly such seeds are heat-treated, but do not depend on it.

REPRODUCTION

Females produce up to 1500 seeds per plant; these travel by wind and last years in soil. The creeping root system allows patches to grow ever denser as young plants emerge. Even tiny pieces give rise to new plants.

ORIGIN

Europe and Asia.

NOTES

Certain weevils can help control this beast, but their help is practical only on a farm-size infestation.

NONINVASIVE ALTERNATIVES

There are no nice perennial thistles, but there are some nice purple coneflowers (*Echinacea* species and cultivars).

LESS-TOXIC CONTROLS

Never let it go to seed. Don gloves and dig out young plants, or repeatedly mow down a patch to prevent flowering and weaken the plants. Follow by smothering the area with black plastic or heavy mulch. Researchers have been testing vinegar and vinegar-based herbicides, in full sun, with some success; apparently, acetic acid causes the topgrowth to dry out and die. You might also try to improve soil fertility and reduce compaction, as this plant prospers in poor soil.

CHEMICAL CONTROLS

Glyphosate is not very effective except perhaps on young plants. Clopyralid can be quite effective; follow label directions exactly.

Convallaria majalis

Lily-of-the-valley

Glossy green parallel-veined leaves grow slowly but thickly, carpeting partially or fully shady areas of fertile, humusy soil. Every spring, they are joined by small stems adorned with tiny white (or pink) bells that waft a sweet fragrance. Small orange-red berries follow the flowers. Plants are generally 4 to 8 inches high and 8 to 12 inches across.

PROBLEM

Even if you want this plant, you may find it a maintenance headache, as other weeds and grass can intersperse with it. Or, it may wear out its welcome, jumping barriers, encroaching on the lawn or other groundcovers, and taking over more than its allotted space.

REPRODUCTION

Via spreading underground stems.

ORIGIN

Europe and Asia.

NOTES

Plants do indeed produce a few seeds; however, plants are self-sterile, and colonies consisting of a single clone will not set seed. Nurseries sell this plant as "pips," which are simply pieces of fleshy, twisty rhizome. Warning: all plant parts are poisonous, containing convallatoxin, probably the most toxic cardiac glycoside.

NONINVASIVE ALTERNATIVES

While not as diminutive or low-growing, hostas like the same conditions, offer similar colors in foliage and flower, and stay where you plant them. *Hosta* 'Tiny Tears', for example, is only 6 inches tall with lavender flowers.

LESS-TOXIC CONTROLS

Yank out unwanted plants (one pull may bring up two or three pips at a time), or dig up larger areas with a shovel. Barriers inserted deep into the ground only work if you install these early in a patch's career.

CHEMICAL CONTROLS

Glyphosate will kill it, but cannot be used if the plants are wending their way among desirable plants.

Cynoglossum officinale

Houndstongue, Gypsyflower

The reddish purple flowers are this weed's most salient feature; they arise from a coarse, hairy rosette in early summer, have five lobes, and are carried from the leaf axils in droopy clusters. The fuzzy, erect stems have long, pointed fuzzy leaves, with both shape and texture suggesting the "houndstongue" common name. The leaves become smaller higher up and nearly clasp the stem near the top. When the flowers pass, distinctive prickly nutlets develop. Roots are thick, black, and tenacious. The entire plant has a funky, musty smell. Flowering plants reach 2 or 3 feet tall; the largest rosette leaves may measure up to a foot long.

PROBLEM
Houndstongue self-sows in overgrazed fields and waste areas, preferring slightly alkaline soil.

REPRODUCTION
Seeds are spread by wind and animals; the stickiness of the seeds allows them to attach to fur.

ORIGIN
Introduced from Europe.

NOTES
Often a biennial, with the rosette developing the first year and flowering and fruiting following in the second season, but a typical patch has plants of various ages. The plant contains liver-damaging alkaloids that are toxic to horses and livestock.

NONINVASIVE ALTERNATIVES
Get similar height, color, summer bloom, and life span from cultivated varieties of mullein, such as *Verbascum* 'Southern Charm'.

LESS-TOXIC CONTROLS
When the rosettes are spotted, dig them up by the roots or cut them off at the crown. At minimum, mow down the plants before flowers have a chance to develop or set seed. Discourage its reappearance by overplanting with desirable plants.

CHEMICAL CONTROLS
Some herbicides, including 2,4-D, picloram, and dicamba, have proven effective for farms and grazing fields but are not recommended for homeowners.

Daucus carota

Queen Anne's lace, Wild carrot

The slim, hollow, ridged stems are erect and branching. The finely textured leaves are pinnate and somewhat hairy. The flat-topped white flowers are technically umbels and become concave, or close inward, as they mature. The white taproot is too tough and bitter to eat, particularly when compared to its domesticated relative. Mature plants attain 2 to 3 feet, and flowerheads are between 2 and 5 inches across.

PROBLEM

This weed eagerly colonizes sunny, open spots.

REPRODUCTION

Seeds, which can remain viable up to five years, cling to everything from socks to pet fur, and are wind-dispersed.

ORIGIN

From Europe and Asia. Has been known and grown since ancient Greece.

NOTES

The common name refers either to Queen Anne (wife of King James I), who used to decorate her hair with it, or to St. Anne, patron saint of lacemakers. Some flowerheads have a single purple floret in the center, representing a droplet of the Queen's blood, according to folklore. Coupled with the larger, sterile outer florets, the purple floret is thought to create a bullseyelike target for pollinating insects. It also distinguishes the plant from similar ones, both safe (such as dill) and toxic (notably poison hemlock). Black swallowtail butterflies are drawn to the flowerheads.

NONINVASIVE ALTERNATIVES

The herb angelica is just as pretty. Related, edible plants include caraway, cilantro, dill, sweet fennel, and parsley.

LESS-TOXIC CONTROLS

Cut off the flowerheads before they ripen seed, using them in bouquets. Dig out entire plants by their long roots, a task made easier when they are young and the ground is damp. Mow down larger patches before they go to seed.

CHEMICAL CONTROLS

None recommended.

Digitalis purpurea

Foxglove

Flowering stalks arise from rosettes, with a few smaller leaves alternating up their length. Blooming commences in early to midsummer; spikes are composed of charming, downward-hanging bells, usually rose-colored and splashed within with white and dotted with dark marks. Mature plants are 3 to 5 feet tall and half as wide; rosette leaves reach up 10 inches long.

PROBLEM

Foxglove is short-lived and often considered a biennial, which simply means that it delays its bloom until its second season. It self-sows with abandon, particularly in moist, fertile soil. Soon you have many plants, perennially, more every year.

REPRODUCTION

Tiny seeds, produced prolifically.

ORIGIN

Introduced as an ornamental from Europe.

NOTES

This plant contains digitoxin, among other glycosides, and has been used for centuries in herbal medicine, particularly as a cardiac sedative but also as a cough suppressant, diuretic, cure for swollen glands, and to treat epilepsy. Occasional overdoses and poisoning deaths render its use too risky. That said, successful extraction of the active ingredient from the leaves made its controlled use possible and relatively safe in cardiac medicine, although nowadays other cardiac drugs seem to have eclipsed it.

NONINVASIVE ALTERNATIVES

Some newer cultivated foxglove varieties such as 'Polka Dot Pandora' are sterile, that is, do not produce viable seed.

LESS-TOXIC CONTROLS

Do not allow your foxgloves to go to seed; instead cut stems for bouquets. Dig out first-year rosettes of unwanted individual plants. If you have an unwanted patch, chop it down with a sharp hoe.

CHEMICAL CONTROLS

Because foxgloves so cleverly intermingle with desirable garden plants, herbicides are too chancy and should not be used.

Dipsacus fullonum

Common teasel

The dried cone, rimmed with bracts, is very distinctive. The inflorescence that precedes it is egg-shaped and has a ruff of tiny purple or pink flowers. Both stems and leaves are prickly, and rosette leaves have a conspicuous white center vein. The plant has a tenacious taproot. Some plants get 6 feet tall.

PROBLEM
Once established, it elbows out existing or native vegetation. It is not easy to eradicate, thanks to its rough texture and deep taproot.

REPRODUCTION
Seeds, up to 2000 per plant, although they tend not to fall far from the plant. Teasel thus spreads to new areas by birds or animals.

ORIGIN
From Europe, Asia, and North Africa.

NOTES
The seeds are an important winter food for some birds, particularly European goldfinch. Florists and craftspeople like to use the dried cones in arrangements and wreaths. Interestingly, a cuplike structure forms where lower leaves meet the stem and can hold rainwater. Botanists speculate that this prevents sap-sucking insects such as aphids from climbing the stem. A recent experiment showed that adding dead insects to these cups increased the seed set, implying partial carnivory.

NONINVASIVE ALTERNATIVES
Consider the much friendlier globe thistle (*Echinops ritro*), whose purple flowers are nice in bouquets, fresh or dried.

LESS-TOXIC CONTROLS
Never let this plant go to seed. Chop it down early in the season and repeat if it regenerates. Dig out entire plants by their roots whenever possible.

CHEMICAL CONTROLS
A few herbicides are approved for use on large infestations in range or pasturelands, but are not warranted in a home-garden setting.

Epilobium angustifolium
Fireweed

Synonym *Chamerion angustifolium*
This handsome wildflower, instantly recognizable by its stately pink-purple spikes, populates many areas but especially prefers full sun and lean, gravely soil. The leaves are long, thin, willowy and alternate up the stalk to just below the flowers. It blooms starting in midsummer. The seedpods are long, thin, reddish, and angle upwards. At maturity, the plant is 2 to 7 feet tall.

PROBLEM
It takes over recently cleared land with a vengeance and even in small, confined areas forms dense patches.

REPRODUCTION
By seeds as well as creeping rootstocks.

ORIGIN
Native in North America, but also from Europe and Asia.

NOTES
Its common name refers to the fact that it is frequently among the first plants to colonize a recently burned-over area. After the great sweeping forest fires in Yellowstone National Park in the late 1980s, this plant was everywhere and widely photographed because its presence was so dramatic.

NONINVASIVE ALTERNATIVES
It is possible to make fireweed into a good garden citizen by planting individuals in deep bottomless pots (like some people do with mint). Tall pink-purple flowers that are carried in spikes or spires but are not quite as vigorous, and make an impact in a garden include phlox, gayfeather (*Liatris spicata*), and obedient plant (*Physostegia virginiana*).

LESS-TOXIC CONTROLS
Cut back, hoe down, or yank out unwanted plants. Chop off flowerheads before they can go to seed.

CHEMICAL CONTROLS
None recommended.

Euphorbia cyparissias

Cypress spurge

There is a certain understated grace to the appearance of this euphorbia. Slender, almost needlelike light green leaves alternate up its stem and the "flowers" (technically bracts), which burst forth in flat-topped clusters at the tops of the stems, are yellow to lime-green. They start in spring, continue on and off through the summer, and color reddish in the fall. Stem juice, like other euphorbias, is milky. Not a tall plant, it typically is between 6 and 12 inches high.

PROBLEM

It forms thick colonies that expand every year and crowd out less aggressive plants. If mowed down and included in hay fed to animals, it may sicken the animals. There are even cases of poisoning among cattle and horses; evidently, it is no problem to sheep.

REPRODUCTION

Creeping roots. Sometimes also by reseeding, although research suggests that the plants are self-sterile.

ORIGIN

Introduced as an ornamental from Europe. A garden escapee in North America.

NOTES

Herbalists have esteemed the roots as a purgative, but overdoses can be fatal. The milky sap, typical of this species, causes an allergic rash in some people. Interestingly, a relative is the holiday poinsettia plant.

NONINVASIVE ALTERNATIVES

Several better-behaved relatives are more popular with gardeners, including white-flowered baby's breath euphorbia (*Euphorbia corollata*). If you like lime-green flowers in your garden and bouquets, try lady's mantle (*Alchemilla*) or annual flowering tobacco hybrids (*Nicotiana* Nikki Hybrids).

LESS-TOXIC CONTROLS

Yank out plants using gloves to protect your hands from the sap, or mow down repeatedly and/or smother after mowing.

CHEMICAL CONTROLS

None recommended.

Euphorbia esula

Leafy spurge

This weedy spurge sports large, broad leaves up to 4 inches long, which alternate up the stem, and an erect profile. The small greenish yellow flowers are carried in small clusters atop the erect or branched stems in late spring and summer. Sap, as is typical of the species, is milky. In mature plants, which typically are 1 to 3 feet tall, the underground root system becomes impressively extensive and may include taproots as deep as 20 feet below the surface.

PROBLEM

A dense-growing, aggressive plant, it is successful at taking over broad areas of dry ground in full sun, displacing grass and native or garden plants.

REPRODUCTION

New buds not only develop at the plant's crown but along the creeping roots. Seeds, once ripe, can eject up to 15 feet from the plant; they also float, which helps them travel via water.

ORIGIN

Introduced from central and eastern Europe, possibly as an ornamental, but more likely the seeds hitchhiked in via ballast or in an oats shipment.

NOTES

The odd flowers technically do not have any petals, but rather bracts. In any event, they produce a lot of nectar and pollen, making them popular with a wide range of insects.

NONINVASIVE ALTERNATIVES

See suggestions under *Euphorbia cyparissias*.

LESS-TOXIC CONTROLS

Chop or mow down patches before or as flowers appear; do not let them set seed. Then smother the area for a season. Farmers have had some success by letting sheep or goats graze leafy spurge; these evidently have no adverse reaction to this plant, while horses and cattle do.

CHEMICAL CONTROLS

None recommended.

Fallopia japonica

Japanese knotweed, Japanese bamboo

Synonym(s) *Polygonum cuspidatum, Reynoutria japonica*
A bushy plant with red-mottled green stems that are erect, hollow and jointed like bamboo, and graceful branches of 4- to 6-inch roundish, heart-shaped leaves. In late summer, panicles of tiny greenish white flowers appear; male and female flowers are on separate plants. Root systems are thick, extensive, and tenacious. Mature plant size is between 3 and 10 feet tall.

LESS-TOXIC CONTROLS
Dig up plants while young, as older ones have daunting root systems that are massive, strong, and intertwined. Cut back the plants repeatedly to weaken and eventually starve the roots. Then smother the area with thick mulch and/or a tarp and leave it in place for at least a year, perhaps longer.

CHEMICAL CONTROLS
To have any hope of effectiveness, herbicide should be applied in late summer or fall to chopped-back plants, before they can send starches down into the roots to fuel next year's crop. That said, glyphosate is often not up to the job.

PROBLEM
In some areas, notably the Northeast and Midwest, this fast-growing, aggressive plant spreads along roadsides and encroaches on yards and gardens. It is very difficult to eradicate.

REPRODUCTION
Seeds, which travel via wind, water, contaminated fill dirt, humans (our shoes), and animals. In addition, creeping, branching rhizomes send up shoots.

ORIGIN
Asia. Introduced from Japan as an ornamental.

NOTES
In parts of Asia, young shoots are steamed and eaten like asparagus. Root extracts are used in a treatment for Lyme disease; resveratrol, thought to slow the aging process, is also present.

NONINVASIVE ALTERNATIVES
Bamboos are also invasive, but can be controlled by growing them in large containers (aboveground or sunk into the garden).

Foeniculum vulgare

Fennel

Synonym *Foeniculum officinale*
Tall, branching, aromatic plant with rather sparse, feathery-thin leaves. Both the hollow stem and the leaves have a bluish cast. The yellow flower umbels appear in midsummer and last through the fall. The carrotlike roots are thin and tapering. Mature plants are up to 4 feet tall.

PROBLEM
Fennel has naturalized on dry hillsides and along roadsides. Its enthusiastic self-sowing tendencies allow it to invade open or neglected areas of yards and gardens.

REPRODUCTION
By seeds.

ORIGIN
Native to the Mediterranean region.

NOTES
This plant is prized for its edible leaves and stems, which have a mild but pungent aniselike flavor. The seeds, whole or ground, are also eaten and can be added to soups, sausage, and baked goods. Fennel has been used as a breath freshener and medicinally to soothe an upset stomach or treat nausea, suppress the appetite, and as a mild diuretic. It is also used in toothpaste, soap, and liqueur. Animal studies have shown that extracts of the seeds are potentially beneficial in the treatment of glaucoma.

NONINVASIVE ALTERNATIVES
Try closely related sweet fennel or finocchio (*Foeniculum vulgare* var. *dulce*), an annual valued for all of the above plus its tasty, swollen, celerylike stem.

LESS-TOXIC CONTROLS
Pull out unwanted plants by their roots, a task that is easier when plants are young or the ground is damp. Do not let mature plants go to seed.

CHEMICAL CONTROLS
None recommended.

Glechoma hederacea

Creeping Charlie, Ground ivy, Gill-over-the-ground

Synonym *Nepeta glechoma*

Creeping, trailing stems bear small roundish to heart-shaped leaves with scalloped edges. In spring, little purple flowers in whorls in the leaf axils cover the plant for weeks. Blooming stems are 3 to 10 inches tall, with an indefinite outward spread, and the leaves are only ½ to 1 inch long.

PROBLEM

A rapid spreader, creeping Charlie can colonize wide areas of a lawn or garden, making it hard to remove.

REPRODUCTION

Roots readily at nodes. Also reproduces by seed.

ORIGIN

From Europe and Asia. Imported as an ornamental or medicinal plant.

NOTES

A member of the mint family. The entire plant has a tart minty-balsamic fragrance. The common name "gill" is from the French word for ferment (*guiller*), and refers to the fact that the leaves were once used in beer-brewing to confer a desirable bitterness. As for medicinal uses, evidently a tea made from the leaves was an effective treatment for scurvy as well as coughs, bronchitis, and even asthma.

LESS-TOXIC CONTROLS

Rip out unwanted plants thoroughly, as even stem fragments can generate new plants; it is easiest to remove plants when the soil is damp after a rain or watering. In a lawn, first pull up runners, then mow close. Act before flowers go to seed.

CHEMICAL CONTROLS

Apply glyphosate in late fall or early spring. Or, apply a post-emergent herbicide, carefully and repeatedly. If you have to sacrifice lawn grass, plan to reseed later.

NONINVASIVE ALTERNATIVES

Related, better-behaved groundcovers for damp ground and partial shade are cultivars of *Lamium maculatum*, such as 'Beacon Silver' and 'White Nancy'.

Gypsophila paniculata

Baby's breath

A bushy, many-branched, yet airy plant. The narrow, blue-green leaves, between 1 and 4 inches long, are mostly basal; in summer, a mature plant produces sprays of dainty ⅛-inch flowers—usually white, sometimes with a pink tinge or fully pink. Over time, the plant forms a deep, thick taproot and grows to between 3 and 4 feet tall and wide.

PROBLEM

Relatively innocuous in a flower garden and providing filler in florist bouquets, this bushy plant's beauty belies its downside. Garden escapees have colonized the dunes along the Great Lakes; their taproots are so deep and stabilizing that they thwart the natural shifting of sand that many native species require.

REPRODUCTION

Via seeds, with most dropping close to the plant and others dispersed by wind or water.

ORIGIN

Native to Europe and Asia. Imported to North America as an ornamental.

NOTES

The flowers dry well and can be used in dried arrangements and wreaths.

NONINVASIVE ALTERNATIVES

So-called baby's breath euphorbia, white-flowered *Euphorbia corollata* 'White Manaus', has been promoted as a heat- and drought-tolerant, well-behaved alternative.

LESS-TOXIC CONTROLS

Do not let your plants go to seed; instead, harvest the flowers for bouquets. Dig out unwanted plants, the younger the better. Or, chop them low and to thwart resprouting, cut a few inches below the soil surface, well into the rootstock. For larger patches, mow low repeatedly or try controlled burning.

CHEMICAL CONTROLS

Picloram is effective, but it is "restricted use."

Heracleum lanatum

Cow parsnip, Pushki, Indian celery

Synonym *Heracleum maximum*

A tall, dramatic member of the parsley or carrot family, this weed features a hollow, grooved, woolly stem lined with large, broad, three-lobed, toothed leaves and topped with flat clusters of white or cream-colored flowers. Flowerheads are 6 to 8 inches across on plants 6 or more feet tall and wide. The plant prospers in moist ground and blooms most or all of the summer.

PROBLEM

The plant is a pernicious weed and if allowed to mature and set seed, it becomes daunting to eradicate. It is a real pest in pastures, where it can ruin the milk of cows that eat it.

REPRODUCTION

Seeds.

ORIGIN

U.S. Pacific Northwest.

NOTES

Larval food source for anise swallowtail butterfly. Roots and young stems are reportedly edible, traditionally steamed or cooked in a stir-fry. However, given that the plant juices contain furocoumarin, the same irritating phototoxin found in the scary relative giant hogweed, this is probably a bad idea. Rashes or blisters can result after exposure to the plant and sunshine or heat. In addition, the flowers resemble those of the poisonous water hemlock (*Circuta maculata*), so be completely sure of your identification before contemplating harvesting or eating: cow parsnip stems are fuzzy or hairy, water hemlock's are smooth. Note, however, that cattle and deer will eat this species.

NONINVASIVE ALTERNATIVES

Various herbs in the same family are worth considering—dill, angelica, and sweet fennel, to name a few.

LESS-TOXIC CONTROLS

Never let this plant go to seed. Cut or mow down small colonies before the flowers mature. Dig out root systems.

CHEMICAL CONTROLS

Herbicides are effective on young plants.

Heracleum mantegazzianum

Giant hogweed, Giant cow parsley

This is a dangerous weed and becomes a massive plant. Erect, hollow, purplish stems are 2 to 4 inches in diameter and covered with bristles. Deeply incised leaves, up to 5 feet across, alternate up the towering stem. Like other members of the carrot family, the plant has white, flat-topped flower clusters (umbels); these can be 1 or 2 feet across. The root system is thick and tenacious. Some plants attain 10 to 15 feet in height and half as wide.

PROBLEM
Because it likes moist, rich soil, it is able to prosper in desirable garden soil. If allowed to grow big, this plant is daunting to remove.

REPRODUCTION
Seeds.

ORIGIN
Originally from Central Asia. Imported to Europe and North America as a horticultural curiosity. The edible seeds (*golpar*) are used in some Iranian recipes.

NOTES
Warning: Protect yourself around all parts of this plant—gloves, goggles, and heavy clothing are necessary. The sap, which contains caustic furocoumarins, in combination with moisture and sunlight, causes burning, itching, and painful blisters, and leaves long-lasting purple scars. If it gets in the eyes, temporary or lasting blindness can occur. Livestock and pigs will eat young plants without any ill effects.

LESS-TOXIC CONTROLS
See warning at right and consider getting professional help. Dig out plants while small. Otherwise, carefully cut off and dispose of flowerheads before they can go to seed, let the plant die back, then try digging it up.

CHEMICAL CONTROLS
Herbicides are effective on young plants.

NONINVASIVE ALTERNATIVES
None.

Hesperis matronalis

Dame's rocket

When not in bloom, this plant is unremarkable, with lance-shaped, serrated leaves alternating up sturdy stems. Early summer brings handsome, four-pet-aled, softly scented flowers in purple, sometimes pink or white. The seedpods that follow are long and slender, 1 to 5 inches long, betraying its membership in the mustard family. An adaptable plant, it tolerates partial shade and most soils, though it likes damp ground best. Mature plants are 1 to 4 feet tall.

PROBLEM
Dame's rocket can quickly colonize and elbow out natives and infiltrate flowerbeds and shade gardens.

REPRODUCTION
Seeds.

ORIGIN
Native to Europe. Imported as an ornamental to the United States by colonists as early as the 1600s.

NOTES
The genus name comes from the Greek *hespera*, which means "eve-ning," and the species name simply means "of matrons," reflecting the fact that the fragrance of "mother of the evening" intensifies at night to attract pollinators. The "rocket" of the com-mon name probably refers to its mem-bership in the mustard family, which includes the salad green arugula, also known as rocket.

NONINVASIVE ALTERNATIVES
The garden phlox (*Phlox paniculata*) offers a very similar flower form, the same colors, and stronger fragrance. In addition, phlox flowers are lusher (have more petals) and thus stand out better.

LESS-TOXIC CONTROLS
Yank out unwanted plants while they are still young. Do not let mature plants go to seed; instead, pick bouquets. You may have to persist for a few seasons if a stand self-sowed, because seeds remain viable in the soil for years.

CHEMICAL CONTROLS
Glyphosate applied in fall is effective.

Hypericum perforatum

St. Johnswort

A bushy, branching plant with clusters of distinctive, brilliant yellow flowers starting in early summer. An inch across, these have five petals (curiously, with black dots on the margins) and a jaunty spray of stamens in the center. The elliptical, opposite leaves are 1 to 2 inches long and, if held up to the light, immediately identifiable because of the many translucent dots. Brown pods develop by fall, dry, and scatter their seeds. Mature plants reach 1 to 2½ feet high and wide.

PROBLEM
This vigorous plant successfully elbows out competition. While this makes it a good groundcover, even in that capacity it can outgrow its welcome.

REPRODUCTION
Seeds (15,000 to 30,000 per plant) and creeping roots.

ORIGIN
From Europe, Asia, and North Africa. Imported to North America by German immigrants in the late 1600s for use as a medicinal herb.

NOTES
The common name refers to the fact that it blooms on or around St. John's Eve, June 24. Derivations from tops and stems are still valued as a treatment for mild depression. Plant parts contain sour sap that livestock avoid; many insects also avoid the plant. Concerns about photosensitivity and toxic reactions limit its usefulness for humans and grazing animals.

NONINVASIVE ALTERNATIVES
Potentilla species and cultivars are of similar habit and sport cheery yellow flowers, but are not aggressive plants.

LESS-TOXIC CONTROLS
Wear gloves to protect your hands from the caustic sap, and yank out unwanted plants by the roots while still small. Chop back before they can go to seed.

CHEMICAL CONTROLS
Kill large unwanted patches with glyphosate or 2,4-D.

Lepidium draba

White top, Whitetop, Hoary cress, Hoary pepperwort

Synonym *Cardaria draba*

Erect, branched, hairy stems are lined with alternate oval or oblong leaves with teethed edges. Showy white flowerheads composed of tiny, four-petaled flowers bloom from early spring into summer and are followed by heart-shaped, inflated seedpods. Root systems grow large, up to 6 feet down and are very tenacious. A member of the mustard family. Thrives in moist, disturbed ground. Mature plants are 3 or more feet tall.

LESS-TOXIC CONTROLS

Dig out young plants and smaller patches—be sure to get all the roots. Attack larger patches by cutting and mowing down, repeatedly, in an effort to starve the root system. Farmers with large infestations have had luck by flooding affected areas for two months.

CHEMICAL CONTROLS

None recommended. Common herbicides are no match for the extensive root system.

PROBLEM

Adaptable and aggressive, this weed overtakes fields, meadows, and waste places throughout North America; it is worst in the Rocky Mountain region.

REPRODUCTION

By seeds, rootstocks, and creeping roots.

ORIGIN

From Europe and western Asia. Probably hitchhiked into the United States country in ballast and/or imported alfalfa.

NOTES

Other species in the genus are also called white top. All are obnoxious. Seedpod shape is the most distinguishing difference.

NONINVASIVE ALTERNATIVES

Any yarrow (*Achillea*), which looks similar with its white flowerheads, is a pussycat compared to this beast.

Lespedeza species

Bush clovers

Three similar species of *Lespedeza*, members of the pea family are tricky to identify correctly, especially when they cross-pollinate. All carry their leaves in leaflets and sport characteristic pealike flowers in upper leaf axils and at their tops. Flowers appear later in the summer and may be purple, pink, or yellow. The fruit that follows is a one-seeded pod. Plant habit varies from erect to densely shrubby to trailing vines. Bushy *Lespedeza bicolor* may be 3 to 10 feet tall and *L. cuneata* is 1 to 6 feet tall, yet the creeping species, *L. repens*, is no more than 2 feet tall but spreads indefinitely. Root systems eventually spread wide and deep.

PROBLEM
The thick growth habit and spreading roots of these plants conspire to exclude most or all other plants. If not arrested while young, the plants are a challenge to eradicate when mature.

REPRODUCTION
Seeds and creeping roots.

ORIGIN
Some are native to North America; others have hitchhiked in from Europe and/or Asia or been imported as ornamentals or for erosion control.

NOTES
Like all legumes, these plants improve the fertility of the soil by fixing atmospheric nitrogen. Bobwhite quails relish their seeds.

LESS-TOXIC CONTROLS
Pull out unwanted plants while they are still small. Mow down established stands repeatedly, before they bloom and can go to seed and in the hopes of starving the extensive root systems.

CHEMICAL CONTROLS
Summer applications of glyphosate, triclopyr, or metsulfuron have been successful in large infestations.

NONINVASIVE ALTERNATIVES
If you like trailing, vining members of the pea family, grow sweet peas (*Lathyrus odoratus*) instead. If you like bushy ones, grow a cultivar of Warminster broom (*Cytisus* ×*praecox*).

Leucanthemum vulgare

Ox-eye daisy

Synonym *Chrysanthemum leucanthemum*
This familiar wild daisy blooms all summer. The 1- to 2-inch flowerheads are carried atop slender but wiry stems. The narrow leaves are dark green; basal leaves are up to 6 inches long, while those that ascend the stems are around 3 inches long at most. Roots are a short, spreading rhizome. Full-grown plants are between 1 and 3 feet tall.

PROBLEM
This daisy grows so quickly and easily that it can invade and take over open areas in just a season or two. Seeds survive a long time in the soil, so the plant can recur even after you thought it was gone.

REPRODUCTION
By seeds (from 100 to 300 per flowerhead) and vegetatively from the rhizomes.

ORIGIN
Originally from Asia, it was imported from Europe as an ornamental. There are no native American daisies.

NOTES
Dairy farmers dislike it because this tough plant crowds out pasture grasses and if their cows eat it, the milk tastes sour.

NONINVASIVE ALTERNATIVES
Cultivated daisies have bigger flowers, a fuller profile, and are not nearly as rampant. Shasta daisy (*Leucanthemum ×superbum*) is a fine choice.

LESS-TOXIC CONTROLS
Do not let it go to seed; instead, pick bouquets. Patrol the garden in late summer and early fall for rosettes of unwanted plants, which are easy to remove when still small. If wild daisy is invading your lawn, this is a likely indication that the soil is compacted and/or too acidic. Mow both grasses and unwanted daisies low, then undertake some soil aeration and perhaps add some lime.

CHEMICAL CONTROLS
Picloram and imazapyr work but these herbicides linger in the soil.

Linaria vulgaris

Butter-and-eggs, Yellow toadflax

This sun-loving, drought-tolerant, summer-blooming plant forms a profile of erect sprays. The stems are lined with alternating, gray-green, almost grassy leaves; the lower ones tend to be opposite or whorled. Atop the stems are flower clusters. The unusual 1-inch spurred blooms are sunny yellow with a yolk-orange lower lip, resembling tiny snapdragon flowers (to which they are related). Small dark capsules that follow hold tiny, black, waferlike, winged seeds that the wind disperses. Roots are tough and pencil-thick. Mature plants are 1 to 3 feet tall.

PROBLEM

Seeds and spreads by creeping roots in dry, open areas, crowding out native or desirable plants. Cattle avoid the plant due to its acrid flavor, eating competing grasses, thus allowing butter-and-eggs to flourish.

REPRODUCTION

Seeds as well as creeping rhizomes and root bits.

ORIGIN

The Mediterranean region. Imported to North America as an ornamental.

LESS-TOXIC CONTROLS

Tough to eradicate unless you extract the entire root system. Tear or dig out unwanted plants, a task easier done when the ground is damp. Mow down flowering plants before they can go to seed. Repeat as needed.

CHEMICAL CONTROLS

None recommended.

NOTES

Studies have shown that the orange "path" on the distinctive flowers' lower lip serves as a "honey guide" for insects. Only bumblebees, hawk moths, and other insects that are heavy enough to push open the flower can get at the nectar and transfer pollen. A similar species is Dalmatian toadflax (*Linaria dalmatica*), with larger flowers (1¾ inches) and oblong, clasping leaves.

NONINVASIVE ALTERNATIVES

Colorful snapdragons (*Antirrhinum majus*) and angelonia (*Angelonia angustifolia*) are relatives; though annuals, they are simple to grow and not invasive.

Lotus corniculatus
Bird's foot trefoil

A low-growing, often sprawling plant with cloverlike leaves (three cloverlike leaflets and two more at the base). The chubby little ½-inch flowers, which carry on all summer, are bright yellow, occasionally veering towards orange or red, and carried in flat-topped clusters of two to eight at the ends of the stems. These are followed by a slender, 1-inch, black seedpod that resembles a bird's foot. Over time, a deep taproot can form, going as deep as 3 feet. The plant, which at maturity is between 6 inches and 2 feet tall, thrives in sandy, well-drained soil.

PROBLEM
The plants form dense patches that exclude desirable plants, and their extensive root systems make them difficult to eradicate. This species has been included in wildflower-meadow mixes, so buyer beware.

REPRODUCTION
Seeds and runners.

ORIGIN
Europe. Introduced to the New World as a forage plant.

NOTES
Evidently it is delicious to grazing animals, whether cattle or deer, elk, and geese. Like other members of the pea family, it fixes nitrogen in the soil.

NONINVASIVE ALTERNATIVES
Try a yellow lupine if you like the color and want the nitrogen-fixing benefit.

LESS-TOXIC CONTROLS
Dig up plants while they are still young, making sure to get all the roots; new ones can generate from fragments left behind. For larger patches, persistent mowing when the plant emerges in spring and again before it goes to seed, season after season, will eventually lead to its demise.

CHEMICAL CONTROLS
Glyphosate is not recommended because some variants are resistant. Clopyralid is successful on this and other legumes.

Lysimachia clethroides

Gooseneck loosestrife

This loosestrife is distinguished from its relatives by the white drooping terminal flower clusters, each 8 to 12 inches long. These tend to droop in the same direction, a striking effect when there is a grouping or large stand; a patch has been likened to a "flock of eager geese dashing by." The tapering leaves are up to 6 inches long and alternate up the erect stems. The root system becomes fibrous and tenacious. Thrives in moist soil, sandy loam, but adapts to other conditions. Mature plant size is 2 to 3 feet tall.

LESS-TOXIC CONTROLS

Dig out unwanted plants while still young and small to contain a colony's spread. Alternatively, take steps to dry out the area, as lack of moisture is fatal. Barriers do not work.

CHEMICAL CONTROLS

Glyphosate may be used, but is not advised where gooseneck loosestrife mingles with desirable plants.

PROBLEM

Although it may get off to a slow start in most gardens, in two or three years, it grows densely and spreads rapidly to form impenetrable thickets. It is especially aggressive in moist sites.

REPRODUCTION

Creeping stems generate additional plants every year.

ORIGIN

Native to Japan and China.

NOTES

The genus name is Greek in origin and refers to peacemaking; the Roman writer Pliny went so far as to claim that when branches of this plant were laid on quarreling, yoked oxen, "perfect reconciliation" occurred.

NONINVASIVE ALTERNATIVES

Bugbane (*Actaea racemosa*) has even more dramatic white flower spires carried in candelabra formations, and it is not nearly as aggressive.

Lythrum salicaria

Purple loosestrife

An attractive plant around 2 to 4 feet tall that favors damp ground and full sun. Clumps of erect stems, lined with opposite or whorled unstalked leaves that are generally between 1 and 4 inches long, are topped with showy, purple to magenta flower spikes by midsummer. Over time, rootstocks become deep and massive.

PROBLEM

This aggressive plant is capable of spreading rapidly and always forms dense stands, effectively shading and thus eventually crowding out native and other wetland plants.

REPRODUCTION

Seeds, plus individual plants produce more stalks with each passing year.

ORIGIN

Introduced from Europe and Asia, perhaps as an ornamental but also probably via ballast and/or animal bedding.

LESS-TOXIC CONTROLS

Do not let it go to seed; instead, cut bouquets. Mowing and burning will check it but probably not eradicate it altogether. Digging it up by its roots is arduous and best attempted only on smaller plants.

CHEMICAL CONTROLS

Glyphosate with a surfactant has succeeded in some areas, but bear in mind the downsides of possible overspray and potential harm to aquatic creatures.

NOTES

Because it is such a handsome plant, purple loosestrife is a popular subject for landscape painters and photographers. Cultivated varieties in various colors, including 'Morden Pink', 'Dropmore Purple', and 'Morden Gleam', were offered by nurseries years ago. The plants were said to be sterile, but all fell out of favor and commerce when it was shown that they could cross-pollinate with wild plants.

NONINVASIVE ALTERNATIVES

Plant gayfeather (*Liatris spicata*) instead; it has the same color range but is not invasive.

Macleaya cordata

Plume poppy, Tree celandine

Synonym *Bocconia cordata*

A big, temperate-climate plant that looks almost tropical and attains between 6 and 10 feet tall and half as wide. Its lower leaves are large, up to 10 inches across, lobed, and heart-shaped, while those that ascend the towering stem are smaller; all are olive green on top and fuzzy gray-white underneath. The cream- to soft-pink colored, fragrant flowers, appearing in mid- to late summer, are carried in terminal plumelike panicles that can be 1 foot long. Roots become a hefty rhizome.

PROBLEM

In full sun and moist, fertile soil, it grows quickly and spreads aggressively.

REPRODUCTION

Suckers come off the creeping underground rhizomes. Also produces seeds that have, mercifully, a short viability of a year or two.

ORIGIN

From Japan and China.

NOTES

Attracts honeybees and songbirds. Fresh or dried, the flowers are nice in arrangements. Sap is toxic and stains clothing. In warm, wet summer weather, the plant may be attacked by slugs and/or disabled by anthracnose.

NONINVASIVE ALTERNATIVES

Consider bugbane (*Actaea racemosa*), which likes similar growing conditions but is not a thug. Bugbane also has a bushy, imposing habit, though it is shorter plant, up to 7 feet tall, and it displays candelabras of white flowers that admittedly are not sweetly scented.

LESS-TOXIC CONTROLS

If you grow it among other plants, thin it every spring and/or keep it in check by digging around the base to break up the spreading roots. Tear out any seedlings while still small. Prevent self-sowing by clipping off all flower plumes before they ripen. Alternatively, raise it in a large pot.

CHEMICAL CONTROLS

Glyphosate is effective.

Mentha species
Mints

There are many mints—peppermint, spearmint, pineapple mint, curly mint, water mint, to name but a few—but they all share the same basic characteristics: square stems, simple, opposite, toothed leaves, and tiny flowers borne in terminal spikes. Flower color is usually purple, sometimes pink or white, and plant fragrance is strong and refreshing. Firm identification can be tricky, as species interbreed readily and nurseries cannot or do not carefully identify and label their plants. Depending on the species and growing conditions, most plants are between 6 inches and 2 feet in height.

PROBLEM
If a mint plant has the partial shade and moist ground it relishes, it spreads very aggressively and resists casual attempts at control. It can invade entire flowerbeds and encroach on lawns in short order.

REPRODUCTION
Reseeds and has invasive, traveling roots.

ORIGIN
Most are native to Europe and Asia.

NOTES
Mint is and has long been prized as an edible plant, used in salads, drinks, jelly, and much more. It is also valued for its many medicinal uses, soothing everything from upset stomachs to insect bites to headaches. It has also been employed in various cosmetics, including soaps and toothpaste, and used as a repellent. In general, leaves are more useful and potent when fresh rather than dried or frozen.

NONINVASIVE ALTERNATIVES
Of all the mints, low-growing Corsican mint (*Mentha requienii*) is reputedly the least rampant.

LESS-TOXIC CONTROLS
Contain the rampant roots by growing your favorite mint in a pot on your porch or deck, or sunk into the garden. Consistently cut back burgeoning plants, putting the harvest to use as you choose.

CHEMICAL CONTROLS
None recommended.

Monarda species

Bee balms

This showy relative of mint tops its tall, leafy stems in midsummer onward with handsome flowerheads that are up to 4 inches across. These are usually ruby red, though there are many cultivated varieties that extend the color range to lavender, pink, and white. Like mint, the stems are square and the foliage is aromatic and dark green. Mature plant size is 3 to 4 feet tall and about half as wide.

PROBLEM
In some climates and in ideal growing conditions of moist, fertile soil, bee balm can become a real thug, growing ever more massive each season and elbowing or shading out its neighboring plants and invading nearby areas.

REPRODUCTION
Seeds and spreading roots.

LESS-TOXIC CONTROLS
Pull out unwanted plants. Move your plants or divisions to a spot where the soil is not as rich and/or is drier. Try containing a rampant plant with a metal barrier or plastic edging sunk down about a foot into the ground.

CHEMICAL CONTROLS
None recommended.

ORIGIN
North America.

NOTES
Bees, butterflies, and hummingbirds visit the flowers. Deer, on the other hand, tend to avoid it, probably due to its strong scent. Traditionally, this otherwise stalwart plant has been susceptible to mildew, which disfigures the leaves later in the growing season, but plant breeders have developed resistant varieties, notably red 'Jacob Cline' and pink 'Marshall's Delight'. Enjoy these in well-drained ground or pots.

NONINVASIVE ALTERNATIVES
If spectacular red flowers in your garden are still your wish, try peonies (*Paeonia*) or cardinal flower (*Lobelia cardinalis*).

Muscari botryoides

Grape hyacinth

The fragrant flowers on this spring-flowering bulb are softer in color than the uber-popular *Muscari armeniacum*, sky-blue, each flower edged in white. The racemes, as the dense clusters are called, generally measure between 1 and 3 inches high on plants 4 to 8 inches tall at best. The long, strappy leaves are mid-green. The plant adapts well to sun or shade, dry or damp soil.

PROBLEM

Its easygoing, adaptable nature allows it to spread freely, often becoming weedy and heading into areas where it is not wanted. The problem is particularly acute for lawns, where it is hard to contain the plants once they invade.

REPRODUCTION

Seeds are produced in autumn, but more commonly, this species expands itself—vigorously—via summer-produced offsets.

ORIGIN

Central Europe and the Mediterranean region.

NOTES

This species has been in cultivation a long time, by some records, as far back as the late 1500s. Its flowers are hermaphroditic (have both male and female organs); the plant is both self-fertile and pollinated by insects. This bulb is very cold-hardy, surviving most winters easily.

NONINVASIVE ALTERNATIVES

Other species in the same genus that are better behaved include pale blue *Muscari pallens* and pretty yellow-flowered *M. macrocarpum*, available from bulb specialists.

LESS-TOXIC CONTROLS

Dig out unwanted plants by the roots. For larger patches, mow down before the flowers go to seed.

CHEMICAL CONTROLS

None recommended.

Ornithogalum arabicum

Star-of-Bethlehem

Whether grown as an early-summer-blooming bulb or for use as a cut flower, star-of-Bethlehem produces richly fragrant, creamy white, cup-shaped blooms that command attention. Individual blooms are a mere 1½ inches across and boast a prominent black ovary in the center. They appear in robust, rounded racemes of between six and twenty-five. Moist soil and full sun allow them to thrive. Mature plants reach 1 to 3 feet tall.

PROBLEM
In milder climates where winter temperature never fall below -10°F, this plant overwinters and produces offsets prolifically. If not checked, it will invade other garden beds and insinuate into lawns as well.

REPRODUCTION
Via offsets.

ORIGIN
Native to the Mediterranean.

NOTES
For best bouquet flowers, pick when the three lowest flowers of a stem are showing color/opening. Warning: all plant parts are poisonous if ingested.

NONINVASIVE ALTERNATIVES
A white-flowered hyacinth, such as *Hyacinthus orientalis* 'White Festival', will also give you fragrance and cut flowers but is not a thug.

LESS-TOXIC CONTROLS
Grow these bulbs in containers, and pot up and give away offsets to gardening friends with a warning about setting them loose in the garden. Dig up unwanted plants in early spring, making sure to get the entire root system and offsets.

CHEMICAL CONTROLS
None recommended.

Oxalis corniculata

Creeping wood sorrel, Yellow wood sorrel

The lightly hairy stems and tiny yellow flowers, ¼ inch in diameter or smaller, emerge from a creeping stem that roots at the nodes. The leaves are divided into three rounded leaflets reminiscent of clover, and come in green or purple. When ripe, the skinny ½-inch seedpod ejects its tiny seeds. The roots (technically stolons) are long, slender, and creeping. Stems can reach 12 inches long and have a sprawling horizontal habit.

LESS-TOXIC CONTROLS
Yank out plants while still young; do not let them go to seed. Knock down larger patches with a sharp hoe, again, before they have a chance to go to seed.

CHEMICAL CONTROLS
Not advised if the creeping plants have intermixed with other, desirable ones. That said, Oxalis-X, a targeted herbicide whose active ingredient is liquid ammonium thiosulfate, is reportedly effective.

PROBLEM
A persistent and prolific weed, it insinuates itself into flowerbeds, lawns, between bricks and paving stones, and open spots with speed and abandon.

REPRODUCTION
Seeds and rootstocks.

ORIGIN
Probably Europe, but unknown.

NOTES
The genus name comes from the Greek word *oxys*, which means "sour." The leaves are rich in Vitamin C and edible, with a sour, lemony tang, but contain oxalic acid, as do all the parts of the plants. Note that the oxalic acid it contains is not safe in large doses.

NONINVASIVE ALTERNATIVES
The so-called purple shamrock (*Oxalis triangularis*) has purple leaves and white flowers and is a popular houseplant. 'Charmed® Wine' is a recent, promising cultivar.

Oxalis stricta

Upright yellow wood sorrel, Sourgrass

Delicate, pale green, cloverlike leaflets adorn an erect growth habit that reaches 6 to 15 inches tall. The yellow flowers bloom all summer and are sometimes reddish towards their base. Distinguished from other *Oxalis* species by the bent stalks that hold the erect seedpods. When ripe and brushed against, the seedpods eject their seeds 10 feet or more. This oxalis grows from a small bulblet. Favors dry, open areas and is drought-tolerant.

LESS-TOXIC CONTROLS
Yank out plants while still young; do not let them go to seed. Knock down larger patches with a sharp hoe, again, before they have a chance to go to seed. Dig out individual plants, making sure to get the entire root system, bulblet and all.

CHEMICAL CONTROLS
Glyphosate is not lastingly effective; fall application of liquid 2,4-D has been successful for some gardeners. Oxalis-X, whose active ingredient is liquid ammonium thiosulfate, is reportedly effective.

PROBLEM
An aggressive and stubborn plant, quickly earning the ire of homeowners and gardeners as it invades both cultivated and wild areas.

REPRODUCTION
Seeds (up to 60,000 per plant) and rootstocks. The plant may root at lower nodes.

ORIGIN
North America.

NOTES
Like all members of the genus, this species contains oxalic acid, which is not safe in large doses, and its edible leaves are rich in Vitamin C. Alternatives include *Oxalis perdicaria*, with a low, spreading habit, and *O. grandis*, with bigger flowers and purple-edged leaves.

NONINVASIVE ALTERNATIVES
It is wise to confine any appealing cultivated oxalis to a container.

Pastinaca sativa

Wild parsnip

This short-lived perennial sometimes behaves like a biennial: in the first season, it develops a rosette of large leaves and a hefty white to yellowish taproot. The leaves are toothed, rough-textured, and furry underneath. In the second season, or later, the plant sends up a deeply grooved, stout stem. Stem leaves are carried in big leaflets of five to fifteen. The pale yellow flower clusters appear in early to midsummer. Adaptable, but likes full sun and fertile soil best. Mature plants are 2 to 5 feet tall.

PROBLEM
Wild parsnip tends to invade an area in stages. Once the population builds, however, it spreads rapidly and crowds out indigenous plants.

LESS-TOXIC CONTROLS
Act early in a plant's life. Using a sharp shovel or spade, cut the entire root just below ground level. This prevents resprouting. In some soil types, in wet conditions, the plants can easily be pulled out of the ground by hand. Never let this plant go to seed; cut or mow it back beforehand.

CHEMICAL CONTROLS
Glyphosate and 2,4-D are most effective when spot-applied to first-year rosettes.

REPRODUCTION
Seeds.

ORIGIN
From Europe. Introduced as an edible, which then escaped.

NOTES
This is the wild form of the garden parsnip. When wet, the leaves produce an allergic skin reaction in some people that is exacerbated by exposure to sunlight. The resultant itching and blistering are reminiscent of exposure to poison ivy or a burn injury. The best remedy in such situations is to retreat indoors and wash the area well.

NONINVASIVE ALTERNATIVES
Garden parsnips, available in seed packets in early spring locally or from mail-order seed houses. Note that they need cool to cold fall weather to develop desirable sweeter flavor.

Physalis alkekengi

Chinese lantern

In spring, this plant is nothing more than a medium-size, rounded-bushy herb with green, ovate leaves alternating up erect stalks. The white flowers, borne in the axils, do not stand out much. The inflated, orange-red, papery "Chinese lantern" calyx that follows in late summer captures attention. Mature plants are between 18 and 24 inches tall.

PROBLEM

Gardeners may love the look of the lanterns, but if growing them in a traditional flowerbed or garden, soon rue the day they welcomed this invasive plant. The plants spread alarmingly quickly via underground stems, sending up new shoots all over the place and often surprisingly far from the original site.

REPRODUCTION

Seeds and creeping rootstocks.

ORIGIN

Japan and southeastern Europe.

NOTES

Stems with orange lanterns are popular in dried fall flower arrangements. The genus name is derived from *physa*, which means "bladder" and of course refers to the large calyx/lanterns.

NONINVASIVE ALTERNATIVES

Honesty (*Lunaria annua*) is a handsome plant for fall flower arrangements as well, and not nearly as aggressive.

LESS-TOXIC CONTROLS

Cut stems before they can go to seed, using use them in arrangements. Because even root pieces can regenerate, unwanted plants need to be dug up completely. If you have a big patch, mow it low before it goes to seed, then using a garden fork, patiently sift though the entire area extracting the roots. If you love the lanterns, raise plants in a large container or tub instead.

CHEMICAL CONTROLS

Glyphosate is effective, but repeated treatments may be necessary.

Pinellia ternata

Pinellia, Crow-dipper

Synonym *Pinellia tuberifera*

This small green woodland plant has trifoliate leaves and a flower typical of plants in the arum family (Araceae), a slightly hooded green spathe, with a protruding, slender spadix, like Jack-in-the-pulpit. Long white stems generate from small, ¼ inch, round underground corms or bulbils, a formation some horticulturists call "mouse tails." The plant prospers in fertile, well-drained soil and full sun to partial shade. Mature size is between 5 and 8 inches high.

PROBLEM
It grows aggressively and spreads rapidly, overtaking other garden plants and invading lawn areas. Eradication requires digging because the root systems are several inches below the soil surface and if you only yank off the leaves, the plant simply generates more.

REPRODUCTION
Via bulblet offsets.

ORIGIN
Native to China, Korea, and Japan.

NOTES
The plant is poisonous when raw, but when processed and cooked has been used in traditional Chinese medicine for treating obesity, for controlling nausea and vomiting, and for reducing mucus or phlegm.

LESS-TOXIC CONTROLS
Dig out the plants by the roots and discard.

CHEMICAL CONTROLS
None recommended.

NONINVASIVE ALTERNATIVES
Similar plants that like comparable growing conditions but are better behaved are Jack-in-the-pulpit (*Arisaema triphyllum*) and green dragon (*A. dracontium*).

Plantago major

Plantain, Broad-leaved plantain

Easily recognizable by its rosette, which is composed of broad, spade-shaped, strongly ribbed basal leaves. In summer, erect spiky stalks lined with tiny whitish green flowers arise from the center, eventually turning into tightly packed seed capsules. Rosettes are generally up to 12 inches across, flower stalks arising 6 to 18 inches above.

PROBLEM
This weed is an aggressive and successful spreader. If not arrested, it can fill in broad areas to exclude all other plants, including lawn grass, forming a ragged-looking groundcover.

REPRODUCTION
Seeds, which are wind-pollinated, and new shoots from roots.

ORIGIN
Introduced from Europe and Central Asia.

NOTES
Contains compounds that are useful in the treatment of cancers and infectious diseases. A poultice made from astringent leaves is prized for an impressive array of medicinal uses, including easing inflammation, itching, infection, wounds, sores, and burns. The seeds and the roots are also valued for numerous other therapeutic and medicinal uses. Related species include English plantain (*Plantago lanceolata*), with leaves more slender and flowerhead bushy, and seaside plantain (*P. juncoides*), with slender, fleshy leaves and a longer inflorescence.

LESS-TOXIC CONTROLS
Yank or dig out unwanted plants by the roots before they go to seed, easiest when the ground is damp; they are too low-growing to be beaten back by mowing. Try heavy mulching or allowing surrounding plants to shade it out. Since plantain thrives in compacted, lean soil, take steps to improve an infested area before overplanting with a more desirable plant or lawn grass.

CHEMICAL CONTROLS
Glyphosate is effective.

NONINVASIVE ALTERNATIVES
If you want a durable green groundcover, an alternative to lawn grass, consider pachysandra.

Potentilla recta and *P. norvegica*

Wild potentilla, Rough-fruited cinquefoil

Like other cinquefoils, these two have foliage displayed in leaflets of five, or, at times, seven or nine; margins are toothed. The stems are hairy and erect. The terminal, pale yellow flower clusters sparsely cover the plants in summer. Individual flowers are bigger than those of some related species, between ½ and 1 inch across. Both species have hairy seedpods, as reflected in one of their shared common names. They like limestone and poor-quality soils. Mature plant size is 1 to 2 feet tall.

PROBLEM
Few animals, wild or domesticated, seem interested in eating these plants, so they have been free to spread. Their ability to send up vertical stalks means they can outcompete lower-growing plants for pollinators. In open, sunny areas, they thrive and ultimately elbow out competing plants.

LESS-TOXIC CONTROLS
Yank out or hoe out plants while still young; do not let them go to seed. Undertake soil improvement and replant the area with desired plants.

CHEMICAL CONTROLS
None recommended.

REPRODUCTION
Seeds.

ORIGIN
Introduced from Europe.

NOTES
Potentilla is a large and weedy genus. You may also encounter common cinquefoil (*Potentilla simplex*), flowers and leaves arise from runners on separate stalks, long, rooting stolons; silverweed (*P. anserina*), creeping habit, mix of leaflet sizes; Canadian dwarf cinquefoil (*P. canadensis*), creeping habit, silvery-downy stems; or prairie cinquefoil (*P. arguta*), clump-forming, with stalks topped with small yellow flowers. All of these spread via rooting runners.

NONINVASIVE ALTERNATIVES
Garden (cultivated) potentillas derived mostly from *Potentilla fruticosa* are pretty and well behaved. These include cherry-pink flowered 'Miss Wilmott', red-flowered 'Gibson's Scarlet', and yellow-flowered 'William Rollison'.

Ranunculus ficaria

Lesser celandine, Fig buttercup

Easily identified by its long-stalked, heart-shaped leaves of varying sizes, this pesky groundcover produces yellow flowers in springtime. The flowers also show a lot of variation, some with five petals, some with many more. Fruits are long, thin capsules. In late summer, plants tend to die back. Drying stalks contain a bright orange dye. Many small bulblets form aboveground; the plants also have underground tubers. Thrives in damp shade. Full-grown plants are 2 to 6 inches high with a sprawling habit.

PROBLEM

Once established, it forms a dense carpet that shades out competing native plants or, if allowed into a shade garden, vies for space and resources with spring bulbs and perennials.

REPRODUCTION

The vigorous tubers produce new rosettes every year. Also reproduces via seed.

ORIGIN

Native to Europe and probably imported to North America as an ornamental.

LESS-TOXIC CONTROLS

Dig out unwanted plants completely in spring or summer, while the plants are still visible; be careful to extract all bulblets.

CHEMICAL CONTROLS

Glyphosate is effective, but beware of exposing any amphibians. Apply it in late winter or early spring.

NOTES

Resembles the native plant marsh marigold (*Caltha palustris*), but that plant is more often seen along streams, ponds, and wet ditches, plus it lacks the bulblets and tubers described above. The poet William Wordsworth admired this plant for its bright, early blooms; an image of it is carved on his gravestone. The plant is reputed to have medicinal uses, for everything from removing warts to treating gall-bladder problems.

NONINVASIVE ALTERNATIVES

The native American plant, goldenstar (*Chrysogonum virginianum*) or, if you like your yellow buttercup-ish flowers taller, try globeflower (*Trollius*).

Ranunculus repens

Creeping buttercup

This buttercup grows from a short, thick, bulblike base, sending up low, creeping hairy stems (stolons) that root and then form new rosettes at the nodes— just like strawberry plants. The leaves, as is typical of this genus, are three-lobed; they often exhibit pale blotches and might remind you of hardy geranium leaves. The abundant small, 1 inch or so, flowers are bright shiny yellow, with five to seven petals; these bloom all summer and often into fall. Leaves and flowers connect to the creeping stems by long stems (petioles). This plant thrives in moist ground and is 1 to 3 feet tall.

PROBLEM
Creeping buttercup grows exponentially from the creeping stems, forming large colonies that exclude all other plants. An invader of lawns, it also is a daunting problem in any damp, sunny spot.

REPRODUCTION
By runners but also via seeds, which have been shown to remain viable in the soil for years.

ORIGIN
Introduced from Europe, possibly as an ornamental groundcover, or in forage hay.

NOTES
Plant parts are poisonous if ingested; cattle avoid these plants.

NONINVASIVE ALTERNATIVES
The native American plant, goldenstar (*Chrysogonum virginianum*) or, if you like your yellow buttercup-ish flowers taller, try globeflower (*Trollius*).

LESS-TOXIC CONTROLS
Hand-pull plants diligently and with care, trying to get up all the creeping roots; this task is easiest earlier in the season and when the ground is damp. If this weed is in your lawn, take steps to improve the lawn's health, which can lead to this weed's decline: aerate, avoid compaction, add lime, and so forth.

CHEMICAL CONTROLS
Some herbicides, notably 2,4-D, are effective, but should be avoided around wetlands, ponds, and streamsides.

Rhaponticum repens

Russian knapweed

Synonym(s) *Centaurea repens, Acroptilon repens*
This bushy, branching, perennial knapweed forms an extensive root system over time, up to 8 feet deep, and can live up to 75 years. It does best in damp soil, full sun, and tolerates alkaline and salty ground. The urn-shaped flowers are small, up to ½ inch across, pinkish purple with cream-tipped bracts; they bloom in summer. Basal leaves are deeply lobed and 2 to 4 inches long; numerous upper leaves are thin and about 1 inch long. The mature plant is between 2 and 3 feet tall.

PROBLEM
A large patch might very well be just one plant with many clones, making eradication a challenge. Tilling and cultivating only chop up the roots, which can regenerate.

REPRODUCTION
Creeping roots and seeds.

ORIGIN
Accidentally introduced to North America from Asia around 1900 in alfalfa seed.

NOTES
It releases chemicals into the soil that inhibit the growth of other plants. It is harmful or toxic to horses, causing chewing disease, but apparently is tolerated by cattle and sheep.

NONINVASIVE ALTERNATIVES
None.

LESS-TOXIC CONTROLS
Dig out plants by their roots while young, if possible. Cut back or mow down more-established plants before they can go to seed. Keep after them, eradicating newcomers as they appear. Avoid spreading seeds by carefully checking your clothing, pet fur, and anything else that might have come in contact with the plants. A couple of biocontrol insects are being tried in rangelands but are not at the disposal of smaller landowners or home gardeners.

CHEMICAL CONTROLS
Treat with clopyralid prior to bloom or in the fall after a light frost.

Rumex crispus

Curly dock, Curled dock

This erect-growing weed has leaves with markedly wavy margins; larger at the base, they are smaller and fewer as they ascend the grooved, rigid stem. The flowers are borne in branching clusters at the stem tops all summer and are reddish green. These give way to brown fruits with heart-shaped wings. Over time, the plant develops a carrot-shaped taproot with brown skin and creamy white flesh. The plant favors rich, heavy soil and prospers in fields, waste places, and the sunny margins of gardens. When mature, plants are between 1 and 4 feet tall.

PROBLEM

Once the taproot has developed, this plant is very tenacious and difficult to eradicate; even if severed, it can generate new plants. This plant is also a prolific self-sower.

REPRODUCTION

Seeds (wind-pollinated) and rootstocks.

ORIGIN

Native to Europe and Asia. Imported to North America as a useful herb.

NOTES

Dock has a long history as a medicinal plant. Leaves were applied to burns, blisters, and nettle stings. The roots serve as a laxative; crushed, they were used by Native Americans to treat boils and abrasions. The leaves are high in Vitamin C, but are so high in oxalic acid that they taste very sour; boiling them helps, or you may eat very young ones in salads.

NONINVASIVE ALTERNATIVES

The leaves of dock's close relative sorrel (*Rumex acetosa*) impart a wonderful lemony taste to salads and cold summer soups, not to mention, it is a more handsome plant.

LESS-TOXIC CONTROLS

Do not let dock go to seed in or near your garden. Dig out plants by the roots using a garden fork.

CHEMICAL CONTROLS

Glyphosate is effective.

Stachys byzantina

Lamb's ears

Synonym(s) *Stachys lanata, S. olympica*

This sprawling plant is grown primarily for its silvery gray foliage, which offers a handsome contrast to other garden plants, particularly purple-, pastel-, and red-flowered ones. Individual leaves are typically about 4 inches long, oblong to lance-shaped, and velvety soft. Stout, woolly flower spikes rise up in spring and summer, studded with small magenta flowers. The plant tolerates most soils except soggy ground and will rot in very damp or humid summers. Full-grown plants are 8 to 16 inches tall and 2 to 3 feet wide.

PROBLEM

In optimal growing conditions, it self-sows and spreads aggressively, over-taking and flopping over adjacent plants. It can be especially rampant in warmer climates.

REPRODUCTION

Seeds and creeping roots.

ORIGIN

Native to Turkey, Iran, and Armenia. Imported to North America as an ornamental.

NOTES

This plant is a member of the mint family. It is popular with bees and butterflies; deer avoid eating it. The genus name, *Stachys*, is Greek for "an ear of grain," referring to the shape of the flower spikes. The species name, *byzantina*, refers to the plant's Middle Eastern origins, including an area that was once part of the Byzantine Empire.

NONINVASIVE ALTERNATIVES

A nonflowering cultivar, 'Silver Carpet', obviously will not self-sow. Or, try the stalwart annual dusty miller (*Senecio cineraria*).

LESS-TOXIC CONTROLS

Cut off flower stalks before they go to seed to prevent self-sowing. Divide overgrown plants, discarding or giving away the extras. Confine plants to designated areas by sinking barriers into the ground several inches deep. Dig up and discard unwanted plants. Do not till—root bits can regenerate.

CHEMICAL CONTROLS

Glyphosate is effective.

Tanacetum vulgare

Tansy

The flowerheads of tansy are the plant's most memorable feature—they are bright orange-yellow and buttonlike, each "button" measuring ½ inch across and displayed with others in a flat-topped cluster. Tansy blooms from midsummer on into fall. The leaves are finely divided into toothed segments, looking somewhat like a fern frond or the foliage of yarrow or Queen Anne's lace, the latter two, its relatives. The entire plant has a strong, pungent, not especially pleasant scent and reaches 2 to 3 feet tall.

PROBLEM
It can invade and take over open areas and becomes rampant in areas of damp soil.

REPRODUCTION
Via seeds and rootstocks.

ORIGIN
Introduced from Europe and Asia as a medicinal herb.

NOTES
The leaves and stem contain tanacetum, an oil that is toxic even in small doses. For centuries, tansy was used to cause abortions, sometimes killing the mother as well. It has proven useful as an insecticide; indeed, its scent protects itself from leaf-eating insects. It also has been used to wrap the deceased or line coffins. It has been successful as a companion plant, where it serves as a natural deterrent to garden pests. Some traditional dyers use tansy to produce a golden-yellow color. Dried flowers are used in wreaths and floral arrangements.

NONINVASIVE ALTERNATIVES
Closely related, pretty, citrus-scented feverfew (*Tanacetum parthenium*, synonym *Chrysanthemum parthenium*) has similar leaves and small daisylike flowers.

LESS-TOXIC CONTROLS
To enjoy it, grow it in a pot, aboveground, or sunk into your herb garden. To get rid of it, dig it up by the roots; larger patches can be mowed repeatedly until the plants give up.

CHEMICAL CONTROLS
None recommended.

Taraxacum officinale

Dandelion

The basal rosette is composed of jagged (irregularly teethed), lobed leaves. Stalks emerge from the center, each bearing a single yellow flowerhead 1 to 2 inches across. The flower opens in the morning and closes in the evening and on overcast days. It ultimately ripens to a white puffball of silky seeds, the tiny seeds being brown or olive-green. The juice in the hollow stems is milky. The plant develops a notoriously deep taproot. Basal leaves are 12 or more inches long; plant height, between 6 and 18 inches.

PROBLEM
Dandelion spreads quickly and abundantly in lawns and gardens, and is hard to eradicate.

REPRODUCTION
Wind-borne seeds and new shoots/rosettes from roots.

ORIGIN
Introduced from Europe and Asia.

NOTES
The "lion" part of the common name refers to the teethed leaves (in French, *dents de lion*, "lion's teeth"). Fresh-picked young leaves are good in salads or sandwiches and a good source of Vitamin A. There are also a host of medicinal uses, from increasing milk production in nursing mothers to treating jaundice and arthritis to providing therapeutic benefits to the liver, kidneys, and urinary tract. The flowers are a good source of pollen and nectar for bees.

NONINVASIVE ALTERNATIVES
Try dark, leafy greens such as kale and spinach.

LESS-TOXIC CONTROLS
Do not let it go to seed; cut off or mow down the plants in the flower stage. Dig out individual plants by the roots; a dandelion fork is wonderfully effective. Leaving behind small or chopped-up bits only leads to more plants.

CHEMICAL CONTROLS
There are many on the market, but 2,4-D applied in the fall appears to be the most effective.

Verbascum olympicum, V. thapsus, V. blattaria, and *V. phlomoides*

Mulleins

These impressive plants develop big rosettes of large, thick, flannel-textured, smooth-edged, lance-shaped leaves and send up tall, erect, woolly stalks lined with more, smaller leaves and topped by a flower stalk. The spikes are a dense cluster of small yellow or white flowers that open from the bottom up. The fruit, a two-parted capsule, contains numerous tiny black seeds. Although technically a biennial, because plants form and overwinter a rosette the first year and bloom the second, mullein commonly has a lifespan of three or more years. Mature plants are 2 to 6 feet tall, with rosette leaves up to 1 foot long.

LESS-TOXIC CONTROLS

Cut them down before they go to seed. Dig out individuals below the relatively shallow crown. Undertake soil improvement/enrichment and overplant with desirable plants.

CHEMICAL CONTROLS

Glyphosate or triclopyr, mixed with a surfactant to help it adhere to the woolly leaves, is effective.

PROBLEM

Mulleins colonize open, sunny spots to the exclusion of native or desirable plants.

REPRODUCTION

Seeds (up to 170,000 per plant), which require light to germinate, but can remain viable decades in the soil until exposed.

ORIGIN

Native to Europe and Asia.

NOTES

The thick, velvety leaves have been put to many interesting uses, from lining shoes, socks, or moccasins for extra warmth to making a tea to treat colds. The flowers and roots have been used in the treatments of everything from earaches to croup. Faded flower stalks have been dipped in grease and used as torches.

NONINVASIVE ALTERNATIVES

Horticulturists have developed self-sterile hybrids that have pretty flowers, notably the multihued 'Copper Rose' and apricot 'Jackie'.

Vinca minor

Myrtle, periwinkle

A rambling groundcover, easily identified by its glossy green, opposite leaves and its springtime show of five-petaled, 1-inch pinwheelish flowers, purple-blue with white centers. Cultivated varieties include ones with bigger flowers, ones with lighter or pink or even all-white flowers, and/or ones with variegated foliage, including gold-splashed or white-rimmed. Tolerates acidic or alkaline soil, dry or wet, though it will expire in downright sodden ground. When mature, plants are no more than 4 to 8 inches tall, with a spreading habit to around 3 feet.

LESS-TOXIC CONTROLS

Pull out by hand if you can, being thorough about tracing down and extracting all runners. Alternatively, rake over an infested area to "fluff up" the runners, then mow and cover the area with a mulch to suppress any return. May be contained and enjoyed in pots and windowboxes.

CHEMICAL CONTROLS

Glyphosate is effective.

PROBLEM

An aggressive spreader in moist shade, it forms a dense, ever-expanding carpet that invades and chokes, or excludes, other plants.

REPRODUCTION

Via underground runners, rooting at the nodes. Only rarely by seeds.

ORIGIN

Introduced from Europe for ornamental and medicinal uses.

NOTES

Unlike some flowering groundcovers, this one tolerates foot traffic, seems impervious to common plant diseases, and chokes out many weeds. The leaves are toxic for animals and the seeds too small to nourish birds. Was once valued as a treatment for diabetes, headaches, and intestinal problems, but modern herbals make little mention of it.

NONINVASIVE ALTERNATIVES

An equally tough but nonaggressive groundcover for similar growing conditions is barren strawberry (*Waldsteinia fragarioides*), however, the flowers are yellow.

Viola species

Violet, Johnny jump-up, Hearts-ease, Wild pansy

There are many violet species and garden (cultivated) varieties, and they can and do cross-hybridize, making firm identification a challenge at times. They are all similar in appearance and growth habit. Leaves are generally dark green, glossy, heart-shaped or triangular, and alternate. The dainty spring-blooming flowers, which may be sweetly fragrant, are symmetrical and have five petals, five sepals, five stamens, and a backward-facing spur. Color varies, from purple to blue to yellow to white, mainly, sometimes with contrasting colors or accenting markings called "whiskers." Little seed-laden capsules follow. Roots are usually thickened rhizomes. Most plants mature at 8 to 10 inches high and wide, though some are smaller.

LESS-TOXIC CONTROLS

Yank out unwanted seedlings before flowers can go to seed, and repeat again in late summer when the second round of seedpods form. When pulling or digging out, be sure to get the entire root system.

CHEMICAL CONTROLS

Triclopyr is effective.

PROBLEM

In decent soil with adequate moisture, violets become thugs, shooting their ripe seeds all over the yard and garden, invading lawns and flowerbeds.

REPRODUCTION

Seeds and creeping roots. In late summer, many species generate self-fertilizing flowerbuds right near the ground, for yet another round of seed dispersal.

ORIGIN

Some species are native; others are European introductions.

NOTES

These flowers have a long and colorful history in poetry and myth, in romance, in medicine, in cosmetics and perfumes, and in the kitchen, where they have been used in jelly, for making violet water, and as candied violets.

NONINVASIVE ALTERNATIVES

Pansies are well-behaved. Or, if you like violets but do not want hundreds, grow them in pots.

6

Grasses and Bamboos

Grasses, bamboos, and their relatives are some of the most successful plants on the planet, and we often have ourselves to blame if these plants are growing too successfully or in the wrong places. It is in the very nature of grasses, bamboos, and similar plants to form broad, monocultural stands. Many have creeping rhizomes, stolons that root, and/or impressive seed production abilities—all in the service not only of survival but also of profuse spread. These reproductive strategies foster dense growth.

The presence of these plants often leads to extra work for and frustration on the part of the gardener or homeowner, not to mention the professional landscaper or golf-green, parkland, or playing-field manager. Our wish for or insistence on a monocultural greensward, for instance, or a weed-free vegetable patch or orchard means that we are always expending effort on excluding plants that want in. If it is a clean slate of open, fertile soil, buried or arriving seeds or rhizome bits are bound to grow before or during our cultivating efforts. If it is an area of neglect, perhaps wet or compacted ground, this, too, is seized upon as an opportunity for ever-resourceful grasses, bamboos, and grassy weeds.

The scope of our horticultural plans is another factor in this familiar battle. We carve out a lawn or garden in a once-wild or reclaimed area and then have to fight to keep out unwanted invaders. Many of the plants in this chapter are simply too expansion-minded (if you will) for our (relatively speaking) modest cultivated patches.

Agropyron cristatum

Crested wheatgrass, Fairway crested wheatgrass

A tufted, cool-season perennial bunchgrass, wheatgrass is used in lawns and for erosion control. Individual blades are up to ¼ inch wide. Seed spikes are short, broad, between 1½ and 3 inches, tapering at the tip. The plant is 10 to 40 inches tall and develops an extensive fibrous root system.

PROBLEM
Crested wheatgrass adapts well to dry conditions and tolerates moderately alkaline soils; it does not prosper in loose sandy soils, heavy clays, or saline soils. It will crowd out native plants. The plant is cold-tolerant and has become a problem in the Great Plains, mostly in the more northerly parts and on into Canada.

REPRODUCTION
Spreads mostly by seed, which remains viable for up to five years. Also spreads by rhizomes and rhizome pieces, so tilling an infested area is a bad idea.

ORIGIN
Native to Russia.

NOTES
Fire-tolerant, so sometimes recommended for fire-prone landscapes. Patches or fields of escaped plants, or those that are allowed to go to seed, attract wildlife. Songbirds will not only eat the seeds but nest in thick stands of this grass.

NONINVASIVE ALTERNATIVES
A less aggressive cool-season grass for lawns in drier sites is the native buffalo grass (*Buchloe dactyloides*).

LESS-TOXIC CONTROLS
Where practical, yank or dig out unwanted plants. Contend with larger areas by mowing early and often, followed by smothering plants with mulch or plastic—tactics calculated to starve the roots. Overplant the area so the grass has a hard time returning.

CHEMICAL CONTROLS
Herbicides approved for grasses, such as glyphosate or dicamba, will kill it; apply according to label directions.

Arundinaria gigantea

Cane, Canebrake, River Cane, Bamboo

A true bamboo, its habit is upright, with lots of tufted, short, bright green stiff leaves at the nodes along the stems. Canes measure up to 1 inch in diameter. Forms dense groups or thickets. Clump size varies with the species, between 2 and 7 or more feet tall and nearly as wide.

PROBLEM
Rich, damp ground encourages rampant growth and spread.

REPRODUCTION
Via underground rhizomes.

ORIGIN
Native to the southeastern United States.

NOTES
Landscapers praise the way this plant confers a lush, tropical look when used for a hedge or screen. Native Americans reportedly used it for fuel, construction, weapons, baskets, jewelry, food, medicines, and even musical instruments (flutes); because wildlife sought shelter in large patches or "canebrakes," stands of these were good hunting areas.

NONINVASIVE ALTERNATIVES
Running bamboos are naturally aggressive and invasive. Try larger ornamental grasses instead if you cannot or do not wish to contain bamboo, or consider clumping bamboo (*Fargesia* spp.).

LESS-TOXIC CONTROLS
May stay in bounds in drier or well-drained ground; otherwise, confine individual plants to a deep bottomless container or grow aboveground in an ample pot. To eradicate unwanted plants, dig out entire rootstock, preferably while the plants are still young and the project is not impossible.

CHEMICAL CONTROLS
Spray with an herbicide labeled for bamboo control, following label instructions to the letter regarding timing and proper application.

Arundo donax

Giant reed

A huge, dramatic plant that is sometimes mistaken for a bamboo although technically it is a perennial grass. Blue-greenish leaves alternate up strong, hollow, upright stems that are 1 to 1½ inches in diameter. Leaves are narrow, flat, and droopy, resembling, at first glance, corn foliage, measuring up to 3 feet long and 1 to 3 inches wide. Technically a big panicle, the late-summer plumes begin reddish brown, and then turn white. A single panicle may be as long as 2 feet. Roots are creeping, knotty rhizomes. Prospers in moist, well-drained soil. Mature plants easily reach 12 to 20 feet high.

LESS-TOXIC CONTROLS

Chop down entire plants low, and then dig them out by the roots; this tactic will work only if you act early.

CHEMICAL CONTROLS

Glyphosate applied to chopped-back stands in fall works, but great care must be exercised because of possible harm to wetland creatures as well as unintended plant targets.

PROBLEM

Giant reed is very aggressive in moist ground and full sun. It clogs ditches, wetlands, roadsides, and open areas, excluding native and desirable vegetation and even changing the course of adjacent waterways. It has few, if any, natural enemies among insects or animals.

REPRODUCTION

Seeds and creeping rhizomes.

ORIGIN

Southern Europe and East Asia.

NOTES

The stiff, hollow stems have been used to make musical instruments (whistles, flutes), trellises, natural fences, fishing poles, thatching, rafts, and so forth. All plant parts contain toxic, unpalatable chemicals, including cardiac glycosides, nerve toxins, and silica.

NONINVASIVE ALTERNATIVES

If you really want this bamboolike look for, say, a windbreak or a natural fence, consider instead a clumping bamboo such as *Fargesia robusta* Green Screen™.

Bromus inermis

Smooth brome

A true perennial bunchgrass, this brome has smooth, usually unbranched stems and sports slender, flat blades no more than ¾ inch wide. It flowers in panicles early in summer; these have up to four stiff branches at each node that stick straight out to the sides or angle up slightly, distinguishing this species from its relatives. The seedheads that follow by summer's end darken to purple and droop slightly. Roots are dark-colored rhizomes that become quite substantial over time. Prospers in full sun in open areas, especially the edges of fields, roadsides, and pastures. Full-grown plants are 1 to 3 feet tall.

PROBLEM
The rhizomes form a dense mat that effectively excludes competition.

REPRODUCTION
Seeds and creeping rhizomes. It adapts easily to different climates and there are now Southern strains and Northern strains; also it can hybridize with native bromes.

ORIGIN
Europe. Introduced for erosion control and as a pasture and forage grass.

NOTES
Foliage is eaten by rabbits and other rodents, plus by elk, deer, and livestock. Unlike in other brome grasses, the spikelets lack awns that can injure the mouthparts and gastrointestinal tracts of wildlife. Gamebirds and some sparrows eat the seeds.

NONINVASIVE ALTERNATIVES
Consider instead the handsome native bunchgrass called little bluestem (*Schizachyrium scoparium*), which adapts well to home gardens in a mixed border, in a meadow garden, even in a big container.

LESS-TOXIC CONTROLS
Mow it down before flowers and hence seeds can form. New seedlings may still germinate, so repeat as needed.

CHEMICAL CONTROLS
Glyphosate, sprayed on unwanted plants in early summer before flowers form, is effective.

Bromus madritensis subsp. *rubens*

Red brome, Foxtail chess

Synonym *Bromus rubens*

An annual cool-season grass with spiky reddish purple, 2- to 3-inch florets that develop in spring. The short, narrow blades develop flat with prominent veins on both surfaces and a lightly furry texture. The plant has a shallow root system and is not shade-tolerant. Seeds germinate in the fall and burst into vigorous growth the following spring, when the flowers develop. Prospers in mild, moist winters and hot, dry summers. Mature plant size is 8 to 20 inches tall.

PROBLEM

Because it tolerates a range of soils, including alkaline and hardpan, red brome easily invades disturbed or neglected areas, crowding out native vegetation and providing fuel for wildfires. Due to its shallow roots, it is unsuitable for erosion control. This plant is a problem in semidesert areas of the West.

REPRODUCTION

Seeds, which are dispersed by water and animals, maybe wind.

ORIGIN

Southern Europe.

NOTES

Eaten by the desert tortoise, the Great Basin kangaroo rat, and sometimes cattle, but its short growing season and sharp florets limit its importance.

NONINVASIVE ALTERNATIVES

Red or purple fountain grass (*Pennisetum setaceum* 'Rubrum') is a handsome reddish grass suitable for gardens, in informal masses or confined to a large container.

LESS-TOXIC CONTROLS

Mowing down unwanted plants only works if done repeatedly; a single mowing inspires development of new culms. Plants are usually killed when cut at soil level once seeds have developed.

CHEMICAL CONTROLS

Pre-emergent herbicides kill the seeds in the soil before they germinate, but this tack will be risky in areas where there are valuable native or garden plants.

Bromus tectorum

Cheatgrass, Downy brome

Probably the most familiar and widely distributed annual pest grass. The thin main stem has long, narrow leaves that are usually covered in short, soft hairs. It germinates in fall or winter, and blooms the following summer before setting seed in panicles heavy enough to cause the stems to droop. Spikelets have long, pointy bristles that extend past the seed. The wine-red flowering stalks and seeds give a stand color. The root system is tangled and fibrous. Cheatgrass thrives in open, sunny areas, and dies back in midsummer. Plants are 18 to 24 inches tall.

PROBLEM
This aggressive spreader monopolizes soil nutrients and moisture, effectively outcompeting native and desirable plants, not just in wild areas, fields, and gardens but also in production nurseries and orchards.

REPRODUCTION
Seeds, which are dispersed by wind, birds, and animals including domestic and wild grazers. Bristles hitchhike on human clothing and socks as well as fur.

ORIGIN
From Europe, Africa, and Asia, probably in contaminated seed.

NOTES
"Tectorum" means roof, from this grass's historical penchant for growing on thatched roofs.

NONINVASIVE ALTERNATIVES
None. However, an "ornamental grass" with handsome seedheads is northern sea oats (*Chasmanthium latifolium*), whose self-sowing tendencies can be managed by mowing it down in late summer before the seeds ripen.

LESS-TOXIC CONTROLS
Smaller stands can be controlled but not eradicated with frequent mowing, before seeds form. Overplanting afterwards, with a native grass or a groundcover, may reclaim the area.

CHEMICAL CONTROLS
On a larger scale, that is, on fields and pastures where cheatgrass is rampant, success has been attained by spraying with glyphosate in concert with applying pre-emergent herbicides, mowing, and even controlled burns.

Cenchrus ciliaris

Buffelgrass, African foxtail grass

Synonym *Pennisetum ciliare*
A perennial warm-season bunchgrass, it starts growth in late winter, forming a shrubby clump of narrow, light-green, rough-textured blades. The purplish, fuzzy "bottlebrush" seedheads form at stalk ends and measure up to 5 inches long; these appear from spring through fall. The roots can reach down 6 to 10 feet, making the plant very drought tolerant and tenacious. Thrives in sandy and well-drained soil in areas with warm, frost-free winters and a summer rainy season. Mature plants are about 1½ feet tall by 3 feet wide.

PROBLEM
It forms dense stands, crowding out native plants, particularly saguaro cactus (*Carnegiea gigantea*), and thus harms native wildlife species, such as mule deer and desert tortoise, and their habitats. Not only is it very flammable, buffelgrass is also able to respond quickly to desert wildfires, filling in newly disturbed areas with seedlings.

REPRODUCTION
Seeds dispersed via wind, water, animal fur, and on clothing and footwear. Also spread by rhizomes.

LESS-TOXIC CONTROLS
Dig out seedlings by their roots. Do not let larger plants go to seed; mow them down early and repeatedly. Digging out larger plants is not practical due to the huge, deep root systems.

CHEMICAL CONTROL
Glyphosate may be effective at killing topgrowth, but will not kill seeds in the soil that can germinate later.

ORIGIN
From Africa and the Middle East, imported for erosion control as well as to increase cattle forage on dry rangelands.

NOTES
It cannot survive flooding or extended subfreezing temperatures.

NONINVASIVE ALTERNATIVES
The ornamental fountain grass (*Pennisetum alopecuroides*) and its cultivars are very attractive and controllable when confined or raised in containers.

Cortaderia selloana

Pampas grass

A giant among perennial grasses, pampas grass forms a bulky fountain of surprisingly sharp-edged grassy leaves. In midsummer, erect stalks arise 1 to 3 feet high, bearing white to cream to soft pink flower plumes up to 20 feet tall; these persist into winter. Roots as well as stems are tough and woody. The plant is very adaptable, growing in acid or alkaline soil, from dry ground to boggy spots. However, it does not tolerate shade well.

PROBLEM

Growth is astoundingly fast—8 feet in one season is not uncommon—and it easily shoves aside other vegetation. The extensive roots monopolize water and soil nutrients. Seed production is prolific, and so this beast spreads with impunity. Eradication is daunting.

REPRODUCTION

Seeds.

ORIGIN

Hails from Argentina, Brazil, and Uruguay.

NOTES

Nurseries offer smaller cultivars. A relative, purple pampas grass (*Cortaderia jubata*), has shorter leaves and fewer plumes, but is also a thug and just as difficult to dig out. Both have naturalized throughout California, in particular, to the extent that many people assume they are native.

NONINVASIVE ALTERNATIVES

Maiden grass (*Miscanthus sinensis*) and its cultivars have big showy plumes too, but friendlier foliage and are easier to manage (assuming, of course, that they are not invasive for you; in dry areas or short seasons, they tend not to be).

LESS-TOXIC CONTROLS

Dig out seedlings when you spot them. Chop down larger plants to the crown with a machete or heavy-duty weed whacker. You can then try to dig out or use a crowbar on the root ball. Some individuals have yanked out big plants by wrapping a rope or chain around the mass, cinching it, and pulling with a tractor or truck.

CHEMICAL CONTROLS

Glyphosate sprayed on the foliage is effective.

Cynodon dactylon

Bermuda grass, Devilgrass

A warm-season, dark to gray-green perennial lawn or turfgrass. Thanks to deep roots, it is drought-tolerant. It has a fine texture, though individual blades are rough-edged. It tolerates poor soil and salt, but is cold-sensitive, mottling yellowish at the first hint of cold and going dormant or brown over the winter months. If they develop, the seedheads are on 1- to 3-inch spikes and are about 2 inches long. Unmowed, this grass can reach 6 inches high.

PROBLEM
It is fast-growing and aggressive, forming mats that crowd out most other grasses and invading garden and other areas and habitats where it is not wanted.

REPRODUCTION
Spreads by runners and rhizomes. By seed, if it is not mowed before it flowers and sets seed; many hybrids are sterile, however.

ORIGIN
From southern Europe, Africa, Asia, and Australia. Imported to the United States via Bermuda as a pasture and forage grass.

NOTES
Earned its common name by becoming invasive and prevalent in Bermuda. Valued in Hindu India, where it is fed to (sacred) cows. It is also nutritious for sheep.

LESS-TOXIC CONTROLS
To contain it as a lawn grass, use a barrier or edging at least 8 inches deep to prevent it from straying. Dig up individual clumps by the roots. Persistent, repeated yanking and digging can stop it. Mulches, alas, only slow it down.

CHEMICAL CONTROLS
Glyphosate is effective when applied in late summer. Or, apply a grass-selective herbicide in early spring.

NONINVASIVE ALTERNATIVES
This will be dictated by your climate and growing conditions—seek advice locally. Buffalo grass (*Buchloe dactyloides*) is often suggested in warmer regions; it is not reliably hardy in the north.

Cyperus rotundus

Nutgrass

Not technically a grass but a sedge, nutgrass has the three-sided stems characteristic of sedges. The dark green leaves are thicker and stiffer than most grasses, and are arranged in sets of three from the base (rather than sets of two as in grass leaves). Flowers are carried in dark reddish to purplish brown spikelets, with few flowers in each cluster. The plant grows from a chain of white, fleshy tubers, with several on a single, horizontal, underground creeping stem (rhizome). Nutgrass favors damp ground but can tolerate a wide range of growing conditions. It usually reaches 12 to 18 inches tall.

PROBLEM

This plant can spread rampantly, forming thick colonies and thriving even in harsh growing conditions. It is a serious problem in agricultural fields and home gardens alike because it outcompetes desirable plants for available water and nutrients, and also because it is allelopathic (the roots release substances harmful to other plants).

REPRODUCTION

Tubers on creeping rhizomes.

ORIGIN

Africa, southern and central Europe, and southern Asia.

NOTES

Because it is so widely distributed and problematic, it has been dubbed "the world's worst weed." Yet it is used in Chinese and ayurvedic medicine to treat a range of conditions, including digestive ailments.

NONINVASIVE ALTERNATIVES

Some true sedges in the genus *Carex* are grown and enjoyed by gardeners.

LESS-TOXIC CONTROLS

Digging, hoeing, and plowing do not work because the roots and tubers are deep, persistent, and able to regenerate from fragments.

CHEMICAL CONTROLS

Glyphosate only works if applied repeatedly as plants resprout. Halosulfuron (brand name SedgeHammer) works if applied repeatedly as plants resprout.

Digitaria ischaemum

Crabgrass

Synonym *Digitaria sanguinalis*
A grass of wide, flat leaf blades and a sprawling, branching, flat-on-the-ground growth habit. Color is pale to flat green and the stems may be purplish. The purplish flowers, if they form, are on a panicle, arranged in three to thirteen "fingers" (that is, in "digitate" fashion). A fast-growing annual, crabgrass germinates in late spring or early summer and dies back by fall. It thrives in infertile, light soil. Plants spread outward to 12 or more inches and form flower spikes 15 or more inches tall.

PROBLEM
An opportunist, crabgrass moves in where there is space, thin grass, and/or poor growing conditions, forming large, dense mats and outcompeting surrounding plants.

REPRODUCTION
Seeds (up to 150,000 per plant in one season). In addition, the plant roots at nodes as it crawls and sprawls.

ORIGIN
Europe. Introduced to the United States in the mid-1800s as livestock forage, and for horses, sheep, and pigs.

NOTES
Plants are allelopathic (secrete chemicals that discourage other plants).

NONINVASIVE ALTERNATIVES
To choose an appropriate lawn grass that will thrive in your yard and climate, seek the advice of a lawn service or good local garden center.

LESS-TOXIC CONTROLS
If a few, yank out by the roots, before they can flower and go to seed. If many, fluff up the plants with a rake before mowing to get a greater number of seedheads. Always remove and dispose of crabgrass clippings. Prevention, of course, remains the best control: improve conditions for desirable lawn grass or other garden plants with regular watering and fertilizing, not mowing too low (no scalping), perhaps aerating.

CHEMICAL CONTROLS
Pre-emergent herbicides specifically labeled for crabgrass control are best applied in early spring. Corn-gluten based ones are best applied to younger plants.

Eleusine indica

Goosegrass, Silver crabgrass, Indian goosegrass, Wiregrass

This is an annual bunchgrass superficially similar to crabgrass. However, it tends to emerge a few weeks later and does not root at the nodes. Instead, it forms a splayed-out rosette that looks like someone stepped on it and flattened the plant. The leaves are dark green, can reach up to ⅓ inch wide, and are flat or folded; near the crown, the leaves are silver or white. Flowers, when they develop, are composed of up to 10 flattened, fingerlike spikes that resemble a zipper, that is, two rows of flattened spikelets occur along each spike. Spikelets emerge from a common point (windmill-like) in mid- to late summer. The root system is fibrous. The plant is not frost-tolerant. When mature, the plant is 1 to 2 feet across.

PROBLEM
This is a pest of poor and compacted lawns and fields. It tolerates close mowing.

REPRODUCTION
Seeds.

ORIGIN
Africa.

NOTES
According to anthropologists, nomads in Arab lands and North Africa used the seeds to make gruel or to grind into flour.

NONINVASIVE ALTERNATIVES
To choose an appropriate lawn grass that will thrive in your yard and climate, seek the advice of a lawn service or good local garden center.

LESS-TOXIC CONTROLS
Yank out plants by the roots, the earlier the better, before they flower and go to seed. Take steps to improve the health of your lawn, mow less closely, and reduce soil compaction by diverting traffic and/or aerating.

CHEMICAL CONTROLS
Consult a lawn service about the possibility of applying a pre- or post-emergent herbicide safely.

Elymus repens,

Quackgrass, Couch grass

Synonym(s) *Elytrigria repens, Agropyron repens*
A perennial, creeping, cool-season grass with long yellowish white, rather fleshy roots, which are actually creeping rhizomes. Blades are flat, ¼ to ½ inch wide, sparsely hairy on top and smooth below, and have small auricles (earlike projections) at the junction of blade and sheath. Seedheads are long, narrow spikelets carried flat to the stems. Though drought- and salt-tolerant, this grass thrives in moist sites. It attains up to 3½ feet in height and spreads out 2 or more feet.

PROBLEM
It grows quickly and extensively, monopolizing water and soil nutrients and crowding out desirable plants, including lawn grasses, which it invades aggressively. It infests crops worldwide.

REPRODUCTION
Creeping rhizomes and seeds.

ORIGIN
Europe, North Africa, and Asia. Imported accidentally in contaminated hay.

LESS-TOXIC CONTROLS
Spot-treat areas of quackgrass with vinegar, mindful that it may only kill the top-growth and not the roots, which you will have to dig out; be thorough in your digging as root fragments can generate new plants. Then prepare the soil and reseed with desirable grass within a week or two.

CHEMICAL CONTROLS
Spot-treat areas of quackgrass with glyphosate, then remove the dead plants, prepare the soil, and reseed with desirable grass within a week or two.

NOTES
Can be used for pasture or hay (it has about the same crude protein content as Timothy-grass, *Phleum pratense*) and erosion control. Certain natural chemicals extracted from quackgrass have been found to have insecticidal properties against mosquito larvae and to harm slugs.

NONINVASIVE ALTERNATIVES
To choose an appropriate lawn grass that will thrive in your yard and climate, seek the advice of a lawn service or good local garden center.

Eragrostis curvula

Weeping lovegrass

This perennial grass is a warm-season bunchgrass, which means that it thrives in summer heat and turns yellow to bronze in winter. It prospers in the South and Gulf Coast states, though it is increasingly widespread. The densely tufted clumps have fine-textured, long, narrow green or gray-green leaves with the tips almost touching the ground (hence the common name). In mid- to late summer, arching, delicate, lavender-gray flower panicles appear. Roots are large and fibrous. The plant is drought-tolerant and can grow in infertile, well-drained soil. Tuft size is 12 to 15 inches high and wide; flowering stalks are 3 to 6 feet high.

PROBLEM
It grows quickly and thickly, has few serious insect or animal pests to slow it down, and is tough and adaptable. Thus, it takes over open areas, edging out native and desirable grasses and other plants and posing a fire hazard during dry months. Its rapid early growth is an important factor in pushing aside other plants.

REPRODUCTION
Seeds.

ORIGIN
From East Africa. Imported for erosion control on highways.

NOTES
The long weeping leaves provide cover for wildlife, and the heavy seed crop is a good food source for birds.

NONINVASIVE ALTERNATIVES
Inquire locally about native grasses, such as big bluestem (*Andropogon geraldii*), prairie dropseed (*Sporobolus heterolepis*), and purpletop tridens (*Tridens flavus*).

LESS-TOXIC CONTROLS
Dig out seedlings in early spring, before they can form flowers and go to seed. Mow down larger plants before they can go to seed. Tilling just spreads it.

CHEMICAL CONTROLS
Glyphosate applied in late summer or fall is effective.

Festuca arundinacea

Tall fescue

A cool-season, cold-hardy bunchgrass that prospers most places except the Deep South and Gulf Coast states. It has a clumping growth habit, that is, no running rhizomes or stolons. The blades are coarse and light green, with prominent veins running parallel their entire length, serrated edges, and glossy undersides. Unmowed stems produce a loose terminal panicle, 4 to 12 inches long with little spikelets, in spring. Seeds mature in early summer. This grass forms deep and extensive roots. Mature plants are up to 6 feet tall.

PROBLEM

It invades marginal soils, such as acidic, poorly drained, or lean ones and ones where stresses occur due to drought and overgrazing. It has overtaken some parts of the Southeast as well as native California grasslands.

REPRODUCTION

Seeds and vegetative expansion; clumps send up additional, sterile shoots.

ORIGIN

Introduced from Europe in the early 1800s as a pasture grass.

NOTES

Tall fescue had developed a symbiotic relationship with a fungal endophyte, which makes the grass tougher, thus discouraging nibbling insects and animals and enhancing resistance to drought and disease. But the alkaloids now within the grass harm horses, livestock, and some wild animals; research continues on "friendly" endophytes.

NONINVASIVE ALTERNATIVES

To choose an appropriate lawn grass that will thrive in your yard and climate, seek the advice of a lawn service or good local garden center.

LESS-TOXIC CONTROLS

Dig out seedlings in early spring, before they can form flowers and go to seed.

CHEMICAL CONTROLS

Glyphosate can be effective, but repeated treatments may be necessary. Large infestations are also sometimes sprayed, and then burned.

Imperata cylindrica

Cogongrass

A real problem in the American South and Gulf Coast, where lack of cold winters allows it to grow rampantly. The leaf blades are usually light yellowish green, with a distinctive, prominent, whitish off-center midrib and razor-sharp serrated edges. Instead of a dense clump, they arise directly from the ground, with thatch around the base. Blooms rise above the foliage in spring to early tsummer, fluffy white dandelion-ish plumes, 2 to 8 inches long. The thick, matted roots are strongly segmented. Plants are between 3 and 6 feet tall and often turn brown in winter. Circular-shaped infestations are common.

PROBLEM
Fast-growing and aggressive, cogongrass overruns open as well as forested areas. Its impenetrable growth habit excludes native and desirable plants, alters wildlife and bird habitats, and can lead to more frequent and intense forest fires.

REPRODUCTION
Spreading rhizomes and seeds, which are dispersed by wind.

ORIGIN
Native to Southeast Asia.

NOTES
It is valued in traditional Chinese medicine as a diuretic and astringent, among other uses.

NONINVASIVE ALTERNATIVES
Handsome *Imperata cylindrica* var. *rubra* or the cultivar 'Red Baron' is considered a lot less aggressive, though you need to watch that established patches do not revert to the species.

LESS-TOXIC CONTROLS
Frequent, low mowing will reduce a stand. Or, till to a depth of at least 6 inches in spring, repeating every six to eight weeks through the summer months. Then put in a fall cover crop of crimson clover or ryegrass; the following spring, plant a perennial grass or shrubs to shade over the area.

CHEMICAL CONTROLS
Glyphosate applied in the fall may beat it back, but watch for a resurgence and retreat as needed.

Microstegium vimineum

Japanese stiltgrass, Nepalese browntop

Although it looks like a small, delicate bamboo, it is actually an annual grass. Skinny, asymmetrical 3-inch-long leaves with a shiny midrib line the stems; growth is distinctive, stiltlike. Slender, hairy spikelets occur in pairs, and then ripen to release copious amounts of seeds in the fall. Root systems are shallow. It leaves a thick layer of thatch after dieback each year in heavily invaded areas, and while leaves decompose quickly, stems do not. Widely adaptable. However, unlike many grasses, it is able to germinate in forested, shady conditions. Mature plants reach 2 to 4 feet tall and have a sprawling habit.

PROBLEM

The prolific seed production, along with dispersal aided by water, creatures, machinery, and humans, has allowed this plant to colonize in the Mid-Atlantic states, particularly in damp ditches, wetlands, and streamsides. It forms dense patches that exclude native and desirable plants.

REPRODUCTION

Seeds (up to 1000 per plant), which remain viable for years. In addition, stems are able to root at the nodes.

ORIGIN

Asia, and evidently inadvertently imported in packing materials.

NOTES

In areas where they are overpopulated, whitetail deer may facilitate this grass's invasion by feeding on native plant species and avoiding stiltgrass.

NONINVASIVE ALTERNATIVES

Inquire locally about native grasses.

LESS-TOXIC CONTROLS

Never let it go to seed. Mow or cut back, repeatedly, preferably in the late summer and fall, when regrowth is not a concern. Small patches may be hand-pulled, easy enough with the shallow roots.

CHEMICAL CONTROLS

Glyphosate, especially when applied in late fall, is effective. Imazapyr applied in the spring has worked.

Miscanthus sinensis

Maiden grass, Eulalia grass, Japanese silver grass, Chinese silver grass

A tall, clumping perennial grass featuring inch-wide green leaves that grow tall, then fountain over at the tops. In mid- to late summer, foot-long fan-shaped inflorescences develop; these begin red or maroon and fade to pink, then silver, then tan as autumn progresses. Meanwhile, the leaves turn tan or brown for the winter. Roots develop into substantial rhizomes. Grows well in sun or shade, in almost any soil. Mature plants are 4 to 12 feet tall.

PROBLEM

This grass is a fast and aggressive spreader, particularly in fertile, moist areas, where it displaces native and desirable vegetation with its sheer bulk and dense growth. It is unchecked by pests and diseases.

REPRODUCTION

Rhizomes and seed (wind-dispersed).

ORIGIN

From China, Japan, and Korea.

NOTES

A candidate for bioenergy production in the United States due to its high yield, effective nutrient cycling, easy propagation, and high genetic variation.

NONINVASIVE ALTERNATIVES

A number of handsome cultivars are available at nurseries for use in mixed borders or as dramatic garden focal points; these are preferable to the species because they are more attractive and less aggressive and/or do not set or ripen viable seed. 'Gracillimus' has slender, weeping foliage and feathery tan flower clusters. 'Zebrinus' has intriguing yellow-banded foliage.

LESS-TOXIC CONTROLS

Mow early, before flowers and seeds develop, and keep after the plants, repeating your assault on resurging seedlings. Digging and cultivating are risky because root bits can generate more plants. Drying out the area might be worth a try.

CHEMICAL CONTROLS

Glyphosate applied in the fall may beat it back, but watch for a resurgence and retreat as needed.

Paspalum notatum

Bahiagrass

The most distinguishing characteristic of this weedy, warm-season perennial grass is its tall, signature Y-shaped seedhead, which occurs throughout the spring, summer, and fall months. Leaves (and flowering stems) are coarse and growth can be sparse. Blades are thin, ¼-inch wide, flat, and hairless, tapering to a fine point; blades are light green, although leaf bases may be purplish. This grass develops a massive, tenacious stolon-root system. Thrives in sandy, infertile, slightly acidic soil. Full-grown plants are up to 30 inches tall.

PROBLEM

Its aggressive root system allows it to spread rapidly, forming dense mats, and to survive drought. It invades desirable Southern turfgrasses and often outcompetes them. Also it generates new seedheads with alarming speed after being mowed.

REPRODUCTION

Seeds and rhizomes.

LESS-TOXIC CONTROLS

Young plants and small infestations can be dug up and disposed of. Mow frequently to prevent seedheads, which return with dismaying speed. Aim for control, if not eradication, by doing some soil improvement and by installing and maintaining a healthy lawn.

CHEMICAL CONTROLS

Spot-treatment with glyphosate can work, but will kill desirable grass. Overplant afterwards with a different grass or groundcover. Other herbicides may work but carry risks and timing is key; consult a lawn service.

ORIGIN

From South America and Mexico. Introduced to North America for forage, turf, and erosion control.

NOTES

Bahiagrass has few insect problems, but it is susceptible to mole crickets.

NONINVASIVE ALTERNATIVES

A number of cultivars have been developed for use as turf grasses. Among these are 'Argentine', 'Paraguay', 'Pensacola', 'Tifton-9', and 'Wilmington'. If growth is thin, overseed.

Pennisetum setaceum

Fountain grass

Synonym *Pennisetum ruppelii*
A warm-season perennial or cool-season annual, medium-size "ornamental" grass. It makes a dense, rounded clump composed of long, slender, arching leaves. These are joined in summer by tall, hollow flowering stems. Flowers are carried in fuzzy, bottlebrush spikes that are 6 to 15 inches long and vary from rose to darker purple. The plant goes dormant in winter or is killed outright by frosts. It performs best in well-drained, even dry soil, and full sun and is exceedingly drought-tolerant. Mature plants typically reach 2 to 5 feet tall and wide.

Problem
Fountain grass self-sows prolifically, grows quickly, and has no serious pest problems. Seed remains viable in the soil for up to seven years. With all this going for it, it spreads opportunistically, pushing out native and desirable plants and, when massed, increasing fire vulnerability.

REPRODUCTION
Seeds.

ORIGIN
Africa, the Middle East, and Southwest Asia. Imported as an ornamental.

NOTES
Popular in dry-climate commercial and home landscaping schemes, as a background or border plant. The plumes may be cut for flower arrangements, though not when dried because they shatter easily.

NONINVASIVE ALTERNATIVES
There are horticultural varieties that do not set seed, including the older, purple-leaved 'Rubrum' or 'Cupreum' with reddish-purple plumes.

LESS-TOXIC CONTROLS
Dig out seedlings early in the season. Cut off flowering stalks before they can go to seed. For larger unwanted plants, chop back repeatedly before they flower, then dig out with a pick or mattock, or wait until the root systems are exhausted and succumb.

CHEMICAL CONTROLS
Try pre-emergent herbicides, and be prepared to repeat treatments as residual seedlings pop up.

Phalaris arundinacea

Reed canary grass

A perennial bunchgrass that forms medium-size spreading clumps. The dark green foliage is flat, ¼ to ¾ inch wide, and gradually tapering; it turns tan in autumn. Flower plumes occur in early summer; color varies but is usually tan. Seeds, produced in huge numbers, are shiny and brown. The roots form formidable mats. Tolerates drought, heat, cold, sun, partial shade, but grows most rampantly in damp ground. Mature size is between 2 and 9 feet tall.

PROBLEM

A fast-growing, tenacious spreader, this grass takes over broad areas, suppressing native and desirable plants. Its root mats can become so substantial that they change the hydrology of some invaded areas.

REPRODUCTION

Underground runners and seeds, the latter dispersed by water, animals, humans, and machines.

ORIGIN

Europe and Asia. Brought to the United States for forage and hay as well as erosion control.

NOTES

An oft-seen variety, ribbongrass or gardener's garters (*Phalaris arundinacea* 'Picta') has white vertical stripes on its leaves. *Phalaris* is derived from the Greek word for "shining," which refers to the plant's polished seeds.

NONINVASIVE ALTERNATIVES

If you like a striped ornamental grass, consider instead Japanese forest grass (*Hakonechloa macra* 'Albo Striata').

LESS-TOXIC CONTROLS

It is possible to grow this grass in a mixed border in a deep bottomless container. If you have unwanted plants, assault them repeatedly by mowing or scything before they can form seeds, then smother the area with plastic or heavy mulch until the root systems succumb and die.

CHEMICAL CONTROLS

Glyphosate has proven effective when applied in early spring, but make sure to choose a formulation meant for use around aquatic habitats.

Phragmites australis

Common reed

Synonym *Phragmites communis*
Technically not a reed, this towering perennial grass prospers in full sun and damp to wet ground. Sturdy canelike stems, up to 1 inch in diameter, have plentiful broad leaves tapering to a point at the ends (resembling corn foliage). In midsummer, dense, feathery flower plumes appear, 5 to 16 inches long, purple to grayish purple. In autumn's cooler weather, leaves drop, stems dry to tan, and the plumes abide. Roots are substantial, deep (up to 6 feet down), spreading rhizomes. Mature plants range from 3 to 20 feet tall.

PROBLEM
This bully forms dense colonies in wetlands, ditches, damp meadows, watersides, even tidal inlets and estuaries where the water is brackish. Native plants and communities are dominated and/or shaded out, habitats are altered, and wetlands are sometimes nearly sucked dry. Research also suggests the plant is strongly allelopathic (secretes chemicals that discourage other plants).

REPRODUCTION
Rhizomes and seeds (wind-dispersed), plus root fragments (carried by water, animals, and even boats) travel to generate new plants.

ORIGIN
Unknown. Genetic variations and regional strains further complicate the issue.

NOTES
It was considered an alien exotic until researchers found ancient North American evidence of it in giant sloth scat.

NONINVASIVE ALTERNATIVES
None.

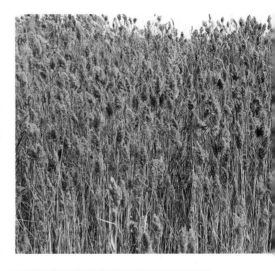

LESS-TOXIC CONTROLS
In smaller infestations, cut back plants and dig up rhizomes. In general, repeatedly cutting down the stalks before they flower eventually weakens and kills a stand, but this can take years.

CHEMICAL CONTROLS
Glyphosate has proven effective when applied in late summer; use only formulations approved for wet areas.

Phyllostachys species

Bamboo, Running Bamboo

Bamboo is technically a large grass. This particular species has the signature culms (large, hollow, woody stems, divided into sections separated by nodes, or joints) and a running, rather than clumping, habit. It spreads via creeping rhizomes, sending up new vertical shoots, often some distance from the mother plant. Green leaves alternate up the culms, on secondary branches, or form fanlike clusters. Some species bloom sporadically. Bamboo thrives in moist, well-drained ground and varies from 3 to 30 feet tall, depending on the species, cultivar, and growing conditions.

PROBLEM
Bamboo spreads alarmingly fast, forming thickets that exclude all native and desirable plants by shading as well as by monopolizing soil nutrients and moisture.

REPRODUCTION
Creeping rhizomes.

ORIGIN
Asia.

NOTES
The edible shoots are often featured in Asian cuisine. Golden bamboo (*Phyllostachys aurea*) is the most widespread and disliked species.

NONINVASIVE ALTERNATIVES
If bamboo is what you want, do research to find one whose appearance and size suit your gardening goals, and then raise it in a big container on a patio or deck, or sunk into the garden soil. Or, investigate clumping bamboos, many of which are tropical and can be enjoyed in mild climates or as a houseplant. The genus *Fargesia* is one of the hardier clumping types.

LESS-TOXIC CONTROLS
Dig out plants with a sturdy spade or mattock; the rhizomes generally are not deep, but do sprawl to the sides. Alternatively, cut off the culms at ground level and chop off new shoots, repeatedly, until the plants weaken and die.

CHEMICAL CONTROLS
Glyphosate applied in early fall can work. If regrowth occurs, repeat.

Sorghum halepense

Johnsongrass

A tall, clump-forming, warm-season perennial grass up to 8 feet tall. The green stems are rosy red near the bottom, with alternating bright green, smooth leaves. These are slender and long, 1 inch wide, up to 2 feet long, with a white midrib. Flowers occur in loose, purplish spikelets in sets of twos or threes. Rhizomes are white to rosy pink, maturing tan. This grass has a weakness: it is not very cold tolerant.

PROBLEM
Rapid, dense growth, spurred by spreading rhizomes, some of which travel as far as 200 feet from the mother plant, prolific seed production, plus regenerating rhizome pieces allow this grass to overtake broad areas to the exclusion of native and desirable crops and plants.

REPRODUCTION
Seeds, which are viable in the soil for up to 20 years. Also spreads via rhizomes and pieces.

ORIGIN
From the Mediterranean region. Introduced to North America as a forage crop.

NOTES
Sometimes this plant is mistaken for corn, but the grass has longer, narrow leaves and the rhizomes are different. The prolific pollen causes allergies in some people.

NONINVASIVE ALTERNATIVES
Related native Indian grass (*Sorghum nutans*) is not a thug. The shorter, blue-leaved cultivar 'Sioux Blues' has a good reputation.

LESS-TOXIC CONTROLS
In smaller infestations, cut back plants and dig up rhizomes (any pieces left behind can regenerate). In general, mowing down the stems before they flower eventually weakens and kills a stand, but this can take years. If you get winter freezes, till up the area in fall to expose rhizomes to the killing cold.

CHEMICAL CONTROLS
Glyphosate applied in the spring can work, but be prepared to deal with resurging seedlings and to repeat the treatment.

Taeniatherum caput-medusae

Medusahead

Synonym *Elymus caput-medusae*

This is an annual "winter" grass, meaning that it germinates in the fall, actually remains green later than most annual grasses, thus standing out. It then over-winters, grows robustly in spring, and flowers. It sets seed by early summer, at which point the plant turns purplish, then tan, and then starts to die back. Leaves are slender and flexible, and the spiky inflorescences are reminiscent of rye or wheat. The seedheads have a layered look and as the awns dry, they twist and splay (the inspiration for the common name). The barbs on the longer awns help them adhere to animal fur, human clothing, and machinery, as well as aiding movement into the soil prior to germination. The plant prospers in well-drained soil, but is widely adaptable. Mature size is 8 to 24 inches tall.

LESS-TOXIC CONTROLS

Do not let this pest go to seed. Chop or mow before flowering, and repeat as new plants germinate.

CHEMICAL CONTROLS

Glyphosate applied in fall or early spring before flowering is effective.

PROBLEM

An aggressive spreader with thick growth, it outcompetes native and desirable plants and increases wild-fire risk.

REPRODUCTION

Seeds, which can remain viable in the soil for years.

ORIGIN

From the Mediterranean region.

NOTES

This plant has infested range- and croplands in the American West, where it is sometimes beaten back with controlled burns in concert with grazing or herbicides. Wildlife and birds do not eat it much, and research has shown that birds do not easily digest the seeds.

NONINVASIVE ALTERNATIVES

If you like grasses with showy flower- and seedheads, shop for an ornamental grass and confine it to a container.

Trifolium pratense
Red clover

Familiar to almost anyone who has a lawn, enjoys sitting on the grass in a public park, or walks pastures and orchards, this sprawling to erect perennial (sometimes biennial) plant has distinctive foliage and flowers. The trifoliate leaves are marked midway with a light green to white V-shaped band. The round to oval flowerheads are rosy pink to purple, measuring anywhere from ½ to 1¼ inches in diameter. Like other legumes, red clover fixes nitrogen in the soil, contributing to soil fertility. The root system is fibrous and, over time, develops a taproot. The plant thrives in moist, well-drained soil. Plant height ranges from 8 to 20 inches.

PROBLEM
This very tenacious and successful plant often invades and completely intertwines with lawn grass and plants in flowerbeds and borders.

REPRODUCTION
Seeds, plus the stems root easily at the nodes.

ORIGIN
Native to Europe, western Asia, and northwestern Africa. Imported to the New World for medicinal uses.

NOTES
Trifolium means "three-leaved," and *pratense* means "found in meadows." Bees help pollinate it. It is edible and also valued for many medicinal uses, from treating menstrual and menopausal symptoms to bronchial and skin conditions. This plant is the state flower of Vermont and the national flower of Denmark.

NONINVASIVE ALTERNATIVES
None.

LESS-TOXIC CONTROLS
Yank out unwanted plants by the roots, before they can go to seed.

CHEMICAL CONTROLS
For large and persistent unwanted infestations, use an herbicide that contains dicamba or clopyralid (more effective than glyphosate). Be prepared to protect all desirable plants and to repeat the application.

Trifolium repens

White clover, Shamrock, Dutch clover

Another widespread clover that has wended its way into lawns and gardens. Since it fixes nitrogen in the soil and outcompetes some other weeds, it is sometimes welcomed. Its small three-part leaves are rounded and often lightly marked in the middle with a rounded to V-shaped, light green or white band. Flowerheads are white, ¾-inch in diameter, thus smaller than those of red clover. The plant forms creeping mats and a fibrous root system. It does best in heavier or clay soils, though it is adaptable. Mature plants are 2 to 6 inches high, with a sprawling habit.

PROBLEM
It is successful in many settings, insinuating itself into lawns in particular and avoiding damage from the mower because it is low-growing. It attracts many pollinating bees, making it undesirable where people sit, play, or walk barefoot.

REPRODUCTION
Seeds and creeping stems (stolons).

ORIGIN
Europe, West Asia, and North Africa. Introduced to North America as a pasture crop.

NOTES
Trifolium means "three-leaved," and *repens* means "creeping." This plant is a favorite of bees and thus beekeepers; it yields a sweet, mild honey.

NONINVASIVE ALTERNATIVES
None.

LESS-TOXIC CONTROLS
Only a small patch or minor encroachment can be successfully removed, and only then if you act before it flowers (and sets seed) and if you get all roots and root fragments. If you seek a low-clover lawn, work to upgrade or maintain a dense turf and avoid high-phosphorus fertilizers.

CHEMICAL CONTROLS
Consult a lawn service about the possibility of safely applying a post-emergent herbicide.

7
Vines

Of all the citizens of the plant world accused of or abhorred for rampant growth, perhaps vines are most often in our crosshairs. Certainly the guiltiest ones are easily noticed, as they run up and over any available support, sometimes moving on to nearby trees or posts, casting thick shade, and then waving a grasping stem in mid-air, as if to growl, "Where next?" Entire roadsides and old buildings may be engulfed and, on the scale of a regular suburban backyard, hedges, shrubs, fences, or even flowerbeds can be threatened.

Here is a wince-worthy description of a rampant vine: "The stems root wherever they touch the ground, helping to stabilize the soil." (It is also true, according to an optimistic real-estate agent, that a 500-square-foot cottage is "cozy.") Among the biggest complaints gardeners, homeowners, and parkland managers have are those questing, ambitious, rooting stems and traveling roots. Of course, they can prevent soil from washing or blowing away, but they also prevent practically any other plant from surviving or prospering. The ground is monopolized, not just the real estate but also soil nutrients and moisture.

Whether in the air, on the ground, or in between, vines live to spread. But think: that is exactly what gardeners ask of them. We want the fence covered, the view of the yard next door hidden. We want the pergola or gazebo draped, the trellis or wall decorated. So sometimes pruning tools must be wielded. Other times, we must acknowledge that the vine is the wrong plant for the spot and try to eradicate it. Either way, let us not forget that expansive growth is their basic nature.

Akebia quinata

Five-leaf akebia, Chocolate vine

A sprawling, twining, woody vine between 20 and 40 feet tall that is semi-evergreen (overwinters in warmer climates and is perennial in cooler ones). The palm-shaped leaves have five leaflets, hence the common name. The 1-inch flowers are rosy to brownish purple and spicily fragrant, hence the other common name, and are either male or female.

LESS-TOXIC CONTROLS
Cut back repeatedly until the roots starve. It is possible to dig up and eradicate the root systems of younger/smaller vines.

CHEMICAL CONTROLS
Cut back the plant as far as you can, then poison the remains with glyphosate.

PROBLEM
A widely adaptable, shade- and drought-tolerant, and cold-hardy plant, it thrives in diverse settings. It can overwhelm desirable trees and shrubs.

REPRODUCTION
Plants spread mostly by vegetative means. Pollination from another plant is necessary for the purple-hued, 2- to 4-inch pods to form, in autumn, and produce seed.

ORIGIN
Hails from Japan, China, and Korea. Imported to the United States as a nursery plant in the mid-1800s.

NOTES
It cannot abide heavy or alkaline soils. The pods and young shoots are eaten in Asia, cooked or raw.

NONINVASIVE ALTERNATIVES
Clematis species and hybrids have similar-size leaves and the vines are far less aggressive.

Ampelopsis brevipedunculata
Porcelain berry

This vigorous, lush-growing vine grabs on with tendrils. Trilobed leaves resemble those of grapevines; fall foliage can be fiery red. Gets its name from its berry clusters, which follow insignificant flowers and are initially yellowish green, maturing in pretty hues of blue and purple. Adapts to most soils, prospers in full sun to partial shade. Attains 20 feet.

PROBLEM
Left to its own devices it can overwhelm a big tree, fence, or small building. The vine has become a problem in urban areas, gardens, and parks from New Hampshire to Wisconsin and south to Mississippi and Georgia.

REPRODUCTION
The berries are full of seeds that are dispersed by birds and small mammals and then germinate in fertile, well-drained ground. Additionally, it has no trouble extending its bounds vegetatively.

ORIGIN
From Northeast Asia. Introduced as a landscape plant.

NOTES
The unique crackled coloration of the berries resembles porcelain, hence the common name. This is due to a copigmentation phenomenon: a mix of anthocyanins, which are found in other dark berries, and flavonols, found in many fruits and vegetables.

NONINVASIVE ALTERNATIVES
'Elegans' has variegated leaves and is not nearly as rampant. Peppervine (*Ampelopsis arborea*) is a native relative with more deeply toothed leaves and berries that end up red to black.

LESS-TOXIC CONTROLS
It can be trained on a fence, arbor, or porch where you can keep an eye on it and never fail to thin and shape it early every spring.

CHEMICAL CONTROLS
If you want to eradicate it, chop it back to the ground in the fall and poison it with an herbicide then and again in the spring as needed.

Calystegia sepium

Bindweed, Hedge bindweed, Wild morning glory

Synonym *Convolvulus sepium*
Related to morning glory, bindweed is much more aggressive. The fleshy, creeping roots are the agents, as they allow the plant to travel. The 2- to 3-inch flowers, pink with white stripes, are produced from mid- to late summer. Leaves are arrowhead-shaped or nearly triangular and up to 5 inches long. Perhaps more than some of its relatives, it prefers and prospers in moist ground. Attains 3 to 10 feet.

LESS-TOXIC CONTROLS
Repeatedly tear out small infestations, digging down to make sure to leave no root fragments. Act before the plants go to seed. You can also smother the area afterwards with a thick mulch to prevent a resurgence, and/or overplant with a fast-growing annual cover crop intended to use available resources and shade out competition. An alternate, interesting suggestion: take the time to remove most or all of the leaves, repeating as necessary through the growing season and next spring, when there will be fewer leaves. Eventually the plant weakens and dies.

CHEMICAL CONTROLS
Herbicides are not a good idea because it is so difficult to isolate the vine from desirable plants.

PROBLEM
Unlike morning glory, this plant is a perennial. It uses its twining stems to insinuate into and engulf native and desirable plants, especially shrubs, hedges, and trees. It is often difficult to eradicate without some harm to the host plant. Bindweed self-sows with abandon.

REPRODUCTION
Seeds and creeping rootstocks.

ORIGIN
North America.

NOTES
Unlike the flowers of other bindweeds and morning glory, the flowers this species do not close up when it rains.

NONINVASIVE ALTERNATIVES
Grow annual morning glory (*Ipomoea* spp.).

Campsis radicans

Trumpet creeper, Trumpet vine

Synonym *Bignonia radicans*
In midsummer, brilliant orange to scarlet, trumpet-shaped flowers cover the plant. They stand out from the lush foliage in terminal clusters of six to twelve, each bloom about 3 inches long. Fruits are pods about 6 inches long. Leaves are compound, up to 15 inches long with 9 to 11 leaflets, deciduous but returning with gusto every spring. The vine uses aerial rootlets to grasp supports. Roots can dive down 3 feet or more and become very thick and tangled. Will grow almost anywhere but thrives in rich soil. Attains 20 to 40 feet.

PROBLEM
A very fast-growing plant, it drapes over anything in its path, including other plants and even trees. Suckers and new growth spring up in unexpected places such as pavement cracks, patio bricks, and the lawn. Colder winters of the North slow it down, but in warmer areas, it can become a daunting pest.

REPRODUCTION
Seeds and suckering, questing roots.

ORIGIN
United States.

NOTES
Hummingbirds adore the flowers. Handling the plant, particularly the stems, causes dermatitis (itching) in some people. In addition, sometimes it attracts ants. The flowers make a mess when they drop.

LESS-TOXIC CONTROLS
If you must grow it, confine it to a large container or site it out of the way. Otherwise, dig out seedlings by their roots while you can. Cutting back or mowing down suckers, repeatedly, discourages spread.

CHEMICAL CONTROLS
Glyphosate applied late in the growing season works, sometimes. For established plants, unfortunately, the battle will be protracted.

NONINVASIVE ALTERNATIVES
Annual trailing nasturtiums (*Tropaeolum* spp.) provide bountiful orange flowers without hassle.

Cayratia japonica

Bushkiller

This exotic perennial vine already has gardeners and land managers on alert in Louisiana, North Carolina, Mississippi, Texas, and other mild-climate areas. Each leaf has five leaflets of up to 3 inches long. Grasping tendrils grow opposite of each leaf. In late summer, umbels of small, salmon-colored flowers develop. These often fall off instead of producing the white, sometimes black, berries, each with up to four seeds within, so self-sowing is evidently not an issue. Instead, the plants spread via root sprouts. Attains 40 to 50 feet.

PROBLEM
It spreads aggressively, ascending, pulling down, and/or shading out native and desirable plants, especially trees and shrubs. It successfully invades disturbed areas including forest margins, fields and pastures, moist river bottoms, and residential areas.

REPRODUCTION
Via questing roots. Seeds are rarely produced.

ORIGIN
Southeast Asia. Allegedly hitchhiked into gardens in nursery plants.

NOTES
Superficially similar to another member of the grape family, Virginia creeper (*Parthenocissus quinquefolia*), but mature leaflets are somewhat smaller and not actually palmate.

NONINVASIVE ALTERNATIVES
Choose Virginia creeper (*Parthenocissus quinquefolia*), then keep it pruned.

LESS-TOXIC CONTROLS
Pull out seedlings as soon as you see them, making sure to get all the roots. Larger plants also must be dug out by their roots—any pieces left behind can regenerate.

CHEMICAL CONTROLS
To treat a larger vine, make your move while it is actively growing. First do your best to disentangle it from whatever it is growing on and cut back, and then paint imazapyr on the cut ends.

Celastrus orbiculatus

Oriental bittersweet, Chinese bittersweet

Green leaves alternate up twining stems; these are roundish, up to 5 inches across, with wavy, toothed edges. The insignificant greenish flowers and consequently the handsome fruit capsules (on female plants, that is) are borne in short side shoots, in flat-topped clusters. In the fall, the leaves turn yellow and the yellow capsules split open to reveal the tomato-red berry within—they may overlap somewhat, then the fruits linger. Prefers full sun, but tolerates all sorts of soils. Becoming a real pest in New England. Attains 40 to 60 feet.

LESS-TOXIC CONTROLS

Pull up seedlings by the roots while they are still small. Larger plants should be tugged down to the ground, and then chopped back at ground level. Persistent, regular cutting will eventually exhaust the roots, resprouting will stop, and the plant will die back.

CHEMICAL CONTROLS

Cut back older vines and treat re-sprouts with triclopyr, taking great care not to harm the plants they may be climbing or adjacent to.

PROBLEM

A garden escapee that runs roughshod over native and desirable plants, particularly along roadsides, at forest and property margins, along trails, and over fences. In trees, it can become a thick-growing plant that shades out both the tree's foliage and plants below.

REPRODUCTION

Seeds, which are dispersed by birds and humans, and suckering roots.

ORIGIN

China, Korea, and Japan.

NOTES

Able to cross with American bittersweet (*Celastrus scandens*), muddying the native genetic pool.

NONINVASIVE ALTERNATIVES

Seek out the native American bittersweet, which has shinier, oval leaves, bigger fall fruits (female plants), and is not as vigorous—though it still must be watched and pruned.

Clematis terniflora

Sweet autumn clematis

Synonym *Clematis paniculata*

A perennial, twining vine reaching 15 to 20 feet tall, with a 6- to 10-foot spread. In late summer and fall, masses of 1-inch, fragrant starry white flowers, borne in panicles on current-season growth, cover the plant. The decorative seedheads that follow this show are rounded puffs with whirls of silvery, feathery hairs. Leaves are opposite, composed of three to five leaflets, each 2 to 3 inches long. Can grow in partial shade.

PROBLEM

Fast growth, the ability to self-sow after all those flowers set seed (in some areas), and a long taproot are a recipe for rampant, tenacious growth and expansion. Escapees invade roadsides, shrubs, trees, forest margins, creeksides, parks, smothering and/or shading out native and desirable plants. Reports are mixed—gardeners in the South often consider it a menace, while those in the Pacific Northwest do not. The difference seems to be whether it sets seed.

REPRODUCTION

Seeds, which are dispersed by wind, birds, water, and animals.

ORIGIN

Japan and China.

NOTES

You may see this plant referred to as "SAC." The native virgin's bower (*Clematis virginiana*) looks very similar.

NONINVASIVE ALTERNATIVES

Some jasmine (*Jasminum* spp.) and moonflower (*Ipomoea alba*) vines have fragrant white flowers and are better behaved.

LESS-TOXIC CONTROLS

Unwanted seedlings should be yanked out in spring, when they first appear. Cut back and dig out larger plants, making sure to get all the deep roots, as even fragments have been known to regenerate.

CHEMICAL CONTROLS

Some have successfully killed this rampant vine by spraying the foliage with glyphosate, others say that does not work at all, and have turned to 2,4-D or triclopyr.

Coccinea grandis

Ivy gourd, Scarlet-fruited gourd

An import from Asia, this sprawling vine is a cucurbit related to decorative gourds (*Lagenaria* spp.). The dark green leaves are ivy-shaped, heavy-textured, and up to 4 inches across. Little white flowers cover the plant in summer, followed by 1- to 3-inch long red fruits (on the female plants). The stems are succulent and the plant develops a deep, tuberous rootstock. It can grow very fast, up to 4 inches per day, maturing at 20 to 30 feet tall. Ample moisture in the soil encourages it.

LESS-TOXIC CONTROLS

Dig up seedlings by the roots. Cut off and dispose of fruit before it can go to seed. Cutting back more-mature vines alone does not work; the plant simply regenerates. Hawaii has experimented with introducing some insects that eat the plant, with mixed results.

CHEMICAL CONTROLS

So far, only triclopyr and dicamba, sprayed on the foliage, have shown effectiveness, followed by applying same to cut stems and young re-sprouts.

PROBLEM

Its fast growth and tenacity allow it to clamber up trees, fences, utility poles and wires, and other supports and then smother them. On most Hawaiian Islands, it is considered a noxious weed, and it presumably poses a threat in any mild climate where it can spread.

REPRODUCTION

Seeds, which are dispersed by birds, animals, and in yard waste. Also spreads by creeping roots.

ORIGIN

Tropical Asia and Africa. Originally introduced as a food crop.

NOTES

The edible leaves are known as Thai spinach, and the shoot tips are used in Asian cuisine. The genus name is sometimes misspelled *Coccinia*.

NONINVASIVE ALTERNATIVES

Grow garden spinach instead.

Convolvulus arvensis

Bindweed, Wild morning-glory

Small, white or pink morning-glory flowers less than 1 inch across adorn this delicate-looking perennial vine. Its arrowhead-shaped leaves are correspondingly small, measuring 1 or 2 inches long. But looks are deceiving, for this plant is not delicate. It sprawls more than it climbs, forming mats of overlapping runners. It sends roots deep into the ground, 10 to 20 feet. Widely adaptable, though it favors full sun and well-drained soil. Up to 12 feet, with a spreading habit.

PROBLEM

It takes over open, sunny areas such as a neglected part of a yard, as well as waste places, fields, and roadsides. There is evidence that it is allelopathic, that is, exudes chemicals into the soil to discourage competing plants. It is a major problem in the West.

REPRODUCTION

Seeds, which are dispersed by birds, remain viable in the soil for 20 years. Also spreads by creeping roots and root fragments.

ORIGIN

Europe and Asia. Probably accidentally imported as a seed contaminant.

NOTES

Its smaller leaves and flowers, and its mat-forming ability help prevent water loss, yet another survival strategy.

NONINVASIVE ALTERNATIVES

Grow annual morning glory (*Ipomoea*).

LESS-TOXIC CONTROLS

Repeatedly tear out small infestations, digging down to make sure to leave no root fragments. Act before the plants go to seed. You can also smother the area afterwards with a thick mulch to prevent a resurgence, and/or overplant with a fast-growing annual cover crop intended to use available resources and shade out competition.

CHEMICAL CONTROLS

Spray glyphosate or 2,4-D prior to flowering.

Coronilla varia

Crown vetch, Purple crown vetch

Synonym *Securigera varia*

A mat-forming perennial weed with trailing stems. Forms mounds 1 to 3 feet high. The 6-inch compound leaves are made up of 15 to 25 pairs of small leaflets, plus one at the top. For most of the summer, the stems are covered with rosy pink (sometimes pale pink, white, or lavender) flower clusters, about 1 inch across; close inspection reveals they are carried on stalks that come off the stems from the leaf axils. These are followed by slim, 2-inch green seedpods that are obscured by the lush foliage. A member of the pea family, this plant fixes nitrogen in the soil. Likes open, sunny spots.

PROBLEM

Its fast, thick growth crowds out, overwhelms, and/or shades out native and desirable plants. In addition, its nitrogen-fixing ability alters habitats that it invades.

REPRODUCTION

Seeds, which are dispersed by animals. Also spreads by underground rhizomes/runners.

ORIGIN

From Europe, Asia, North Africa. Imported for erosion control and as a cover crop.

NOTES

The plants contain nitroglycerides, toxic to horses but apparently tolerated by livestock and wild animals. Seeds also are poisonous.

NONINVASIVE ALTERNATIVES

Other nitrogen-fixing cover crops that are recommended for home gardeners include alfalfa and clover.

LESS-TOXIC CONTROLS

If only a few plants, hand-pulling is an option, but get all of the roots. If you have a big patch, try mowing repeatedly, well before the plants go to seed. Additionally or alternatively, an infestation can be smothered with black plastic or a substantial mulch.

CHEMICAL CONTROLS

Most common herbicides work; spray in late spring for best results.

Cuscuta japonica

Japanese dodder

This is technically a parasitic plant that behaves as an annual. It may be thread-like, or thicker, and is yellow with red dots or markings; whatever chlorophyll it contains is nominal. It lacks obvious leaves but produces tiny pale yellow flowers. Tiny, papery fruit, only ⅛ inch in diameter and containing no more than four brown seeds, follow. Upon germinating, they must find a host or perish. A yellowish stem gropes in the air until it makes contact with a host plant and coils around the stem. Oddly, once attached, its connection to the soil shrivels away, while the rest of it carries on with its life cycle, developing haustoria (suckers) that penetrate the host to extract nutrients and water. Mature size varies, depending on the host plant.

LESS-TOXIC CONTROLS
Alas, eradicating it by hand means yanking out the host plant as well. Act before the dodder forms seed. Destroy/discard everything to prevent spread.

CHEMICAL CONTROLS
Pre-emergent herbicides are effective, or affected plants (host and entwined dodder) may be killed with 2,4-D during the growing season.

PROBLEM
It infects alfalfa, potatoes, and other crops. Homeowners may find it hooking up with their mums, dahlias, petunias, English ivy, and other ornamental plants. At best, the host plant is rendered unsightly; at worst, it is killed. Dodder also produces much seed.

REPRODUCTION
Seeds are dispersed by water, in animal feed, and in manure, and they can remain viable in soil for years.

ORIGIN
Asia.

NOTES
Botanists used to place it in the morning glory family; it is now considered separate (dodder family).

NONINVASIVE ALTERNATIVES
None.

Cynanchum louiseae

Black swallowwort, Dog-strangling vine

Synonym *Cynanchum nigrum*

Its relationship to milkweed is obvious in the fall, thanks to its green, slender, 3-inch long, floss-filled pods, which ripen brown, split open and send forth plentiful seeds. An herbaceous perennial, it ascends by twining or rambles on the ground, forming a matted tangle. The opposite, glossy green leaves are oval-shaped with pointed tips, 3 to 4 inches long and half as wide. The springtime blooms are clusters of purplish five-petaled flowers, ¼ inch across. The root system is a creeping rhizome. This vine adapts to lean, alkaline, salty, gravely and/or dry soil. It attains 3 to 6 feet.

PROBLEM
Favorite invasion sites include fields, lots, and roadsides. This plant crowds out native and desirable plants. Already a concern in Vermont, New Hampshire, and upstate New York, it appears to be spreading to other areas, including California.

REPRODUCTION
Seed, which is dispersed by wind. Also spreads by creeping rhizomes.

ORIGIN
Europe and Asia. Evidently a garden escapee.

NOTES
Although monarch butterflies may lay their eggs on this plant, research suggests that unfortunately the larvae do not survive.

NONINVASIVE ALTERNATIVES
The native honeyvine, *Cynanchum laeve*, is better behaved, or grow milkweed (*Asclepias* spp.) for the butterflies.

LESS-TOXIC CONTROLS
Act before seedpods form. Remove plant crowns and roots, easier of course with smaller ones but worth the effort for any. If seedpods form, cut back the plants while they are still green and dispose of everything; mature, ripe seeds are brown. Repeated cutting and mowing, over two or more seasons, can be effective.

CHEMICAL CONTROLS
Spray plants with glyphosate or triclopyr after flowers form but before seedpods develop.

Dioscorea bulbifera

Air potato, Bitter yam

A deciduous perennial twiner, it plasters supports with its large, oppositely held, heart-shaped, prominently veined leaves, each at least 8 inches long. In early summer, these are joined by round, brown "potatoes" no more than 5 inches across. These are not fruit, but rather aerial tubers capable of generating new plants. The main plant grows from a more substantial underground tuber, up to 6 inches across. Flowering is rare and would occur in late summer on separate male and female plants; if they appear, they are fragrant, green to white pendulous spikes, 4 inches long. Not a cold-hardy plant; mainly present in Florida, the Gulf Coast, and Hawaii. Attains 60 to 150 feet.

LESS-TOXIC CONTROLS

Cut off and dispose of bulbils as they appear. Dig out young plants by the tubers. Tug older, more substantial vines off their supports and cut back at the crown; repeating this process can exhaust and eventually kill the plant.

CHEMICAL CONTROLS

Glyphosate kills the foliage, but unless you dig out the tuber, resprouting often occurs, requiring another round of spraying.

PROBLEM

Super-fast growth allows it to cloak trees, fences, hedges, and roadside embankments, outcompeting and/or shading out native and desirable plants. When the "potato" bulbils fall, they further spread this pesky vine.

REPRODUCTION

Via bulbils, dispersed by falling nearby and by water. Also via rambling stems.

ORIGIN

From Asia and Africa.

NOTES

This species twines to the left and is considered toxic; related plants twine to the right and are eaten and/or used medicinally.

NONINVASIVE ALTERNATIVES

Consider the less aggressive native crossvine, *Bignonia capreolata*, though it will need managing.

Euonymus fortunei
Wintercreeper

Whether it behaves as a thick, clinging, grasping vine or as a marauding groundcover, this plant is a thug. There is a fair amount of natural and selected variation; in addition to the plain species, there are numerous cultivars (of which plantsman Michael Dirr remarks dourly, "from 17 feet away, they all look the same"). Generally speaking, the opposite, evergreen leaves are about 1 inch long at maturity, often with white or golden margins, veins, or blotches; cold weather sometimes adds rose. Flowers are insignificant, not showy, and may segue to tiny pink or red seed capsules that split open to reveal orange seeds. Rootlike holdfasts allow the plant to ascend rough surfaces (brick, concrete, wood) or tree trunks. Not fussy about soil, grows in full sun or shade. Attains 40 to 70 feet tall.

PROBLEM
It grows steadily and thickly, pushing out native and desirable plants and blanketing, sometimes killing, host trees or shrubs. It is also very prone to disfiguring scale infestations.

REPRODUCTION
Seeds, which are dispersed by birds.

ORIGIN
Japan, Korea, China. Imported as an ornamental groundcover.

NOTES
Juvenile leaves look different from mature ones, generally smaller and greener.

NONINVASIVE ALTERNATIVES
Consider bearberry (*Arctostaphylos uva-ursi*), a good-looking, red-berried evergreen groundcover. It sprawls and spreads, but not aggressively.

LESS-TOXIC CONTROLS
Cut back repeatedly until the roots starve. It is possible to dig up and eradicate the root systems of younger/smaller vines.

CHEMICAL CONTROLS
Cut back older vines and spray re-sprouts with glyphosate or triclopyr, taking great care not to harm the plants they may be climbing or adjacent to.

Hedera helix

Ivy, English ivy

If a trellis, tree, fence, wall, building or other support is handy, ivy grabs on with its aerial roots and soon covers it. Otherwise, it forms a thick, sprawling ground-cover. Juvenile leaves are triangularly heart-shaped, glossy-textured, and up to 4 inches across. Given time, and if nobody prunes, an ivy plant becomes woody and generates upright branches with bigger, unlobed adult leaves. Clusters of tiny white star-shaped flowers can occur in summer, followed by blackish berries, which are poisonous. Ivy prospers in moist, well-drained soil on the alkaline side and develops extensive roots; it is valued for its shade tolerance. It attains up to 90 feet tall as a vine, only 8 inches tall when a groundcover.

PROBLEM
Ivy is capable of smothering plants in its vicinity. Should you tear it off a building, it will bring paint or bricks and mortar down with it, thanks to its tenacious aerial roots. Slugs, snails, dodder, leaf spot disease, and other problems can further make a planting a liability.

REPRODUCTION
Mainly via runners that can root at nodes, but also via seeds dispersed by birds.

ORIGIN
Europe, western Asia, North Africa.

NOTES
There are many cultivars to tempt gardeners, including ones with smaller leaves and white or gold markings or variegation.

NONINVASIVE ALTERNATIVES
In mild climates, you could substitute star or Confederate jasmine (*Trachelospermum*). Both species and cultivars have glossy green leaves and scads of fragrant white or yellow flowers.

LESS-TOXIC CONTROLS
Cut vines back repeatedly until the roots starve. It is possible to dig up and eradicate the root systems of younger/smaller vines. Heavily mulch the area afterwards to smother reemergence.

CHEMICAL CONTROLS
Apply a broadleaf herbicide early in the season.

Humulus japonicus

Japanese hops

Synonym *Humulus scandens*

Though fast-growing and able to produce greenish female flowers that look like papery pinecones, this is not the hops used in brewing beer. This twining vine is an annual, but puts on prodigious growth in a season, rapidly ascending a provided support such as a fence, trellis, pergola, or tree. Its rough-textured leaves are 2 to 5 inches long, usually with five deeply cut, pointed lobes. Stems are coated with coarse, hooked prickles. There are bracts where the leaf stems attach to the main stems. Very rampant in fertile soil in full sun, especially in the longer growing season of warmer-climate areas. Attains 20 to 35 feet.

PROBLEM

Japanese hops is increasingly encroaching on open lots and fields, roadsides, neglected areas, where it is able to outcompete and shade out native and desirable plants and self-sow prolifically.

REPRODUCTION

Seeds, which are dispersed by wind and water.

ORIGIN

Japan and China. Introduced as an ornamental.

NOTES

It is a member of the hemp family.

NONINVASIVE ALTERNATIVES

Grow common hops (*Humulus lupulus*), which in addition to being a more attractive and useful plant, is perennial. Just prune it to keep it in bounds. Of European origin, this species has a different chemical makeup and is used in brewing beer.

LESS-TOXIC CONTROLS

Cut back repeatedly until the roots starve. It is possible to dig up and eradicate the root systems of younger/smaller vines. Act before the plants flower. Wear gloves and protective clothing, as the abrasive stems and leaves can cause skin irritation.

CHEMICAL CONTROLS

Spray glyphosate on young leaves in spring, or paint on cut stems in fall.

Jasminum fluminense

Brazilian jasmine

A perennial vine well-suited to mild climates, where it grows lustily to 40 feet. It has fuzzy young stems and opposite, compound leaves on short stalks; each leaf is made up of three 3- to 4-inch-long oblong leaflets, the center one larger than the others. Flower clusters cover the plant every spring, opening in the evening hours; individual blooms are white, about 1 inch across, and are richly scented. The fruit that follows is a round, double-lobed, purple-black berry, about ⅓ inch across.

PROBLEM

Brazilian jasmine grows quickly and thickly, enveloping trees, shrubs, fences, poles, or sprawling on the ground when there is nothing to climb. The result is that native and desirable plants are choked or shaded out. An infested tree, no matter the species, actually looks like it is a Brazilian jasmine tree. The problem is increasing in Florida and the Gulf Coast states, as well as Hawaii.

REPRODUCTION

Seeds (self-sows and is dispersed by birds and mammals, particularly raccoons) and rooting, rambling stems.

ORIGIN

Tropical Africa. Introduced via Brazil to Florida, as an ornamental.

LESS-TOXIC CONTROLS

Cut back repeatedly until the roots starve. It is possible to dig up and eradicate the root systems of younger/smaller vines.

CHEMICAL CONTROLS

Apply triclopyr to cut stems and stumps in fall, and be prepared to re-treat as necessary.

NOTES

Another import, Gold coast jasmine (*Jasminum dichotomum*) is similar in behavior and appearance, but has glossy, pointy leaves up to 4 inches long.

NONINVASIVE ALTERNATIVES

Try common jasmine (*Jasminum officinale*) or Chilean jasmine (*Mandevilla laxa*); both are attractive and less vigorous, but may still require frequent pruning to keep them in bounds.

Lonicera japonica

Japanese honeysuckle

On one hand, this plant's fragrance is so delicious—the creamy white (some-times tinged pink or purple, eventually fading to yellow) tubular blossoms, 1½ inches long, cover the vine for most of the summer. On the other hand, it grows very quickly, dominating plants, supports, structures, roadsides, embankments. Dark green leaves about 2 to 3 inches long are opposite along softly furry, twin-ing stems. Fall color brings purplish black berries ¼ inch in diameter. Thrives in full sun and many soils, from sand to poorly drained ground. In colder climates, it is semievergreen; in warmer areas, it is evergreen. Attains 15 to 30 feet.

PROBLEM

Fast, aggressive growth shades out and smothers native and desirable plants in its path.

REPRODUCTION

Seeds, which are dispersed by birds. Also by underground rhizomes and by trailing branches that can root at nodes.

ORIGIN

Japan, China, and Korea. Imported as an ornamental, a wildlife plant, and for erosion control.

NOTES

Bees and butterflies love the flowers. Although the berries nourish birds, the leaves feed rabbits and deer, and lush plants provide shelter for these creatures. Ultimately the monoculture inhibits habitat diversity.

NONINVASIVE ALTERNATIVES

Some of its cultivars are touted as being less aggressive and hav-ing equally fragrant, more attractive blooms, such as white-flowered 'Halli-ana', but even these need to be pruned and managed so they do not outgrow their bounds.

LESS-TOXIC CONTROLS

Repeatedly tear out small infestations, digging down to make sure to leave no root fragments. Act before the plants go to seed.

CHEMICAL CONTROLS

Spray glyphosate in the fall while foliage lingers but after other plants have gone dormant. Re-treat as needed.

Lygodium japonicum
Japanese climbing fern

Deceptively dainty, this plant's lacy-looking fronds measure between 4 and 8 inches long, with numerous small pinnae (fertile ones are three times divided). Collectively, they grow densely. Twining green, reddish, or tan stems are rather wiry and difficult to break. The plant thrives in moist ground, in sun or shade. It is not cold-hardy and thus is found mainly in warm climates of the South and Florida, where it remains green year-round. In somewhat colder areas, such as Texas, it browns in the fall and generates new growth the following spring. Attains 10 to 50 feet high, or more.

PROBLEM
Garden escapees aggressively cloak forests, marshes, ravines, roadsides, and the like, blocking sunlight from shrubs and trees they may ascend as well as native and desirable plants below.

REPRODUCTION
Spores, which are wind- and water-dispersed, like in other ferns, plus extensive creeping rhizomes.

ORIGIN
Asia and tropical Australia. Imported as an ornamental.

NOTES
Sometimes marketed to gardeners and hobbyists as a houseplant, basket plant, or terrarium candidate. Closely related Old World or small-leaf climbing fern (*Lygopodium microphyllum*) is rampant in central and South Florida.

NONINVASIVE ALTERNATIVES
To enjoy this plant or its relatives, raise it in a container.

LESS-TOXIC CONTROLS
Yank out small plants as soon as spotted, taking care to follow and extract the creeping underground roots (or they will regenerate). Act early in the growing season, before spores can form.

CHEMICAL CONTROLS
First tug down and cut back stems as far as you can, then spray remaining foliage with glyphosate. Act early in the growing season, before spores can form.

Merremia tuberosa

Spanish arborvine, Wood rose, Hawaiian woodrose

Synonym *Ipomoea tuberosa*

The jaunty yellow flowers of this twining vine look like yellow morning glories—because it is in the same family. The blossoms open each morning and close each evening or when the weather is overcast. They measure from 2 to 2½ inches across and are usually carried in stalked clusters of three to nine blooms. The seedpods, when the growing season is long enough for them to form, look like small wooden roses, hence the common name. Seeds are the size of marbles and only germinate in moist conditions. The palmate leaves have five to seven lobes. Technically a perennial and capable of becoming woody and quite sprawling over time, it is a novelty annual in colder climes. Prefers plentiful light and moist soil. Attains 20 to 70 feet tall.

LESS-TOXIC CONTROLS
May be grown in a greenhouse, or set outdoors in a container for the summer. Collect and discard seeds before they can ripen. Tear out in-ground plants while still small.

CHEMICAL CONTROLS
Spray glyphosate on young leaves in spring, or paint on cut stems in fall.

PROBLEM
Aggressive growth and prolific seed production allow this plant to invade neglected and natural areas, overwhelming and shading out native and desirable plants. It is a growing problem on several of the Hawaiian Islands and is being watched in Florida, Texas, and other Gulf Coast states.

REPRODUCTION
Seeds, which can remain viable for years.

ORIGIN
From Mexico and Central America.

NOTES
The dried seedpods are used in wreaths and dried-flower arrangements. The seeds are poisonous.

NONINVASIVE ALTERNATIVES
Try instead golden-flowered Carolina jessamine (*Gelsemium sempervirens*).

Parthenocissus quinquefolia
Virginia creeper, Woodbine

In fall, palmate leaves, in leaflets of five with toothed edges, turn ruby-red or wine-purple. Blue-black berry clusters, on red stems, add dramatic contrast on into the cold winter months. Summer color is dark green (new spring growth has a bronze tinge). Tiny clusters of greenish white flowers hide under the leaves. Close inspection reveals tendrils, each ending in "holdfasts," adhesive-like tips that help stems cling to trees, walls, and other supports. Adapts easily to almost any growing conditions. Attains 30 to 50 feet tall.

PROBLEM
This fast, thick grower overwhelms trees and shrubs and shades out native and desirable plants. Lacking support, it rambles along the ground or over rocks, dirt piles, and stumps, monopolizing space and resources.

REPRODUCTION
Seeds, dispersed by birds. Also, stems can root at nodes.

ORIGIN
North America.

NOTES
Sometimes mistaken for poison ivy, which has leaflets in threes. Nonetheless, its oxalic acid content does give some people a painful, itching rash. The acid content in the berries also renders them unpalatable or toxic to animals and humans.

NONINVASIVE ALTERNATIVES
This really is the only vine with such spectacular fall color. If you like the blue berries, porcelain berry (*Ampelopsis brevipedunculata*) has pretty ones, but alas, it, too, can be invasive in many areas.

LESS-TOXIC CONTROLS
Repeatedly tear out small infestations, digging down to make sure to leave no root fragments. Act before the plants go to seed.

CHEMICAL CONTROLS
First tug down and cut back stems as far as you can, taking care to protect your skin with gloves and heavy clothing. Spray remaining foliage with glyphosate.

Persicaria perfoliata
Mile-a-Minute vine

Synonym *Polygonum perfoliatum*
This annual has earned its hyperbolic nickname, as it grows up to 6 inches per day, with an ever-upward habit. Yet it has a deceptively delicate look, with thin green stems and pale green, triangular leaves 1 to 3 inches across. Underneath these are long stems as well as little barbs, or curved prickles, that help clutch supports. Also along the stems are "ocreae," little round, cup-shaped leafy structures from which the flowers and berries emerge. The tiny white flowers are inconspicuous, but the deep blue berrylike, pea-size fruits, carried in clusters, are very distinctive. Fairly adaptable, but prefers full sun and damp ground. Attains 20 to 50 feet.

PROBLEM
Unchecked by predators and sowing prolifically, this pest plant is on the move. It smothers trees, shrubs, posts, fences, power lines, and roadside areas, choking and shading out native and desirable plants. Frost kills it, but if seeds have ripened, it will be back.

REPRODUCTION
Seeds, which are dispersed by water, birds, animals, and possibly ants, can remain viable in the soil for years.

ORIGIN
East Asia, China, Taiwan.

NOTES
Some land managers and nurseries are calling this vine "the kudzu of the North." Although it is not used as an ornamental, it becomes a problem for homeowners when it jumps the fence from an overgrown lot next door.

NONINVASIVE ALTERNATIVES
If you want to occupy the soil, replace with annual morning glory vines (*Ipomoea* spp.). They are so much nicer.

LESS-TOXIC CONTROLS
Before the plants go to seed and before the barbs harden, yank out unwanted plants by their roots. Then watch for and remove emerging seedlings. Wear protective gloves and clothing if the barbs are irritating.

CHEMICAL CONTROLS
First tug down and cut back stems as far as you can, then spray remaining foliage with glyphosate or triclopyr.

Pueraria montana var. lobata

Kudzu

"The weed that ate the South" flourishes where the growing season is long and the winters mild. Leaves are palmately lobed and typically about 7 inches across, composed of three ovate or diamond-shaped leaflets, with the central one being larger than the other two. A member of the pea family, kudzu generates fragrant purplish racemes up to 10 inches long; flat, brown, fuzzy seedpods follow. The root system develops a tuber/deep taproot. Adapts to almost any soil or setting. If there is no support to ascend, it forms massive groundcovering mats. Attains 70 feet or more.

LESS-TOXIC CONTROLS

Dig out emerging plants by the roots. Repeated mowing may eventually starve them. Also, goats and pigs will eat the plants and roots.

CHEMICAL CONTROLS

First tug down and cut back stems as far as you can, then spray remaining foliage with glyphosate or triclopyr. Most effective in the fall when the plants are sending food reserves down into the roots. Repeat. The object is to kill the roots.

PROBLEM

Super-fast growth of a foot a day plus no significant pests or diseases make for a virtually unstoppable plant. It is found mostly in fields and along roadsides and forest margins. For homeowners, it is a daunting foe.

REPRODUCTION

Rambling roots and runners, plus seeds, which are rarely viable, actually.

ORIGIN

China, Japan, and Pacific Islands. Imported as an ornamental and for erosion control and forage.

NOTES

Leaves are used in paper-making, vines for basket-making, and starchy roots are edible. It has many uses in traditional Chinese medicine. Although it is not used as an ornamental, it becomes a problem for homeowners whose properties abut wild fields and forests.

NONINVASIVE ALTERNATIVES

None.

Smilax rotundifolia

Greenbriar, Catbrier

This is a thorny, woody, evergreen plant. Its pliable green stems, laden with stout thorns, are like flexible rolls of green barbed wire. Leaves are rounded, heart-shaped, prominently veined, with a glossy, leathery texture; they measure 2 to 5 inches across. Tiny yellowish green flower clusters occur in spring on female plants, barely noticeable except for a light but foul scent (pollinators are carrion flies). Clusters of blue-black berries, with a slight waxy coating, follow; these often persist through the winter months. Roots are woody and fibrous and become extensive over time. The plant climbs via tendrils and forms tangled thickets. It thrives in moist ground and tolerates shade. Attains 40 feet or more.

LESS-TOXIC CONTROLS

Dig out emerging plants by the roots. Repeated chopping back or mowing eventually starves the plants, but this process can take several years.

CHEMICAL CONTROLS

Spray leaves with glyphosate starting in spring and repeating at two-week or monthly intervals as needed, or treat cut stems in late summer or early fall.

PROBLEM

Once established, greenbriar drapes supporting trees and shrubs, shading out other native and desirable plants below. Its thick growth and prickly nature make eradication a challenge, especially when it invades garden shrubs or trees.

REPRODUCTION

Seeds, which are dispersed by birds and small mammals. Also spreads by rambling stems.

ORIGIN

North America.

NOTES

A thicket provides shelter for birds (especially catbirds), rabbits, deer, and others.

NONINVASIVE ALTERNATIVES

Where coverage with a perennial vine is wanted on a fence, trellis, or tree, consider a clematis.

Toxicodendron radicans and *T. pubescens*

Poison ivy and Poison oak

If you live in the East, you know poison ivy; if you live in the West, you know poison oak. These two closely related deciduous vines or rambling shrubs share certain characteristics: shiny, compound leaves in three leaflets, clusters of white berries on female plants, and grasping, hairy mature stems (the hairs are actual aerial rootlets). Foliage turns red in the fall. That of poison oak resembles small, blunt-lobed oak leaves. The irritating oil, urushiol, is contained in all plant parts. Widely adaptable, but thrives in fertile ground. Varies from 6 to 60 feet tall, depending on setting.

PROBLEM
Rampant growth outcompetes or shades out native and desirable plants in open and marginal areas.

REPRODUCTION
Seeds, dispersed by birds, and rambling stems.

ORIGIN
North America.

NOTES
Songbirds and game birds eat the berries with no ill effects. Formerly classified in genus *Rhus* along with poison and nonpoisonous sumacs, moved to its own genus; debate remains about whether these two plants are variants of the same plant.

NONINVASIVE ALTERNATIVES
None.

LESS-TOXIC CONTROLS
With proper protection and careful cleanup for yourself and any cutting tools used, tear out, cut back, or mow down these plants in late fall or very early spring. Additionally or alternatively, smother plants with a thick mulch.

CHEMICAL CONTROLS
Treat cut-back stems and stumps with glyphosate or triclopyr, repeating as needed.

Wisteria floribunda

Wisteria, Japanese wisteria

Famously beautiful and famously burly with age, this vine has long been valued for its lush foliage and trailing racemes of (usually) purple flowers. The pinnately compound leaves, composed of 13 to 19 leaflets, can reach 15 inches long; they are bright green in season and fade to yellow and fall off in autumn. Scented racemes are 8 to 20 inches long, eventually giving way to velvety brown pods about 6 inches long. Mature plants develop thick, woody stems and become very heavy. Best in moist, well-drained soil and full sun. Very long-lived. Typically attains 20 to 30 feet high on man-made supports, up to 50 feet high in a tree.

PROBLEM

The heaviness and rampant vegetative growth of a neglected plant can bring down its support, whether trellis, arbor, or outbuilding, and can harm the health of a tree by greedily taking sun and resources. Branches can also wedge off a roof or pry off gutters.

REPRODUCTION

Seeds and rambling roots and suckers.

ORIGIN

From Japan.

NOTES

Closely related to the also-troublesome, rampant-growing Chinese wisteria (*Wisteria sinensis*), which has shorter leaves and shorter racemes. It has been noticed that the stems of Japanese wisteria climb clockwise, while those of Chinese climb counter-clockwise.

NONINVASIVE ALTERNATIVES

The native American wisteria (*Wisteria frutescens*) has smaller, pale-purple racemes and is not as big or vigorous in growth.

LESS-TOXIC CONTROLS

For wanted plants, support with metal, not wood, and keep well-pruned and properly fertilized; research how or hire an experienced arborist. Remove unwanted seedlings by the roots. Repeatedly cut back unwanted plants until they starve.

CHEMICAL CONTROLS

Paint cut stems and stumps with glyphosate or triclopyr.

8

Shrubs

For a homeowner or gardener to call a shrub invasive is, in effect, to realize that you made a bad choice. Maybe a nursery sold you something it should not have. This is less likely at local nurseries, which tend to be knowledgeable about what does well in your area and thus make for happy customers. It can happen, though, when you buy from a national-chain box store's garden center. It can also happen if you shop by mail and either you or the supplier neglected to double-check whether the shrub is a good choice for your area and growing conditions. Either way, bad bushes are planted deliberately and it usually does not take more than a season or two for you to regret the decision. Perhaps it sends out unwelcome runners or suckers, or its fruit (berry, drupe, whatever) seeds all over the yard.

It is also entirely possible that an invasive shrub is an uninvited guest. Flowering shrubs inevitably produce seeds and often these are carried into your garden or even its less-watched outskirts, by birds, wildlife, or water. Seeds or viable root fragments can stow away in a delivery of topsoil or hitchhike in with a pot-grown plant. The plant sprouts, and before you know it, it turns out to be a pest.

No matter how a pesky shrub arrives, you should take arms sooner rather than later. Dig it out (if the root system is not too daunting, while it is still rather small), cut or mow it down, or even resort to herbicides. There is no room in most people's yards for something as large as an unwanted bush.

Alhagi maurorum

Camelthorn

Synonym(s) *Alhagi camelorum, A. pseudalhagi*
A member of the pea family, it has the characteristic leaflets and summertime flowers (pink to maroon) followed by brown-reddish pods (which are constricted between the individual seeds). One to 2-inch-long pointy yellow thorns are arrayed along the stiff branches. The multistemmed shrub is between 2 and 4 feet tall, albeit with a massive, creeping root system that can extend over 6 feet deep and up to 20 feet wide.

PROBLEM
It has gained a foothold in the arid western United States, but needs moisture to germinate, grow, and spread, so favors riverbanks, canals, and irrigation ditches.

REPRODUCTION
Ripe seeds are hard-coated but germinate in damp ground. Sometimes these are spread by wind and weather or after being eaten by livestock, but plants spread more easily by runners/clones.

ORIGIN
Native to the Mediterranean and Russia. Now established in temperate climates.

NOTES
Numerous and varied medicinal uses, including diuretic, expectorant, laxative, antiseptic properties; also mentioned for the treatment of rheumatism and piles. The sap of the plant is cited in the Qur'an as a source of the resinous gum called "sweet Mann."

NONINVASIVE ALTERNATIVES
None.

LESS-TOXIC CONTROLS
Digging out is usually not practical. Avoiding tilling/cultivation and taking steps to dry out an infested area may contain the spread.

CHEMICAL CONTROLS
Herbicides (including glyphosate) ought to be effective, but few are presently labeled for control of this pest plant and great care would have to be taken that none leaches into any nearby water or your water table.

Alnus glutinosa

European alder, black alder

Often a large multistemmed plant reaching 40 to 60 feet high, can grow as wide as tall and attain a pyramidal profile. Its toothed leaves are rounded; juvenile leaves and twigs are sticky. In fall, 4-inch catkins (male flowers) appear in clusters of three or four. When fertilized, the smaller, ¾-inch female catkins harden into the characteristic alder "cones." Older bark is dark brown to black.

PROBLEM

This alder favors areas of full sun and moist to wet ground, including ditches, damp backyards, and streamsides. It has become problematic along the Eastern seaboard as far south as Tennessee and as far west as Minnesota.

REPRODUCTION

Fertilized female catkins/cones contain the seeds, but these tend not to germinate unless they land in damp soil.

ORIGIN

From temperate areas of Europe and Asia. Imported to the New World in the late 19th century.

NOTES

Native Americans used to boil fresh alder bark (any species) for a tea that induced vomiting. Dried, powdered bark has been used to staunch bleeding from minor cuts and wounds.

NONINVASIVE ALTERNATIVES

Try one of the native alders, smooth (*Alnus serrulata*) or speckled (*A. incana*); these may grow less lustily and less densely. Or, consider a moist-soil-loving birch such as paper birch (*Betula papyrifera*) or black birch (*B. nigra*).

LESS-TOXIC CONTROLS

Smaller plants can be cut back and their stumps dug out. Alternatively, draining a damp area or diverting water away causes them to falter.

CHEMICAL CONTROLS

Larger plants, once cut back severely, can be treated carefully with an herbicide to kill the remaining stump and rootstock.

Aralia elata

Japanese angelica-tree, Japanese aralia

A large shrub or chunky tree related to our native devil's walkingstick (*Aralia spinosa*), though it is a bigger plant and, if not pruned otherwise, usually multi-stemmed. Like its cousin, it has stout stems with prickles—though not as many. Also, like its cousin, it has huge compound leaves (bi- to tri-pinnately arranged), up to 40 inches long—with much more downy undersides, however. Plush creamy white flower panicles are carried like feathers above the foliage in late summer, giving way eventually to a bounty of purple fruit. Fall leaf color can be yellow to wine-purple. The tree adapts to a wide range of growing conditions and grows 20 to 40 feet tall, 15 to 30 feet wide.

LESS-TOXIC CONTROLS

Do not let plants go to seed. Chop down unwanted plants and dig out the roots or they will resprout. Watch for and dig out unwanted seedlings.

CHEMICAL CONTROLS

Cut back a targeted plant down to a stump, and then paint it with glyphosate.

PROBLEM

No pests or diseases trouble it and it grows quickly under the right conditions, forming dense thickets that overrun and shade out native and desirable plants from forests, woodland edges, fields, roadsides, garden margins. It is displacing the native aralia.

REPRODUCTION

Seeds, which are dispersed by birds. Also spreads by suckers.

ORIGIN

Japan, Korea, and Manchuria.

NOTES

The native devil's walkingstick sports a pyramidal inflorescence with a long central axis, while the inflorescence of this one has a short central axis with long branches spraying outward.

NONINVASIVE ALTERNATIVES

The native bugbane (*Actaea racemosa*) is a smaller but somewhat similar-looking and trouble-free plant—and it lacks thorns.

Ardisia crenata

Coralberry, Christmas berry

This is a medium-size shrub or small tree for milder climates. It is often multistemmed, often growing in clumps. Mature size is up to 6 feet tall. Foliage is glossy dark green, thick-textured, and has scalloped margins; leaves are about 8 inches long. The white or pinkish flowers are borne in axillary clusters. These are followed by bright coral-red berries that hang or droop on the plant. The evergreen leaves and bright berries make it a standout in the fall and winter months.

PROBLEM
It ends up shading out and/or crowding out native and smaller plants.

REPRODUCTION
Seeds, which fall and germinate close to the plant, create thick colonies.

ORIGIN
Japan and India. Introduced as an ornamental.

NOTES
Birds and raccoons eat the berries, distributing them far and wide.

NONINVASIVE ALTERNATIVES
Most holly (*Ilex*) bushes (for example, the Meserve hybrids) are a fine alternative, but bear in mind that you need both male and female plants to have red berries. Beautyberry (*Callicarpa americana*) is an appealing shrub with fall and winter interest; the berries are purple, however.

LESS-TOXIC CONTROLS
Cut down and remove trees, if possible while they are still small and certainly before their seeds ripen. Then overplant the area with a thick groundcover, in the hopes of discouraging any remaining seedlings. Larger shrubs can be cut back and the area monitored for seedlings, which should be removed immediately.

CHEMICAL CONTROLS
On seedlings and smaller plants, glyphosate (with a surfactant, due to the thick glossy nature of the leaves) is effective. Larger ones will succumb to 2,4-D or triclopyr.

Ardisia elliptica

Shoebutton ardisia, Inkberry

This is a small tree or large shrub to 20 feet tall found in mild climates, notably (for now) Florida and Hawaii. It has plentiful leathery green leaves alternating on the stems, each one 3 to 6 inches long and reddish when young. Small, drooping flower clusters develop in the leaf axils; they are composed of tiny, pink, star-shaped flowers. These ripen to small, drooping fruit clusters that begin red and soon turn dark purple to nearly black (the inspiration for "inkberry").

PROBLEM
The plant spreads readily thanks to the many creatures that enjoy eating the berries. It also grows and matures quickly. Because it is shade-tolerant, it can thrive where other plants may not. It crowds out native vegetation.

REPRODUCTION
Seeds (one per fruit), dispersed by dropping nearby, by birds, and by raccoons and opossums.

ORIGIN
Native to Southeast Asia, India, and New Guinea. Imported to North America as an ornamental shrub.

NOTES
From Florida gardens, it has managed to invade tree islands in the Everglades and other open areas. The berries will stain your fingers and skin dark purple.

NONINVASIVE ALTERNATIVES
A close relative, the native marlberry (*Ardisia escallonioides*) is a durable and attractive alternative with white flowers followed by dark purple fruit.

LESS-TOXIC CONTROLS
Yank out seedlings as soon as you spot them.

CHEMICAL CONTROLS
Glyphosate is effective on groupings and seedlings, but should not be used around water. Individual plants can be cut down and their stumps painted with glyphosate or 2,4-D, or the bark may be treated with triclopyr mixed with oil.

Berberis thunbergii

Barberry, Japanese barberry

A much-branched, rounded, dense shrub 3 to 6 feet tall, 4 to 7 feet wide. Leaves are borne in clusters along the tangled branches and are small and variable, about ½ inch long. The reddish brown stems are angled or grooved, often with sharp, ½-inch-long spines beneath each leaf cluster. Tiny yellow flowers cluster under the foliage. Orange-red berries, about ⅓ inch long, are also on the twig undersides, borne singly, and often persist through winter. Leafs out early in spring and turns vivid red, orange, and/or reddish purple in autumn. A tough, drought-tolerant plant.

PROBLEM
This species forms prickly masses that are daunting to hikers, landscapers, and homeowners. Many creatures, including wild turkeys and grouse, eat the berries and help the plants' spread. One plant soon becomes a thicket.

REPRODUCTION
Via seeds and creeping roots. Branches can root at nodes.

ORIGIN
Imported from Japan as an alternative to common barberry.

LESS-TOXIC CONTROLS
Thanks to a shallow root system, this shrub can be ejected from the ground using a hoe or mattock. It is best, of course, to make your move while the plant is still young.

CHEMICAL
Cut back a targeted plant, and then paint the stump with glyphosate.

NOTES
When common barberry (*Berberis vulgaris*) was found to harbor wheat rust, this relative was introduced. Horticulturists have developed scores of cultivars with enhanced fall color and different growth habits. Among them, 'Crimson Pygmy' is compact and small; 'Erecta' has a more upright habit.

NONINVASIVE ALTERNATIVES
If you want a colorful but thorny hedge, consider shrub roses (*Rosa* species and hybrids). For spectacular fall color, try smokebush (*Cotinus coggygria*).

Caragana arborescens

Siberian pea-shrub

This pea-family shrub has a rather sparse, oval profile that is taller than broad at 15 to 20 feet tall and 12 to 18 feet wide. The pinnately compound leaves consist of 8 to 12 leaflets that are fresh bright green. Sharp little ¼-inch spines develop along the stems, making the entire plant bristly. The sweetly scented flowers are yellow and carried either solo or up to four in a cluster. Seedpods that follow are small at 1½ to 2 inches long and contain between three and five peas. When ripe, they burst open and shoot the seeds up to several feet away. The root systems can end up fairly extensive. It is a tough plant, adapting to lousy soil, salt and alkalinity, cold, drought, and wind; insects are not very interested in it. Like all legumes, it is a nitrogen-fixing plant.

PROBLEM
This plant seems to relish poor growing conditions and establish itself quickly, elbowing or shading out other plants.

REPRODUCTION
Seeds.

ORIGIN
Hails from Siberia and China.

NOTES
Thanks to its medium-to-fast growth rate, it has been used as a windbreak plant. Hummingbirds like the flowers. The pods are edible, best steamed/cooked. Some cultivated varieties are less prickly and denser in habit.

NONINVASIVE ALTERNATIVES
Similar-size, casual shrubs that can be used as windbreaks or hedges and that are not as troublesome include serviceberry (*Amelanchier*) and chokeberry (*Aronia*).

LESS-TOXIC CONTROLS
Do not let plants go to seed. Chop down unwanted plants and dig them out by their roots. Watch for and remove unwanted seedlings.

CHEMICAL CONTROLS
Treat a stump with glyphosate or triclopyr.

Cistus ladanifer

Gum rock rose, Crimson spot rock rose

Synonym(s) *Cistus ladaniferus, C. ladanifer* var. *maculatus*
This is a cousin of the landscape shrubs so popular in mild climates, especially in California. A compact grower, it produces fragrant 4-inch evergreen leaves that are dark green on top, light gray-green below, smooth-edged, and opposite on the stems. Stems are sticky due to being coated with many small resinous hairs (not thorns). The 3- to 4-inch flowers are white, with a boss of yellow stamens in the center and one mahogany spot on each of five petals. Petals are the texture of crepe paper. The plant blooms in early summer. Like all rock roses, it prospers in full sun and is drought-tolerant. Mature plant size is 3 to 5 feet tall and wide.

PROBLEM
A tough and opportunistic plant, it escapes cultivation and runs rampant in open, sunny spots of poor soil, crowding and/or shading out smaller desirable or native plants.

REPRODUCTION
Seeds, which can remain dormant in the soil for years.

ORIGIN
Native to the Mediterranean region.

NOTES
The fragrant leaves are a source of a resin called gum labdanum, used for perfumed products and flavorings. In Spain, where this rock rose has invaded fields and grasslands, it is called *jara pringosa*, meaning "sticky shrub." The plant may have allelopathic ability (the resin and/or roots appear to inhibit adjacent competing plants).

NONINVASIVE ALTERNATIVES
Choose a cultivated variety of rock rose. Or, consider groundcovering roses, which take up about the same amount of space, discourage trespassers with their thorns, and have pretty flowers.

LESS-TOXIC CONTROLS
Cut back and dig out unwanted plants.

CHEMICAL CONTROLS
None recommended.

Cotoneaster species

Cotoneasters

Among this large group of berried, often low-growing, sometimes congested landscape shrubs and groundcovers are a few that have worn out their welcome or escaped into lots and fields—in particular, *Cotoneaster buxifolius*, *C. microphyllus*, *C. pannosus*, and *C. lacteus*. The tiny, tough, usually evergreen leaves line stiff, arching or sprawling stems. The insignificant white flower clusters are followed by the small ¼- to ½-inch orange to red berries, which crowd along the stems. The plants can be fast-growing and long-lived. Mature size varies, but typically is from 1 to 3 feet tall and 4 to 6 feet wide.

PROBLEM

Cotoneasters self-sow prolifically and get help with dispersal from many birds (notably cedar waxwings and robins), opportunistically taking over broad areas. The sprawling, rangy habit makes extraction tricky. Established plants also seem to be a magnet for litter, which is trapped and held in their branches.

REPRODUCTION

Seeds.

ORIGIN

Originally from China, some via Europe.

NOTES

Despite the species' overall toughness, some species and cultivars can be ruined by fireblight, a bacterial disease characterized by sudden blackening and wilting of twigs and branches. Mealybugs also are a problem for some plants.

NONINVASIVE ALTERNATIVES

Not all cotoneasters are created equal. Do some research on species and varieties appropriate for your area and climate; be sure to check out new and improved nursery cultivars.

LESS-TOXIC CONTROLS

Wade into a large plant or patch before it goes to seed and lop off as many branches as you can, then dig out what remains, roots and all.

CHEMICAL CONTROLS

None recommended.

Cytisus scoparius

Scotch broom, Common broom

A mounded, largish deciduous shrub of slender bright-green leaves and wand-like stems. Impressive when in bloom in late spring and early summer; though individual, sweet-pea-shaped flowers are 1 inch or less long, they cover the stems, singly or in twos. Color is usually bold yellow, sometimes creamy white or red. Small 1- to 2-inch pods follow. The plant adapts well to poor and sandy soil, loves full sun. The roots fix nitrogen in the soil, and forge deeply into the soil, aiding the plant's drought tolerance. Full-grown plants reach 5 to 10 feet tall and wide, or wider.

PROBLEM

Scotch broom grows quickly and self-sows, the pods literally exploding when ripe and sending the seeds several feet. Thus it forms large colonies that elbow or shade out more desirable plants. Meanwhile, the older plants experience dieback in the middle or die out altogether after a few years, giving a patch an overall ratty appearance. In addition, the seeds have been shown to remain viable in the soil for decades.

REPRODUCTION

Seeds.

ORIGIN

Central and Southern Europe/Mediterranean area.

NOTES

Gets its common name from the fact that the twigs were used in its native Europe to make brooms.

NONINVASIVE ALTERNATIVES

The related Warminster broom (*C. ×praecox*) has a more compact habit, is more cold-hardy, and is generally a more handsome, manageable plant.

LESS-TOXIC CONTROLS

Do not let it go to seed; instead, cut stems for bouquets or filler in mixed flower arrangements. Cut plants to the ground, and then dig up. In the coming years, monitor the area for seedlings as they appear and tear them out.

CHEMICAL CONTROLS

Treating cut-down plants with triclopyr is effective, as is attacking small plants (4 to 6 inches tall) with 2,4-D.

Elaeagnus umbellata

Autumn olive

A medium to large, spreading shrub, with slightly thorny stems, that becomes dense and tough with age. Mature size is usually 3 to 12 feet tall, but can reach 30 feet. The leaves are glossy green on top and silvery gray below, between 2 and 4 inches long and 1 inch wide. The shrub flowers heavily in spring and fruits heavily in summer and fall. Small, ½-inch flowers are fragrant, creamy white to yellow, funnel-shaped. Fruits begin silvery and turn red. The plants tolerate poor and saline soil, some shade, and are drought-tolerant.

PROBLEM

A rampant grower and prolific self-sower (with plenty of help from birds), this weedy shrub takes over and out-competes and shades out other plants.

REPRODUCTION

Seeds.

ORIGIN

From China, Korea, and Japan. Imported as an ornamental.

NOTES

It is related to the also-weedy Russian olive (*Elaeagnus angustifolia*), which has narrower leaves, thornier stems, and yellow, more dry and mealy fruits. The roots of both species have the ability to fix nitrogen in concert with soil bacteria, which enriches the soil and thus changes the sites wherever they grow.

NONINVASIVE ALTERNATIVES

Dense-growing, drought-tolerant, berry-forming shrubs that are not nearly as weedy include species and cultivars of holly (for instance, *Ilex verticillata*, *I. glabra*, *I. ×meserveae*) and doublefile viburnum (*Viburnum plicatum* var. *tomentosum*).

LESS-TOXIC CONTROLS

Hand-pull seedlings as soon as you see them. Cut down established plants and dig out by the roots, if practical.

CHEMICAL CONTROLS

Glyphosate painted on cut stumps is effective; do this in late summer.

Euonymus alatus

Winged euonymus, Burning bush

A spreading, mounding shrub with dark green foliage much of the year, but ablaze with cherry-red fall color. The most distinguishing characteristic, however, is the four prominent brown corky-textured wings that line the green (sometimes brown) stems. The abundant leaves are 1 to 3 inches long and very finely teethed. The yellow-green, four-petaled flowers, barely noticeable because they are so tiny, bloom in spring and lead to small orange-red fruits that are also often obscured by the foliage. Develops a fibrous, shallow root system. A tough, resilient, slow-growing plant, adapting to almost all soils except soggy ones. It ultimately reaches 15 to 20 feet tall and wide but usually is around 8 to 10 feet.

PROBLEM
When it outgrows its garden bounds or escapes into fields and lots, its adaptability allows it to outcompete desirable and native plants.

REPRODUCTION
Seeds, mainly dispersed by birds.

ORIGIN
Asia. Introduced as an ornamental.

NOTES
The nursery industry has long embraced this plant, especially for hedges and mass plantings. There are numerous quality cultivars, especially the popular, dense-growing 'Compactus'. The species name is sometimes misspelled as *alata*.

NONINVASIVE ALTERNATIVES
Consider blueberry (*Vaccinium*) or chokeberry (*Aronia*) species and cultivars, which also have berries and brilliant fall color.

LESS-TOXIC CONTROLS
Due to the fairly shallow roots, seedlings are somewhat easy to yank out. Cut back larger unwanted plants to the ground, and then dig out the root system.

CHEMICAL CONTROLS
Paint cut stumps with glyphosate.

Frangula alnus

Glossy buckthorn, Alder buckthorn

Synonym *Rhamnus frangula*
An open, spreading, rather gangly-looking large shrub. The branches are long and arching. Alternating up them are shiny, oval 3-inch leaves (hairy underneath), with distinctive upcurved veins. Foliage is dark green, but fall color is a lackluster greenish yellow. The bush blooms in spring, producing small, stem-hugging, light green flower clusters that attract many bees. Around midsummer, ¼-inch red berries (technically drupes) adorn the plant. These darken to purple-black by fall. Tolerates cold, prefers moist soil. When mature, the bush is around 10 to 12 feet tall by 8 to 12 feet wide.

PROBLEM
Due to its adaptability, fast growth, and ability to spread, spread it does, forming impenetrable thickets in open and unused areas, shading and choking out all competition.

LESS-TOXIC CONTROLS
Tear out seedlings by the roots, and watch for more to appear, as seeds may be dormant in the soil. Repeatedly mow or cut down bigger plants, in the hopes of eventually exhausting the root systems.

CHEMICAL CONTROLS
Paint cut stumps with glyphosate.

REPRODUCTION
Seeds, which are dispersed far and wide by birds.

ORIGIN
From Europe and Asia. Imported as an ornamental.

NOTES
Two horticultural cultivars are for sale in some places, despite the plants' bad reputation and presence on invasives lists: 'Columnaris' has a narrow, tall profile; 'Aspenifolia' has narrow leaves that give it a ferny texture. Two other, related species are also problematic and invasive: common buckthorn (*Rhamnus cathartica*) and dahurian buckthorn (*R. dahurica*).

NONINVASIVE ALTERNATIVES
Nonpesky, better-looking shrubs that have berries and attract birds including many viburnum species and cultivars, including doublefile viburnum (*Viburnum plicatum* var. *tomentosum*) and the dwarf *V. opulus* 'Nanum'. Consult a local nursery.

Hibiscus syriacus

Rose-of-Sharon, Shrub althea

A flowering shrub with a loose vase-shaped growth habit; it blooms on new (current season's) wood. The 2- to 4-inch flowers have five petals, usually white or violet with red or purple middles. The palmate, three-lobed leaves are around 2 to 4 inches across; the plant leafs out late in spring and there is no fall color to speak of. The brown fruit, less than 1 inch in diameter, is a five-valved capsule. Thrives in moist, well-drained soil, tolerates cold winters. Mature plants are 8 to 12 feet tall, 6 to 8 feet wide.

LESS-TOXIC CONTROLS

Tug out unwanted seedlings, the earlier the better. If this is a perennial problem, try underplanting the main shrub with a dense groundcover such as pachysandra. Cut down unwanted bigger plants and dig out the root systems.

CHEMICAL CONTROLS

Glyphosate may be effective on cut stumps with repeated applications.

PROBLEM

Seeds germinate readily when they fall from the plant, creating a thicket of seedlings and often succeeding in making a planting ever-denser. Plants can also self-sow all over a yard and garden, and jump the fence.

REPRODUCTION

Seeds. Self-seeds prolifically in some places.

ORIGIN

From China and India. Introduced as an ornamental.

NOTES

Many cultivated varieties are a clear improvement on the species in flower and even foliage quality, but habit always tends to be multistemmed and rather rangy. This plant is the national flower of South Korea.

NONINVASIVE ALTERNATIVES

Triploid varieties are touted as sterile (do not set seed). Among the best is the lovely, prolific, white-flowered 'Diana'.

Ilex aquifolium

English holly

This holly becomes a big, rangy shrub or a tree. The easiest way to tell it from other hollies is its leaf, which is spiny-margined, especially when younger. The leaves vary from 1 to 3 inches long, and from a mere ¾ inch wide to 2½ inches wide. Otherwise, the leaves have the familiar heavy, waxy texture and lustrous-green color. The insignificant little white flowers bloom in the leaf axils in late spring. The fruit—assuming a male pollinator is available—is round and orange to red, about ¼ inch in diameter. Over time, this holly develops a deep and extensive root system. Does fine in sun or in shade but needs well-drained soil to prosper. Mature size is 15 to 50 feet tall, up to 15 feet wide.

PROBLEM

When it escapes into forests and fields, it grows aggressively and creates heavy shade that inhibits native plants.

REPRODUCTION

Seeds. Also spreads by suckering. Trailing branches may root at the nodes.

ORIGIN

Western Asia, Europe, and North Africa. Imported as an ornamental.

NOTES

Bees pollinate the flowers. Though poisonous to people, the berries are relished by many birds.

NONINVASIVE ALTERNATIVES

Try other hollies with friendlier foliage and better growth habits, such as winterberry (*Ilex verticillata*) or inkberry (*I. glabra*).

LESS-TOXIC CONTROLS

Cut off berries as they appear so they cannot reseed in your yard or nearby or be moved about by birds. Pull seedlings as soon as spotted. Cutting back to the roots, alas, usually results in resprouting, though if you do this repeatedly and persistently, you may win.

CHEMICAL CONTROLS

Glyphosate applied to a fresh-cut stump, in late summer, will kill it.

Ligustrum species

Privets

There are many different species of privet—among them *Ligustrum amurense, L. lucidum, L. obtusifolium, L. ovalifolium, L. vulgare, L. sinense,* and *L. japonicum.* What they all have in common is a multistemmed habit and small, opposite, ovalish shiny green leaves that make them popular as hedge, screen, or foundation plants. The creamy white flower panicles appear in late spring to early summer. The fruit, technically a drupe, is usually small, ¼ inch or so, oval, and purple to black; carried in clusters, it may be produced in great numbers and can persist into the winter months. Most privets thrive on neglect and are widely adaptable, tolerating everything from full sun to shade. Plant size varies from 5 to 10 feet tall and wide.

PROBLEM

With help from birds, seedlings sprout far and wide, forming impenetrable thickets. In addition, because they leaf out early, privets shade out seedlings of smaller desirable or native plants. The worst offenders are Chinese privet (*Ligustrum sinense*) and common privet (*L. vulgare*).

REPRODUCTION

Seeds.

ORIGIN

Asia and Europe.

NOTES

There are no native privets; all are introduced. Though bees like privet flowers, most people find the scent unappealing or even offensive.

NONINVASIVE ALTERNATIVES

In mild climates, substitute cherry laurel (*Prunus caroliniana*) or manzanita (*Arctostaphylos*). In colder areas, try hollies (*Ilex*) or upright cotoneaster.

LESS-TOXIC CONTROLS

Very small seedlings can be yanked out as soon as spotted. Chopping or mowing down stands does not work well; the plants just regrow.

CHEMICAL CONTROLS

Glyphosate is effective on the leaves in summer or painted on stumps in late summer to early fall.

Lonicera maackii

Amur honeysuckle

An upright, spreading, rather large and leggy shrub with multiple stems, this honeysuckle leafs out early and fades back in the fall. In summer, the foliage is dark green. Leaves are unique among honeysuckles because they end in a long point. One-inch flowers open white and turn cream then yellow, soon followed by a ¼-inch red berry that persists all winter. This species is more shade-tolerant than other honeysuckles and can live under tall trees. Also tolerates alkaline soils. When full grown, plants are 12 to 15 feet tall and wide.

PROBLEM
This fast and aggressive grower forms thickets if unchecked. Birds eat the berries and deposit them widely. The bush will grow almost anywhere and soon wears out its welcome with its rampant, weedy ways.

REPRODUCTION
Seeds.

ORIGIN
From Korea and China. Imported as an erosion-control plant.

NOTES
A few garden cultivars are offered by some nurseries, including pink-flowered 'Erubescens' and 8- to 12-foot 'Rem Red'. The common name refers to the Amur River, which forms the border between the Russian Far East and Manchuria in China where this plant is native. "Maackii" is derived from Richard Maack, a 19th-century Russian naturalist.

NONINVASIVE ALTERNATIVES
Better, fast-growing, casual-profiled, shade-tolerant shrubs include forsythia, weigela, and red osier dogwood (*Cornus sericea*).

LESS-TOXIC CONTROL
Do not let plants go to seed. Tear out seedlings as they develop. Dig out bigger plants by the roots, or try cutting them down repeatedly until all root reserves are depleted and the plant dies.

CHEMICAL CONTROLS
Glyphosate applied to a fresh-cut stump, in late summer, will kill it.

Lonicera morrowii, L. tatarica, and *L. xylosteum*

Shrubby honeysuckles

Nonnative shrubby honeysuckles are dense, twiggy, tangled bushes, over time forming a daunting mass. They leaf out earlier in spring and hang onto their foliage longer in fall than native honeysuckles. Typically, they have blue-green summer foliage, usually smooth, though Morrow's leaves are downy; fragrant flowers in peduncled pairs of creamy white, yellow, or pink, depending on the species; and the 1/4-inch red berries develop later the summer. These shrubs tend to be relatively shallow-rooted and are 6 to 12 feet tall and wide.

Problem

Early leafing out and the ability to hang onto their leaves later into fall give shrubby honeysuckles a competitive advantage not only over other honeysuckles, but also over most plants. From seedling stage on up through adulthood, these bushes are thugs. They grow quickly and thickly, to the exclusion of most other plants.

REPRODUCTION

Seeds, which are dispersed mainly by birds.

ORIGIN

Western Europe and Asia. Imported as ornamentals and/or as wildlife plants.

NOTES

Deer eat honeysuckles—a rare case where a gardener might want to encourage deer to visit. Goats do, too, evidently, if you live in a place where you can have them.

NONINVASIVE ALTERNATIVES

For a fragrant-flowered shrub with a casual profile that is not a thug, consider spicebush (*Lindera benzoin*).

LESS-TOXIC CONTROLS

Pull or dig out seedlings and young plants. Cut down bigger plants repeatedly, spring and fall, for several seasons (up to five years) and you should succeed in disabling and eventually killing them.

CHEMICAL CONTROLS

Glyphosate—sprayed on the leaves in summer, or painted on fresh-cut stumps in late summer or fall—has proven effective.

Myoporum laetum

Lollipop tree, Mousehole tree

Really more of a large shrub than a tree, this import has evergreen leaves that are white- or yellow-speckled; the spots are actually oil glands. The flowers occur in clusters from midspring to midsummer; blooms are white, five-lobed, sport small, reddish brown spots and are 1 inch or less across. When they pass, numerous bright red ¼- to ½-inch berries form and persist into fall. The plant is drought-tolerant and is cold-hardy only to about 25°F. Mature plants reach 20 to 30 feet tall and are half as wide.

PROBLEM
In mild climates, notably California, where it is considered a pest, it grows quickly and densely, excluding desirable and native plants. It is especially rampant in moist soil.

REPRODUCTION
Seeds, which are dispersed far and wide by birds.

ORIGIN
New Zealand. Imported as an ornamental.

NOTES
The Māori would rub the leaves over their skin to repel mosquitoes and sandflies. The chemical compounds in the leaves are toxic even to livestock, evidently damaging the liver. In cultivation, however, it is susceptible to a variety of insect pests that can really disfigure a planting, including thrips, aphids, scale, and spider mites.

NONINVASIVE ALTERNATIVES
Sweet bay (*Laurus nobilis*) or toyon (*Heteromeles arbutifolia*) are much better evergreen shrubs for California and other mild-climate areas.

LESS-TOXIC CONTROLS
Cut off the flowers before they go to seed. Tear out seedlings while they are still small. Chop down hedges, repeatedly (stumps will resprout), until the root systems are starved and the plants give up.

CHEMICAL CONTROLS
Glyphosate painted on a fresh-cut stump is effective.

Nandina domestica

Heavenly bamboo, Sacred bamboo

Not a bamboo at all, though it has an upright if spreading habit. It is a medium- to fine-textured shrub, especially popular for hedges, screens, and groupings. Its growth tends to be consistently handsome and uniform, with plentiful evergreen leaves (pinnately compound) that are reddish bronze when young, dark green in summer, and reddish in winter. The pinkish white late-spring flowers are carried in lush, branched, terminal clusters, 8 to 15 inches long. Fruit is a bright red berry about ⅓ inch in diameter, again carried in panicles and remaining on the plants for months. A very adaptable plant, prospering even in shade. Mature plant size is 6 to 10 feet tall and 4 to 10 feet wide.

PROBLEM

Because it is untroubled by pests and diseases and grows and spreads quickly, it forays into places where it is not welcome, crowding out other plants. If it forms a thicket or colony, it becomes difficult to remove.

REPRODUCTION

Seeds, suckers, and spreading rhizomes.

ORIGIN

From China and India. Introduced as an ornamental.

NOTES

The nursery industry has produced scores of cultivated varieties that are superior to the species, with more compact (less leggy) growth habits and improved foliage color.

NONINVASIVE ALTERNATIVES

For red berries on a noninvasive evergreen plant, consider hollies (*Ilex*).

LESS-TOXIC CONTROLS

Pull out seedlings and keep a lookout for more, as seeds remain viable in the soil for a few years. Dig up unwanted small plants.

CHEMICAL CONTROLS

Glyphosate painted on a fresh-cut stump is effective, as is glyphosate or triclopyr sprayed on the foliage.

Rhamnus cathartica

Buckthorn, Common buckthorn

A large, fast-growing bush or small tree composed of stout, spiny branches and dark glossy-green foliage. The leaves are light green underneath, ovate to elliptic, have lightly serrated edges, and measure between 1 and 3 inches. Fall color just fades to a dull yellow. Male and female flowers appear on separate plants. The flowers, which appear clustered in umbels in late spring, are small and yellow-green, eventually giving way on the female plants to black berrylike drupes, each ¼ inch in diameter. A tough customer, it adapts to poor soil and partial shade. Mature size is 18 to 25 feet wide and tall.

PROBLEM

Not an especially attractive plant to begin with, it invades quickly and aggressively where it can and outcompetes and shades out adjacent, existing plants.

REPRODUCTION

Seeds, which are dispersed by birds.

ORIGIN

Europe and Asia. Imported to North America for use in hedgerows and for wildlife.

NOTES

It is a host plant for a rust (*Puccina coronata*) that decimates oat crops. In large field- or pasture-size infestations, it has been possible to burn out the plants, but this tack is not practical on a smaller scale.

NONINVASIVE ALTERNATIVES

Shrub roses can also form a thorny deciduous hedge or barrier but are not aggressive or troublesome.

LESS-TOXIC CONTROLS

Pull out small seedlings as soon as spotted. Digging or yanking out bigger plants is risky because you might bring buried seeds to the surface, and they will germinate and retake the area.

CHEMICAL CONTROLS

Glyphosate painted on a fresh-cut stump is effective, as is glyphosate or triclopyr sprayed on the foliage.

Rhodotypos scandens

Jetbead, Black jetbead

Forms a loosely mounded shrub with slightly arching branches. Leafs out earlier in spring than most *Rhodotypos* species, with medium to dark green foliage in summer, fading yellow by fall. The prominently ribbed leaves have serrate edges, are opposite, and are between 2 and 4 inches long. Flowers are white and 1 or 2 inches across. Small drupes, each one about ⅓ inch long, develop in clusters of three or four, follow and persist through fall and into winter in some areas. These begin red but become black and shiny, hence the common name. Tolerates all sorts of growing conditions, including shade and poor soil. Plants typically attain 3 to 6 feet tall and are somewhat wider.

PROBLEM

Because it is so adaptable, has a fast growth rate, and is untroubled by insect pests, it is able to colonize almost anywhere.

REPRODUCTION

Seeds, which are dispersed by birds. Also spreads via rhizomes.

ORIGIN

From central China and Japan.

NOTES

Though birds eat the berries, they are poisonous to animals and humans, containing a potent cyanide-like chemical, amygdalin (laetrile). This plant is a member of rose family, which you can see in the flowers (though, oddly, jetbead's flowers only have four petals).

NONINVASIVE ALTERNATIVES

Try a white-flowered floribunda (cluster-blooming) rosebush instead, such as 'Iceberg'.

LESS-TOXIC CONTROLS

Tear or dig out small plants by the roots. Cut back bigger plants and colonies, repeatedly, until the root systems die—this can take a few years.

CHEMICAL CONTROLS

Kill new growth in the spring with glyphosate, or paint glyphosate or triclopyr on freshly cut stumps in the fall.

Rhus typhina

Sumac, Staghorn sumac

This is a loose, sprawling shrub, occasionally a small tree, with lots of suckers. Most recognizable in the fall, when the pinnately compound leaves turn vibrant orange and crimson. Summer color is bright green. Similarly, the dense flower panicles, up to 8 inches long and always bigger on the male plants, are greenish for the summer but once in fruit, in the fall, turn into dramatic crimson clusters of hairy drupes. Stems are coated with velvety soft hairs, hence the common name. Similar smooth sumac (*Rhus glabra*) has smooth stems. Both tolerate almost any soil except the very wet. Staghorn sumac attains 10 to 25 feet tall or taller.

PROBLEM

A fast growth rate and extensive suckering lead to extensive stands of clones. In addition, the plant sows prolifically. Once it gains a foothold anywhere, it is very hard to eradicate.

REPRODUCTION

Seeds, which are dispersed by birds and other wildlife. Also spreads via suckers.

ORIGIN

North America.

NOTES

Soak the fruit clusters in water and strain for an acidic red tea known as "Indian lemonade." Warning: a related plant, poison sumac (*Rhus vernix*), causes dermatitis as bad as poison oak and ivy; it is less common and grows in wet areas.

NONINVASIVE ALTERNATIVES

Get spectacular fall color for much less trouble with one of the many small cultivars of Japanese maple.

LESS-TOXIC CONTROLS

Chop or mow down the plants, repeatedly. Eventually the root systems become exhausted and/or the seedlings get shaded out by other plants, and the sumac dies.

CHEMICAL CONTROLS

Treat cut-back stubs and trunks with glyphosate in late summer or fall.

Rosa multiflora

Multiflora rose

The only rose everyone hates. More prickly than thorny, with a fountaining habit of long, grasping canes. The leaves are bright green in summer and become lackluster yellow in fall. The fragrant flowers are borne in heavy clusters; individual blooms are five-petaled and about 1 inch across. The hips that follow are round to egg-shaped and about ¼ inch in diameter. Tolerates poor soil and some shade. A single plant can become 10 feet tall and wide or wider.

PROBLEM

Multiflora rose is very fast-growing and soon forms a daunting, sprawling thicket. Unlike its beautiful domesticated cousins, it seems impervious to the usual rose pests and diseases.

REPRODUCTION

Seeds, which are dispersed far and wide mostly by birds but also by mammals, can remain viable in the ground for up to 20 years. Canes on the ground can and do root.

ORIGIN

Japan and Korea. Originally imported for and touted as a good rootstock for ornamental roses.

NOTES

It has also been used for erosion control, in wildlife shelterbelts, and in freeway plantings.

NONINVASIVE ALTERNATIVES

Almost any other rose is nicer. If you want thorniness (as for a boundary planting), there are many shrubby choices that have lovely blooms and better manners. If you like single white roses, 'Simplicity' is a fine choice.

LESS-TOXIC CONTROLS

Wearing protective clothing and gloves, cut back all canes to the ground, then dig out the roots—easier earlier in the season, before growth really gets going.

CHEMICAL CONTROLS

Cut canes can be painted with glyphosate or triclopyr. Or, spray glyphosate on the bushes in summer after flowerbuds appear.

Rosa rugosa

Beach rose, Rugosa rose

A coarse-looking, very prickly rosebush that forms a dense, mounded shape. The dark green foliage is heavy-duty, with a rough, wrinkled texture. Flower color varies from white to pink to rosy purple, with only five petals and a boss of stamens in the middle. Fragrance is rich and spicy. It flowers most of the summer and often into fall. The hips are urn-shaped, about 1 inch long, and orange-red. Rugosa rose grows well in difficult settings, including beach sand and dunes (both roots and foliage are salt-tolerant), embankments, and open and disturbed areas. It is also cold-tolerant and can survive southern Canadian winters. Attains 4 to 7 feet high and wide.

LESS-TOXIC CONTROLS

Dig out little seedlings. For established plants, cut back and then dig out, including all the roots, to prevent regeneration.

CHEMICAL CONTROLS

Cut canes can be painted with glyphosate or triclopyr. Or spray glyphosate on the bushes in summer after flowerbuds appear.

PROBLEM

Seedlings can and do pop up opportunistically, eventually forming thickets that exclude native and desirable plants.

REPRODUCTION

Seeds, which are dispersed by birds and mammals. Also spreads by root suckers.

ORIGIN

Japan, China, and Korea. Imported as an ornamental.

NOTES

This plant has become so prevalent along the seashores of the Northeast (planted or seeded in) that many people think it is native. There are many improved cultivars, bred for better blooms, mostly; pink-flowered 'Frau Dagmar Hastrup' is among the best.

NONINVASIVE ALTERNATIVES

Check out the similar but better-looking, better-mannered Explorer Series of shrub roses, developed in Canada. 'Henry Hudson' is white; 'William Baffin' is strawberry-pink.

Scaevola sericea var. *taccada*

Beach naupaca, Sea lettuce, Hawaiian half-flower

Synonym *Scaevola taccada*
This is a durable, succulent rounded shrub or small tree 6 to 16 feet tall and wide. Individual leaves are light green, spoon-shaped, and between 5 and 9 inches long and 1 to 4 inches wide. Flower clusters occur in the leaf axils. Each is white, pink, or pale lilac, marked with purple streaks, about 1 inch across, and sports five petals arranged in a semicircle (as is characteristic of the species). Tiny ½- to ¾-inch green berries follow, eventually turning white. Not a cold-hardy plant, it is widespread in Hawaii and on Florida sand dunes and coastal habitats.

PROBLEM

Plants form dense colonies that push out and shade out native and desirable plants.

REPRODUCTION

Seeds, which are dispersed by sea birds and pigeons, or by water and tides. Trailing stems root where they touch the ground.

ORIGIN

From the Western Pacific and Indian Ocean area. Likely introduced from Hawaii for erosion control and as a low-maintenance coastal landscaping plant.

LESS-TOXIC CONTROLS

Hand-pull seedlings as soon as spotted. Cut off flowers before they can go to seed. Dig out larger plants, making sure to get the entire root system so the plants cannot regenerate.

CHEMICAL CONTROLS

Cut back to the crown and paint with triclopyr.

NOTES

The corky interior of the fruit allows it to float on salt or fresh water. Seeds remain viable in seawater for up to a year, but can only germinate in fresh-water areas.

NONINVASIVE ALTERNATIVES

The similar beachberry or inkberry (*Scaevola plumieri*) is less aggressive and is native.

Solanum viarum

Tropical soda apple

A nasty, shrubby perennial whose stems and leaf veins bristle with spines ½ to 1 inch long. The large, hairy-textured leaves, up to 8 inches long and 6 inches wide, alternate along furry stems and resemble big oak or fig leaves. Tiny, five-petaled white flowers with yellow stamens appear in clusters in late summer and fall. After the flowers fade, the fruits that give the plant its common name develop: round, mottled green, eventually turning yellow, and about 1 inch in diameter, they look like tiny watermelons. A single fruit may hold up to 400 reddish brown seeds. The plant tolerates poor and sandy soil. Mature size is 3 to 6 feet tall and wide.

PROBLEM
A fast, aggressive grower, it invades open areas, forms prickly thickets, and excludes native and desirable plants. Its large leaves also shade out competition.

REPRODUCTION
Seeds, which are dispersed by birds, wild animals, and livestock.

ORIGIN
Native to Brazil, Paraguay, and Argentina. Probably introduced accidentally in contaminated hay or seed.

LESS-TOXIC CONTROLS
Dig out seedlings and small plants, making sure to get all the roots. Then watch for regrowth or sprouting seeds and keep after them. For bigger colonies, mow down repeatedly, acting before seeds can form.

NOTES
The fruit is poisonous to humans. It contains solasodine, a source of steroids. The species is in the same plant family as potatoes and tomatoes.

CHEMICAL CONTROLS
Paint cut-back stems and/or regrowth with glyphosate or triclopyr.

NONINVASIVE ALTERNATIVES
None.

Spiraea japonica

Japanese spirea

Of all the spireas, this one is perhaps the most ragged-looking and variable. A medium-size shrub 3 to 7 feet tall and wide, its reddish brown branches are fuzzy when young and smoother when mature. The alternate light green leaves range from 1 to 3 inches, with serrated margins; these fade away and fall in autumn. The flat-topped, frothy, rose-pink flowerheads, carried at the ends of the branches, may be anywhere from a few inches across to up to 12 inches across. Small lustrous seed capsules contain numerous tiny seeds. This spirea adapts to all sorts of conditions, but prospers in full sun and moist, well-drained soil.

PROBLEM
It forms dense thickets that keep out all other plants, invading open areas, meadows, and the perimeters of woods.

REPRODUCTION
Seeds, which are dispersed by birds, wildlife, and water, can last for many years in the soil.

ORIGIN
Japan, Korea, and China. Imported as an ornamental.

NOTES
This shrub blooms on current season's growth, so if you are trying to control or shape a plant, late winter or early spring is the time to prune it back.

NONINVASIVE ALTERNATIVES
Take a look at other spireas at a good local nursery; there are many improved, worthwhile cultivars within related species.

LESS-TOXIC CONTROLS
Pull out seedlings. Dig out young plants by the roots; if you miss some, likely the plants will regenerate. Cutting plants down alone will not eliminate them, in other words.

CHEMICAL CONTROLS
Kill new growth in the spring with glyphosate, or paint glyphosate or triclopyr on freshly cut crowns in the fall.

Taxus cuspidata

Japanese yew, Spreading yew

A multistemmed conifer often valued as a tough, adaptable, low-maintenance hedge or foundation plant, sometimes growing to tree size. Some plants attain 40 feet high and wide, but most are much less, say, 10 feet high and wide. The needles are ½ to 1 inch long, dark green above and tinged yellowish underneath. The bark is thin, scaly, reddish brown; inner bark is reddish purple. Male and female flowers are produced on separate plants. When fruit (a berrylike structure called an "aril") develops, it is tiny (⅓ inch long), open at the end, and bright red. The root systems can become quite substantial. Few bugs or creatures trouble it, it adapts well to sun or shade, and it does well in most any soil as long as the soil is well-drained.

PROBLEM
Escaped from cultivation, it has appeared in young forests, woodland edges, and open areas, excluding native and desirable plants. Established plants are very tenacious.

REPRODUCTION
Seeds.

ORIGIN
Japan, Korea, and Manchuria.

NOTES
The entire plant is toxic to animals (dogs, horses) as well as humans.

NONINVASIVE ALTERNATIVES
A relative, European yew (*Taxus baccata*) is often preferred. Or, try hemlock (*Tsuga canadensis*), which fulfills the same roles in a home landscape (that is, hedge or foundation plantings), has a softer profile, is not poisonous, and does not spread.

LESS-TOXIC CONTROLS
Pull out seedlings. Dig out young plants by the roots before they get too big and unmanageable.

CHEMICAL CONTROLS
Colonies and larger plants can be eradicated by chopping them down to stumps, then painting the stumps with glyphosate or triclopyr.

Viburnum dilatatum
Linden viburnum

A nonnative viburnum of uneven quality. Growth is often open and leggy. The opposite dark-green leaves are lustrous, with a hairy texture, and vary from 2 to 5 inches long and half as wide. Although they linger on the plant late into fall, the leaves have a dull color that varies from red to red-brown. The shrub flowers heavily in spring, with 3- to 5-inch creamy white flat-topped clusters. The bright ⅓-inch red berries (technically, drupes) adorn the plant in fall, and although they may persist into winter, they start to shrivel and fade in color. This viburnum prospers in moist ground and reaches between 8 and 10 feet tall and wide.

PROBLEM
Birds who eat the berries have spread this particular species into wild and open areas, where it forms heavy thickets to the exclusion of native and desirable plants. Also, it seems to be impervious to the nonnative viburnum leaf beetle that can decimate other viburnums.

REPRODUCTION
Seed, which are dispersed by birds.

ORIGIN
From East Asia.

NOTES
Related species that can also become troublesome when they escape gardens include *Viburnum lentago*, *V. plicatum*, and *V. sieboldii*.

NONINVASIVE ALTERNATIVES
Grow instead one of the many worthy native species, such as *Viburnum dentatum*.

LESS-TOXIC CONTROLS
Pull out seedlings. Dig out young plants by the roots before they get too big and unmanageable.

CHEMICAL CONTROLS
Kill new growth in the spring with glyphosate, or paint glyphosate on freshly cut stumps in the fall.

Viburnum lantana

Wayfaring tree

Despite the common name, not actually a tree, but a multistemmed, rangy shrub that grows leggy with age. The opposite, ovate, rough leaves are dark gray-green on top, fuzzy underneath, with serrated margins, and measure between 2 and 5 inches long. Flat-topped flower clusters are 3 to 5 inches across, white with yellow stamens, which give them a creamy-white look. The fruit (technically, drupes) are ⅓ inch long and strikingly colored—they begin green, turn yellow, change to cherry red, and darken to black, often with some or all of these colors represented in a cluster. Prefers well-drained sites, is more drought-tolerant than many of its kin, and tolerates sweet (alkaline) soil. Mature shrubs are 10 to 20 feet tall and wide.

PROBLEM
Birds that eat the berries have spread this particular species into wild and open areas, where it forms heavy thickets to the exclusion of native and desirable plants.

REPRODUCTION
Seeds.

ORIGIN
Europe and western Asia.

NOTES
If you want this plant, choose one of the improved cultivars, such as 'Mohican', introduced by U.S. National Arboretum. Its habit is much more compact than that of the species, up to 9 feet tall and wide, the foliage is a handsome dark green, and the drupes retain their gorgeous orange-red color for weeks in the fall.

LESS-TOXIC CONTROLS
Pull out seedlings. Dig out young plants by the roots before they get too big and unmanageable. Prevent spread by cutting off the inflorescences.

CHEMICAL CONTROLS
Kill new growth in the spring with glyphosate, or paint glyphosate on freshly cut stumps in the fall.

NONINVASIVE ALTERNATIVES
Consider a native species, such as nannyberry (*Viburnum lentago*).

Viburnum opulus var. *opulus*

European cranberry bush, Guelder rose

A medium-size, multistemmed, rounded bush that, with age, develops arching branches that hang to the ground. The dark green maplelike leaves are opposite. When autumn comes, they may color like other viburnums, but often they will simply fade and fall off. The white, flat-topped flowerheads measure between 2 and 3 inches across, and sport both sterile and fertile flowers for a pinwheel effect (similar to a lacecap hydrangea). The bright red berries (drupes) that follow are ¼ inch in diameter, shriveling to dark red and persisting on the plant through the winter. Thrives in full sun and moist ground, but adaptable to less-ideal conditions. Susceptible to aphid infestations. Mature plant size is 8 to 15 feet tall, 10 to 15 feet wide.

LESS-TOXIC CONTROLS

Pull out seedlings. Dig out young plants by the roots before they get too big and unmanageable. Prevent spread by cutting off the inflorescences.

CHEMICAL CONTROLS

Kill new growth in the spring with glyphosate, or paint glyphosate on freshly cut stumps in the fall.

PROBLEM

It has been displacing native plants in wetlands, particularly in the Midwest; it also invades roadsides and forest edges. Reportedly it interbreeds with the native highbush cranberry (*Viburnum opulus* var. *americanum*), which could lead to a truly invasive plant.

REPRODUCTION

Seeds.

ORIGIN

Europe, northern Asia, and North Africa. Imported as an ornamental.

NOTES

An older, time-tested dwarf cultivar, 'Compactum', has a denser habit, is better-looking in leaf, flower, and fruit, and is a more appropriate size for most home landscapes.

NONINVASIVE ALTERNATIVES

Try instead the native beauty, oakleaf hydrangea (*Hydrangea quercifolia*).

Vitex agnus-castus

Chaste tree, Monk's pepper

A fast-growing big bush or small tree, it has dramatic fragrant flowers, which appear in early summer on new wood (current season's growth), in long, up to 18-inch, branched clusters. Blooms are pale purple and radiate a sweet scent; they occur at stem ends as well as in leaf axils. Foliage is opposite, palmate (five to seven leaflets per leaf), and dark gray-green in color, fuzzy gray underneath. Not hardy in the north. Mature size is 8 to 10 feet tall and half as wide.

PROBLEM

Where it has escaped into wild areas, including forest edges, fields, and open lots, it grows quickly and out-competes native and desirable plants.

REPRODUCTION

Seeds.

ORIGIN

Southern Europe and western Asia.

NOTES

The flowers attract many bees. The berries and decoctions made from them were believed, in ancient Europe, to be an anaphrodisiac, used for quelling lust for monks and others, hence the common names. It also has a long history of treating various gynecological conditions; modern extractions have been successful in treating symptoms of PMS (premenstrual syndrome).

NONINVASIVE ALTERNATIVES

The native buckeyes, white-flowered *Aesculus parviflora* and red-flowered *A. pavia*, also have fragrant flowers and are not aggressive.

LESS-TOXIC CONTROLS

In colder climates, winter will kill it back to the ground, but it often resprouts. To control its spread, remove the flowers before they go to seed. To eradicate it, cut it down repeatedly until it no longer resprouts. Dig up seedlings and smaller plants by the roots.

CHEMICAL CONTROLS

Kill new growth in the spring with glyphosate, or paint glyphosate on cut-back crowns.

Vitex rotundifolia

Beach vitex, Chasteberry, Pohinahina

Running horizontal stems travel outward, rooting at the nodes and sending up new stems. Young stems are green but mature woody, brown, and fissured. The 1- to 2-inch semiwaxy, opposite leaves are ovate, dark green above, lighter below; they are fragrant, and more so when crushed, the scent reminiscent of eucalyptus. The light purple 1-inch flowers are both terminal and axillary. The ¼-inch drupes that follow change from yellow to blue-black. Prospers in poor, sandy, and well-drained soil, colonizes beaches and dunes in the mild-climate Southeast. Mature plant size is 1 to 2 feet tall, spreading out 15 feet, though 60-foot stems have been reported.

LESS-TOXIC CONTROLS
Due to deep roots and an often-fragile dune environment, digging up all but the smallest plants is tricky. However, chopping back stems to the crowns, repeatedly, eventually weakens the plants and they die back; use a sharp machete.

CHEMICAL CONTROLS
Seedlings and resprouted plants may be killed with an application of triclopyr.

PROBLEM
Fast, rapacious growth means that this plant takes over large areas to the exclusion of native and desirable plants. In South Carolina, it has been dubbed "the kudzu of the beach."

REPRODUCTION
Seeds, which are dispersed by water—the drupes float—and runners. Even stem fragments can root.

ORIGIN
China, Japan, and Korea.

NOTES
Has invaded important beach (loggerhead) turtle egg-laying sites. The leaves contain an oil, rotundial, which shows promise as a mosquito repellent.

NONINVASIVE ALTERNATIVES
Not too many plants will prosper in similar conditions and not become a pest, but low-growing potentillas and bush honeysuckle (*Diervilla lonicera*) are worth considering.

9
Trees

If you are asking yourself how in the world a plant as large as a tree can be called invasive, then probably you have not had to contend with one of the characters described in this chapter. Trees are every bit as invasive as other plants, and in today's smaller yards, not something a homeowner cares to tolerate.

Invasive trees wear out their welcome in a variety of ways: generating an excess of fruit/seeds, suckering, allelopathic characteristics to their roots or leaf litter that harm or kill plants in their vicinity, or sprawling, greedy root systems. Some exhibit more than one of these qualities.

If you do not intervene when the plant is a sapling, or if you inherit a mature problem tree, dealing with it can be daunting indeed. Removing flowers to discourage the setting of fruits and dissemination of seeds is not often practical. Constantly chopping off unwanted suckers is a chore. Girdling, whereby trunk bark is deliberately damaged to disable and kill a tree, could be worth a try, though you might do wise to hire an arborist experienced in this technique. Cutting it down entirely may be your best option, with or without the professional assistance, muscle, and/or equipment of an arborist, but then you will be left with a stump, seedlings, or suckers that continue to pop up after the mother plant is vanquished. So stump removal or on-site grinding, though a big job, might be in order as well.

In short, tall pest plants are trouble to have and trouble to eradicate.

Acacia auriculiformis

Black wattle, Earleaf acacia

A multistemmed tree, it is thorny and has a crooked, rangy growth habit. Small clusters of yellowish flower spikes appear in profusion in spring and summer and are followed by flat, ½-inch pods. Thin, sickle-shaped leaves (technically "phyllodes") resemble those of eucalyptus. Tolerates poor soils, whether dry or waterlogged, and has proven useful for reforesting and erosion control. Attains 98 feet.

PROBLEM
In South Florida, in particular, it has invaded pinelands, scrub, and hammocks, displacing native vegetation and threatening to shade out rare plants. Developers and homeowners should not spare these trees when clearing areas.

REPRODUCTION
Seeds, which are mainly dispersed by birds.

ORIGIN
Australia and New Guinea. Widely grown in India, Southeast Asia, and parts of Africa. A popular roadside shade tree in Singapore.

NOTES
Its wood is good for making tools, furniture, and paper. In India, the wood is commonly used for charcoal and as firewood.

NONINVASIVE ALTERNATIVES
Some tree-size species of *Acacia* like the same growing conditions, also have yellow flowers, and may not turn out to be as aggressive, notably mimosa (*A. dealbata*) and Queensland silver wattle (*A. podalyriifolia*).

LESS-TOXIC CONTROLS
Cut the tree down and remove or kill the stump or at least any suckering branches that appear.

CHEMICAL CONTROLS
Treat the stump with glyphosate.

Acer ginnala

Amur maple

Synonym *Acer tataricum* var. *ginnala*

A smallish, multistemmed tree. A handful of named cultivars are still offered by some nurseries. Yellowish white flowers in spring. Fall color is yellow and red. It prospers in cooler climates, and adapts well to sun and part-shade and a range of soil pH levels. It grows easily and quickly, especially in moist soil. Mature plant size is between 15 and 25 feet tall and wide.

PROBLEM

This tree is becoming a problem in the Midwest, especially in Illinois and Missouri, where it displaces native shrubs and understory trees in open woods and shades out native grasses and herbaceous plants in open areas.

REPRODUCTION

Grows easily from seeds in small keys (samaras), which it produces prolifically.

ORIGIN

Originally hailing from northern and central China, Manchuria, and Japan.

NOTES

Unlike most maple species, this one has fragrant flowers with a light, sweet scent. Among maples, it is exceptionally cold-hardy.

NONINVASIVE ALTERNATIVES

The very similar Tatarian maple (*Acer tataricum*) is said to be slower-growing, or substitute the similar-size American hornbeam (*Carpinus caroliniana* subsp. *virginiana*), Pagoda dogwood (*Cornus alternifolia*), or one of the larger, multistemmed viburnums.

LESS-TOXIC CONTROLS

Cut the tree down and remove or kill the stump or at least any suckering branches that appear.

CHEMICAL CONTROLS

Treat the stump with glyphosate.

Acer negundo

Box elder,
Ash-leaved maple

This unappealing maple tends to have a ragged, lanky profile and may be multi-stemmed. Because it grows so fast, its wood is weak and brittle. Also, unique among maples, male and female trees are separate. Females produce long chains of "maple keys" (samaras), while male trees flower in much smaller, flat-topped clusters. Leaves are pinnately compound, usually three to five leaflets, sometimes up to nine. Fall color is bland. The trees are short-lived. Thrives in moist soil and full sun. Mature size is up to 50 feet tall and wide.

PROBLEM
A fast-growing, weak, unattractive tree that fills up space that could be occupied by and/or shades out bet-ter-quality plants. Box elder spreads rampantly.

REPRODUCTION
Seeds, which are wind-dispersed. Also spreads by suckers and root shoots.

ORIGIN
Native to the United States and southern Canada.

NOTES
It is a host to the pesky boxelder bug, which lays its eggs on it. The bugs do not appear to disable the trees. Their tendencies to congregate and to shel-ter in our homes are what make them unwanted. In addition, they smell bad and can be hard to eradicate.

NONINVASIVE ALTERNATIVES
Japanese maples and cultivars thrive in the same locations and are superior in every way.

LESS-TOXIC CONTROLS
Remove samara chains from female plants before they ripen. Cut back and dig out seedlings as soon as spotted. For larger trees, cut down then remove the stump if possible. Where possible, drying out the site is another option, which at least slows growth.

CHEMICAL CONTROLS
Paint the stump with glyphosate.

Acer platanoides

Norway maple

Another maple that does not endear itself, the round-headed, densely branched Norway maple has a shallow root system that is notoriously greedy and also makes the tree less stable in windstorms or floods. The dark green leaves tend to be larger than those of sugar maple, up to 7 inches across. Fall color is disappointing, usually pale yellow fading to tan. This tree flowers heavily in spring, yellow-greenish clusters about ⅓ inch across. Plenty of winged seeds (samaras) follow and persist into fall and winter. It is also susceptible to leaf scorch and anthracnose. Though it is widely adaptable and pollution-tolerant, its liabilities can outweigh its benefits. Attains 40 to 50 feet, or more.

PROBLEM

Norway maple has a deserved reputation as a thug in some settings—its shallow, wide-ranging root system monopolizes soil nutrients and moisture to the detriment, especially, of lawns and groundcovers. Research suggests it may also be allelopathic (produces a toxin that discourages other plants).

REPRODUCTION

Seeds, which are wind-dispersed, and suckers.

ORIGIN

Norway, of course, and temperate Europe.

LESS-TOXIC CONTROLS

Cut back and dig out seedlings. Cut down larger trees and remove the stump, if possible. Watch for and cut back new seedlings and sprouts.

CHEMICAL CONTROLS

Paint the stump with glyphosate, and then watch for resprouting.

NOTES

The wood has been used by instrument-makers (luthiers), including in the making of the famous Stradivarius violins.

NONINVASIVE ALTERNATIVES

The nursery industry offers numerous improved cultivars that might be worth considering. Arguably, the best one is red- to purple-leaved 'Crimson King'. If you seek a substantial, shade-tree maple, the sugar maple (*Acer saccharum*) is a much better choice.

Ailanthus altissima

Tree-of-heaven

Fast-growing and adaptable, this deciduous tree withstands pollution and dreadful soil. In late spring, 2-foot-long, pinnately compound leaves composed of up to 25 leaflets each alternate up stout stems. Young twigs are furry, while mature stems are smooth. Male and female flowers usually occur on separate plants; these are yellow-green, carried in 8- to 16-inch long panicles in early summer. Male flowers smell bad. The fruit that follows in late summer to fall is yellow to orange-red samaras, which brown and remain through winter. Mature plant size is 80 feet or more.

PROBLEM

Tree-of-heaven insinuates itself into empty lots and pavement cracks, forest and road margins, and the like, where it establishes a tenacious thicket that excludes native and desirable plants. It also emits allelopathic chemicals into the soil to discourage other plants. Its powerful roots have been known to damage building foundations and breach underground pipes.

REPRODUCTION

Seeds and suckers.

ORIGIN

Central China and Taiwan.

NOTES

Trees often harbor beneficial insects, light green lacewings. Various plant parts are important in Chinese medicine, although their quassinoid content can be harmful, especially to the heart. The tree has also been used in silk-making.

NONINVASIVE ALTERNATIVES

None.

LESS-TOXIC CONTROLS

Chopping back does not work well, because new sprouts soon appear. Seedlings can be dug up, but if you leave behind any root fragments, they will generate new plants.

CHEMICAL CONTROLS

Glyphosate can be effective, but timing is key—apply to a cut stump in summer or early fall, or spray on the leaves as they emerge in spring.

Albizia julibrissin

Mimosa, Silk tree, Persian silk tree

Not a big tree, and sometimes multistemmed, mimosa grows quickly to a vase-shaped profile with a flattened, umbrella-like crown. It leafs out later than other deciduous trees, with double-compound leaves up to 20 inches long; individual leaves have up to 25 pinnae, each with 40 to 60 leaflets. Fragrant clusters of pink, 1-inch, powder-puff flowers give way to 5- to 7-inch long, thin, straw-colored pods. The tree is short-lived and susceptible to destructive insect pests and a fungal wilt disease. When the flowers pass, leaves drop, pods fall, and/or the weak, brittle wood breaks off, the tree creates a mess. It adapts to a wide range of growing conditions in mild-climate areas. Ultimate height and width is 20 to 40 feet.

PROBLEM

Mimosa self-sows prolifically, creating dense stands that exclude native and desirable plants. Like other legumes, it fixes nitrogen in the soil, thus altering its habitat. The wilt disease mentioned above disfigures plants that then produce many suckers.

REPRODUCTION

Seeds, which can remain viable for 50 years, and suckers.

ORIGIN

From central China, Japan, and the Middle East.

NOTES

Hummingbirds, honeybees, and butterflies relish the flowers.

NONINVASIVE ALTERNATIVES

Similar-size, superior flowering trees include redbud (*Cercis canadensis*), flowering dogwood (*Cornus florida*), and fringe tree (*Chionanthus virginicus*).

LESS-TOXIC CONTROLS

Pull out seedlings as soon as spotted. Remove pods from established trees before they can ripen. Cutting back bigger trees does not work because the stumps resprout or sucker from the roots.

CHEMICAL CONTROLS

Treat a cut stump with glyphosate, or spray the foliage with glyphosate or triclopyr in spring after it leafs out.

Bischofia javanica

Bishopwood, Javawood

A dense evergreen tree suitable for mild climates. Glossy greenish bronze leaves are opposite, composed of three leaflets. Male and female flowers are produced on separate plants, though the greenish yellow, petal-less blooms, nestled in leaf axils, are tiny, barely noticeable. However, the females develop blue-gray berrylike fruit clusters. Twigs and leaves contain a milky sap, as is typical in the euphorbia family. Mature tree size is 30 to 70 feet tall.

PROBLEM

In the moist soil it likes best, it grows and spreads rampantly, crowding and shading out native and desirable plants. Seedlings pop up in sun or shade. Bishopwood has been used as a street tree in South Florida and has escaped into the wild, where it has invaded threatened tropical hardwood hammock and cypress plant communities.

REPRODUCTION

Seeds, which are dispersed by birds and water.

ORIGIN

Asia and Pacific Islands. Imported to Florida as an ornamental.

NOTES

In its native Asia, the wood is used in building and furniture, the bark for a red dye, the fruit in winemaking, the edible seeds as a source of lubricant, and the roots medicinally.

LESS-TOXIC CONTROLS

Since female trees are the source of all those seeds, control them first. Remove the fruit clusters before they ripen. Watch for and dig out seedlings as soon as you spot them. Cut down trees altogether and either remove the roots or be vigilant in cutting back new sprouts.

CHEMICAL CONTROLS

Paint stumps with triclopyr, or spray a mix of triclopyr and oil around the lower trunk.

NONINVASIVE ALTERNATIVES

Crape myrtle (*Lagerstroemia indica*) grows in similar settings, has handsome foliage and flowers, and is a lot less troublesome.

Broussonetia papyrifera
Paper mulberry

Synonym *Morus papyrifera*
Rather variable in leaf and profile, and thanks to its appetite for suckering, this tree can become an unattractive nuisance. Related to mulberries but less woody. Generally wider than tall, it forms a broad to rounded crown and is thick with dull green foliage. Some leaves are very lobed, others are not, edges are teethed, tops are rough-textured, while undersides are lightly fuzzy. Male flowers are like catkins, while females are ½-inch balls. If both sexes are present, the female trees will produce (edible) wine-red to red-orange drupes in bunches. The root systems are extensive but notoriously shallow. Tolerates heat, drought, and alkaline soil. Up to 50 feet tall and wider.

PROBLEM
Escaped plants grow quickly and form a thicket of suckers and stems, outcompeting and shading out native and desirable plants. A good storm can uproot them, however, leaving behind a mess.

REPRODUCTION
Seeds and suckering roots.

LESS-TOXIC CONTROLS
Watch for and dig out seedlings as soon as you spot them. Cut down trees altogether, and either remove the roots or be vigilant in cutting back new sprouts. Note that the sap is very sticky and can ruin clothing.

CHEMICAL CONTROLS
Chop back the thicket, then wade in and paint the stumps with glyphosate.

ORIGIN
China and Japan.

NOTES
The bark fiber can be used to make paper; in the Polynesian islands, it is used to make cloth. Some people are very allergic to the pollen.

NONINVASIVE ALTERNATIVES
The native red mulberry (*Morus rubra*) is a good-looking, nonsuckering alternative; males produce no fruit.

Casaurina equisitifolia

Australian pine

Although it looks like a soft, wispy pine, this tree is not a pine and is actually deciduous. Its branchlets resemble soft pine needles, 4 to 8 inches long, in bundles of five to twenty. The reddish brown to gray bark is brittle and peels. The tree generates small, hard, pointy brown conelike fruits, about ½ inch in diameter, with winged seeds inside. The root system is thick yet shallow. This pine is not cold-tolerant, but has made successful inroads on Southern beaches and dunes, as well as roadsides and fields. Mature size is 40 to 100 feet tall, depending on the setting.

PROBLEM

It is very fast growing and becomes a bully where it invades. Its dense profile shades out other plants, its roots release allelopathic chemicals that inhibit other plants, and it sheds a lot of needles and fruits to create an inhibiting carpet underneath its branches. Its shallow roots are easily uprooted in hurricanes and thus allow a great degree of beach erosion during these events.

REPRODUCTION

Seeds, which are wind-dispersed.

ORIGIN

Malaysia, southern Asia, Oceania, and Australia. Imported to Florida in the late 1800s.

NOTES

Its roots fix nitrogen, which allow it to grow in areas of poor soil such as on sandy beaches. It was introduced for this reason.

NONINVASIVE ALTERNATIVES

The sea grape (*Coccoloba uvifera*) is a better choice for sand and soil stabilization.

LESS-TOXIC CONTROLS

Watch for and dig out seedlings as soon as you spot them. Meanwhile, remove or rake out the "cones" to discourage more from germinating.

CHEMICAL CONTROLS

Glyphosate is effective on cut stumps, painted on trunks, and sprayed on foliage.

Crataegus monogyna

English hawthorn, Single-seed hawthorn

A small deciduous tree, it spreads via its berries, which birds relish. Like other hawthorns, it has stout spines along its branches. Leaves are dark green and have three to seven lobes. The sweetly scented white flowers are borne in clusters and fade to pink. The one-seeded (hence the common name) red berries, each about ½ inch in diameter, develop by late summer and hang on the tree into winter. Plants tend to form dense thickets, with branches low to the ground. Established plants are drought-tolerant and 20 to 30 feet tall.

PROBLEM

Dense thickets of this plant along property margins, roadsides, and even in woodland settings displace native and desirable plants, altering the existing habitat and physically blocking movement of animals and people.

REPRODUCTION

Seeds which are dispersed by birds and mammals. Also spreads by stump sprouts.

ORIGIN

Europe, western Asia, and North Africa.

NOTES

This is the plant, along with relative *Crataegus laevigata*, that forms so many of those daunting bristly hedgerows in rural England.

NONINVASIVE ALTERNATIVES

A relative, *Crataegus viridis* 'Winter King', is a fine landscape tree in many settings.

LESS-TOXIC CONTROLS

Watch for and dig out seedlings as soon as you spot them. Larger specimens can be killed if you cut down not only the entire tree, but also the crown of the plant several inches below the surface (part of the main roots). Early summer, when the trees are investing energy in topgrowth, is the best time to do this.

CHEMICAL CONTROLS

A mix of triclopyr and oil applied to a stump or painted on the main trunk will kill it.

Cupaniopsis anacardioides

Carrotwood, Tuckeroo tree, Beach tamarind

A fast-growing evergreen tree that prospers in mild climates and poor and damp soils. The densely produced foliage is compound, with four to ten oblong leaflets 4 to 8 inches long. Small greenish white flowers appear in early spring in the leaf axils and are followed by the plant's most memorable aspect, the colorful fruit. The fruit is a yellow three-lobed capsule that bursts open to reveal red or orange fleshy tissue in which three shiny black seeds are embedded. The gray outer bark peels to reveal orange inner bark, hence the common name. Mature trees can be up to 35 feet tall.

PROBLEM

When it escapes, it is aggressive. It is a threat to Florida mangroves and their critical role in coastal ecosystems, and to other native plants. In California, carrotwood is evidently not yet a significant escapee; in Texas, it is being watched by concerned resource managers.

REPRODUCTION

Seeds, which are distributed widely by birds and small mammals.

ORIGIN

Australia, Indonesia, and Papua New Guinea. Imported as an ornamental or street tree.

NOTES

The fruits are produced unequally; some trees are prolific, while others are barren.

NONINVASIVE ALTERNATIVES

The cherry laurel (*Prunus laurocerasus*) also has dense evergreen foliage, is tough and adaptable, and is not invasive. Its fruit, a little dark purple drupe, is not as distinctive.

LESS-TOXIC CONTROLS

Cutting off the fruit before seeds ripen may offer some measure of control. Dig out seedlings, and cut back and dig up larger specimens.

CHEMICAL CONTROLS

Triclopyr has proved effective as a basal bark treatment and cut-stump treatment; glyphosate is less effective.

Elaeagnus angustifolia

Russian olive

Sometimes loved, sometimes loathed, this silver-leaved small tree grows fairly quickly to establish a loose, rounded, open profile. Those leaves are small, smooth-edged, and slim, usually about ½ inch wide and up to 3 inches long, displayed alternately on the branches. Thorns may be present. Stems, buds, and leaves have a dense covering of silvery to rusty scales. Small, scented, creamy white flowers lodge in the leaf axils in late spring. The distinctive fruit is yellowish and drupelike. A very tough and adaptable plant, it does best in well-drained, sandy soil in the drier areas of the American West and Midwest. When full-grown, plants are 12-20 feet high and wide.

PROBLEM
Left to their own devices or escaped from cultivation, these trees form dense thickets that overwhelm native and desirable plants in open areas and along streams and canyons. The roots are able to fix nitrogen in the soil, thus an incursion alters the habitat it invades.

REPRODUCTION
Seeds, which are distributed by many different birds, and some root suckering.

ORIGIN
Southern Europe and Central Asia. Imported as an ornamental tree.

NOTES
Has a remarkable tolerance for soil salts, making it a good choice for roadside, highway, and seaside landscaping.

NONINVASIVE ALTERNATIVES
Other gray-leaved small trees to consider include the native silverberry (*Elaeagnus commutata*), silver buffaloberry (*Shepherdia argentea*), and cultivated willows (*Salix*).

LESS-TOXIC CONTROLS
Watch for and dig out seedlings as soon as you spot them. Cut down trees altogether, and either remove the roots or be vigilant in cutting back new sprouts.

CHEMICAL CONTROLS
Cut down trees in late summer and paint the stumps with glyphosate.

Eucalyptus globulus

Tasmanian blue gum, Blue gum, Common eucalyptus

While Tasmanian blue gum is hardly the only problematic eucalyptus around, its qualities and management issues are certainly representative of all the fast-growing, introduced species. The erect trunks tend to shed their bark, and the branches are brittle. Leaves are dark green and sickle-shaped, 6 to 10 inches long, and produced in heavy, pendulous masses. Small creamy white to yellow flowers appear in late winter to early spring. The 1-inch seed capsules are blue-gray and warty-textured. The entire plant is aromatic. Mature plant size is 150 to 200 feet tall.

PROBLEM

A greedy and messy plant, it requires deep soil and plenty of elbowroom. It then stifles native and desirable plants not only by monopolizing soil moisture and nutrients, but also by its profuse and probably allelopathic leaf, bark, and seed litter at its feet. Its high oil content makes it a hazard in forestfire-vulnerable areas.

REPRODUCTION

Seeds, which are wind-dispersed, and sprouts.

ORIGIN

Australia. Imported for use as wind-breaks, railroad ties, and fuel wood.

NOTES

Oil extracted from the leaves has many uses, including perfume, flavoring, disinfectant/antimicrobial, pesticide, and cough suppressant. Hummingbirds like the flowers.

NONINVASIVE ALTERNATIVES

The native Engelmann oak (*Quercus engelmannii*) is recommended for similar sites and uses.

LESS-TOXIC CONTROLS

Watch for and dig out seedlings as soon as you spot them. Cut down trees altogether, then either eject the roots or be vigilant in cutting back new sprouts. Eucalyptuses are vigorous resprouters.

CHEMICAL CONTROLS

Cut down trees in the fall, brush away all sawdust, and immediately paint on glyphosate or triclopyr.

Ficus microcarpa

Laurel fig, Indian laurel fig, Chinese banyan tree

Synonym *Ficus retusa*

This evergreen tree for mild-climate areas is most common in California and Florida, where it has escaped cultivation in places. It has a weeping profile, with long drooping branches cloaked in small, 2- to 4-inch long leaves. Yellowish to rose new leaves are always coming on, which gives a tree a duo-tone look. Trunk wood is light gray and there are dangling aerial roots. Sap is milky. The fruits, or figs, develop only if the plant is pollinated, and are tiny, ½ inch in diameter, starting out green and ripening to red. The tree cannot tolerate frost. It is usually 15 to 30 feet tall, occasionally much taller.

PROBLEM

A strong, fast-growing plant, it can survive on little or no soil when young. It overtakes other trees, shades out native and desirable plants, and can insinuate into and damage sidewalks, buildings, rain gutters, culverts, and bridges. Additionally, it may be pest-plagued: thrips damage new growth—the leaves look stippled, curl up, die, and fall.

REPRODUCTION

Seeds are dispersed by many different birds and by ants.

ORIGIN

Southern Asia. Imported as an ornamental and street tree.

NOTES

The tree became a much greater problem once its natural pollinator, a fig wasp (*Eupristina verticillata*) joined it, and seedlings started popping up everywhere.

NONINVASIVE ALTERNATIVES

Try a magnolia instead, such as native sweetbay (*Magnolia virginiana*).

LESS-TOXIC CONTROLS

Seedlings can be pulled. Larger ones can be chopped back or cut down, but watch for regenerating sprouts and keep after them.

CHEMICAL CONTROLS

Paint stumps with triclopyr.

Melia azedarach

Chinaberry

An impressively fast-growing deciduous tree that has spread itself all over the South in lots, waste places, and roadsides. Not cold-hardy. Forms a dome-headed profile of stiff, coarse branches and is weak-wooded. Foliage is alternate and bipinnately compound, overall 1 to 3 feet long and half as wide; individual leaves are mainly smooth and have serrated edges. Fall color is yellow. It blooms in spring in long, loose clusters of light purple fragrant flowers. The fruits that follow are dangling ½-inch yellow drupes that persist on the tree if not eaten. It tolerates a wide range of growing conditions, including poor soil. When full-grown, the tree is between 30 and 50 feet high and wide.

PROBLEM
Because it is untroubled by pest and diseases, and because it is so fast-growing, with the help of birds and various animals, it has invaded many locations. Once established, it monopolizes a site, excluding native and desirable plants.

REPRODUCTION
Seeds, which are dispersed by birds and animals, and root suckers.

ORIGIN
Northern India, central and western China. Imported as a shade tree.

NOTES
The bark, leaves, fruit, and seeds are poisonous for humans. Crushed seeds have been used by native fishermen to stun freshwater fish.

NONINVASIVE ALTERNATIVES
The mild-climate ash tree, flowering ash (*Fraxinus dipetala*), is about the same size, also has yellow fall color, and is not weedy.

LESS-TOXIC CONTROLS
Hand-pull seedlings as they appear, and keep a lookout for more. If you dig up seedlings or larger plants, be thorough in getting the root system out, because even small pieces can regenerate.

CHEMICAL CONTROLS
Paint fresh-cut stumps and lower bark with triclopyr.

Morus alba

Mulberry, White mulberry, Silkworm mulberry

Forms a dense, twiggy, unkempt-looking profile. The glossy green leaves are lobed or heart-shaped, with serrated edges, and vary from 2 to 7 inches long and wide. Spring brings yellowish green, separate male and female catkin flowers that are followed by heavy pollen production. Blackberry-like drupe fruits, about 1 inch long, are light purple (sometimes pale pink, sometimes darker purple). When they fall or are excreted by birds, they stain sidewalks, patios, even clothing. Widely adaptable to almost any setting except soggy ground. Most mature plants are 20 to 40 feet tall and wide; some reach 60 feet.

LESS-TOXIC CONTROLS
Watch for and dig out seedlings as soon as you spot them. Cut down trees altogether and either remove the roots or be vigilant in cutting back new sprouts. Note that the sap is very sticky and can ruin clothing.

CHEMICAL CONTROLS
Chop back the thicket, then wade in and paint the stumps with glyphosate.

PROBLEM
Mulberry grows quickly, invading and crowding out native and desirable plants. It is susceptible to sooty canker disease, which disfigures and eventually kills the trees. It also hybridizes with and transmits disease to the native red mulberry (*Morus rubra*).

REPRODUCTION
Seeds, which are dispersed by birds and animals.

ORIGIN
Imported to the United States from China for the silkworm industry (which failed).

NOTES
The fruit, while edible, is not especially tasty, exhibiting kind of a watery sweetness. Leaves have been used to feed silkworms as well as livestock. Leaves and root bark have long been used in traditional Asian medicine.

NONINVASIVE ALTERNATIVES
A cultivar called 'Chaparral' is fruitless and has an attractive pendulous habit.

Paulownia tomentosa

Princess tree, Empress tree, Royal paulownia

Very fast-growing, putting on 8 to 10 feet in a single season and thus having weak, brittle wood. Forms a rounded crown, dense with large, light green, heart-shaped leaves up to a foot across. It flowers before the leaves emerge, in 8- to 12-inch-long, richly scented upright panicles; individual blossoms are about 2 inches long, purple with some darker or yellow markings, reminiscent of foxglove. Little brown seed capsules follow. Leaves drop in autumn (no fall color). Prominent, olive-sized brown flower buds form in autumn and winter over if cold weather does not kill them. Adapts to difficult growing conditions and poor soil, but grows lushly in moist, well-drained ground. Attains 30 to 60 feet high and wide when mature.

PROBLEM
It can self-sow a lot, giving it an unkempt look and entry into lots, roadsides, streamsides, and other marginal areas. Its dense growth and shallow surface roots inhibit growth underneath, lawn grass and ground-covers in yards, and native or desirable plants elsewhere. It regenerates from roots and stems.

REPRODUCTION
Seeds (thousands per capsule) and suckers.

ORIGIN
From China.

NOTES
It is named for Anna Pavlovna, who was the daughter of Russia's Czar Paul I.

NONINVASIVE ALTERNATIVES
Catalpa trees, *Catalpa speciosa* or *C. bignonioides*, have similar leaves and flowers, a slower growth rate, and are arguably more attractive.

LESS-TOXIC CONTROLS
Seedlings can be pulled. Larger ones can be chopped back or cut down, but watch for regenerating sprouts and keep after them.

CHEMICAL CONTROLS
Paint cut stumps with glyphosate. Spray foliage or treat large trunks with glyphosate or triclopyr.

Populus alba

White poplar, Silver-leaved poplar

A wide-spreading, profusely suckering deciduous "tree" that often ends up more like a thicket. Bluntly lobed leaves, 2 to 5 inches long, are dark green above and furry white below; there is no fall color show. Woolly fuzz, which you can rub off with your thumb, coats the stems. Young bark is whitish or greenish gray with some dark splotches. Male and female flowers are produced on separate plants, with the males having longer, 2-inch catkins. Fluffy little white seeds develop in summer. Overall, the wood is weak and brittle. The plants shed a lot of leaves, twigs, and other debris. A widely adaptable plant but prospers in moist ground. Becomes 40 to 70 feet tall and wide, sometimes bigger.

PROBLEM

If its suckering, weedy profile, aggressive growth, vulnerability to various diseases, and tendency to be messy do not endear it to homeowners and land stewards, the ability of its questing roots to invade water and sewer lines and septic tanks will be a turnoff.

REPRODUCTION

Seeds, which are wind-dispersed. Also spread by suckers.

ORIGIN

Southern Europe and Central Asia.

LESS-TOXIC CONTROLS

This is a battle against suckers. Cut or mow them down to get to the main trunk, then cut that off. Then keep after regenerating suckers.

NOTES

Some individuals have used the tree's suckering ability to advantage, planting white poplar as a windbreak or hedgerow.

CHEMICAL CONTROLS

Paint glyphosate on cut stumps and cut-back suckers, or spray foliage, branches, and suckers carefully and thoroughly with glyphosate or triclopyr.

NONINVASIVE ALTERNATIVES

All poplars and cottonwoods have similar drawbacks, but if you want one, consult with a reputable local nursery. You might consider a birch instead.

Pyrus calleryana

Callery pear

If this short-lived, weak-wooded, poorly branched tree is not disfigured or broken by winter storms, it matures into a decent-looking if lollipop-shaped, medium-size plant with many thorny branches. Ultimate height is 25 to 50 feet. The oval-shaped, glossy, dark-green leaves have scalloped edges, are up to 3 inches long, and cloak the tree well. Fall color is wine-red. The showy white flower clusters, composed of individual blooms about 1 inch wide, appear very early in spring and have an unpleasant, pungent scent. When the blooms avoid being nipped by a late frost, small, round, hard, green-brown fruits develop; these are not edible.

PROBLEM

Its fast growth and thorny nature make this tree an unwelcome invader in fields, empty lots, roadsides, woodland edges, fencerows, under power lines, and at the base of gutters. Thickets of it crowd out native and desirable vegetation.

REPRODUCTION

Seeds, which are dispersed by birds, particularly starlings, and small animals.

ORIGIN

Korea and China. Imported to confer some fireblight resistance into commercial pears.

NOTES

'Bradford', the cultivar originally used successfully as a rootstock and pollen donor for orchard trees, turns out to have structural weakness (it splits due to too many closely positioned branches) and has been superseded by superior cultivars.

NONINVASIVE ALTERNATIVES

If you want a handsome, early-blooming tree, try redbud (*Cercis*) or serviceberry (*Amelanchier*).

LESS-TOXIC CONTROLS

Pull or dig out unwanted seedlings and saplings. Cut down larger ones.

CHEMICAL CONTROLS

Paint glyphosate or triclopyr on cut stumps.

Quercus acutissima

Sawtooth oak

It is hard to imagine an objectionable oak, but this import is starting to wear out its welcome. When young, it has a dense, broad habit that develops into an oval or rounded profile with age. The bark is very deeply ridged, almost corky on older trees. The leaves are often compared to those of a chestnut tree—long and narrow, with serrated edges (actually marked with little bristles)—but these are skinnier, generally up to 7 inches long and 2 or so inches wide. Inch-long acorns have fringed caps; these the tree produces in huge numbers, though in alternate years. It is widely adaptable and withstands lousy, compacted soil, air pollution, and drought. Full-grown trees are 35 to 50 feet tall.

PROBLEM

Escapees invade native forests, fields, and roadsides, showering their many acorns, and elbowing out native and desirable plants. It seems to be impervious to insects and disease.

REPRODUCTION

Seeds (acorns), which are dispersed by wildlife.

ORIGIN

Japan, Korea, and China.

NOTES

The large acorn production is a boon to wildlife, including squirrels of course, but also deer and turkeys. Gobbler sawtooth oak (*Quercus acutissima* 'Gobbler') is valued for its early and plentiful food for turkeys in particular. Because of its natural toughness, sawtooth oak has also been deliberately planted in highway medians.

NONINVASIVE ALTERNATIVES

There are many native oaks suitable for home landscapes; choose a locally adapted one based on advice from a reputable local nursery.

LESS-TOXIC CONTROLS

Pull or dig out unwanted seedlings and saplings. Cut down larger ones.

CHEMICAL CONTROLS

Paint glyphosate or triclopyr on cut stumps.

Robinia pseudoacacia

Black locust, Common locust

This fast-growing, ragged-looking tree's habit is naturally tall and upright, with deeply furrowed bark and a narrow, oblong crown. The dark, blue-green leaves are pinnately compound (up to 19 leaflets) and long at up to 14 inches. The slender, often zigzag stems have pairs of sharp little spines at the nodes. Richly fragrant 4- to 8-inch-long racemes of white flowers adorn the tree in late spring, followed in autumn by dark flat seedpods 2 to 4 inches long. Is very drought-tolerant, adapts to all but soggy sites, and fixes atmospheric nitrogen in its soil. Mature size is typically between 30 and 50 feet tall, and can be taller.

PROBLEM
Not only does it grow quickly, it self-sows and suckers prolifically. The result is often dense, prickly, stubborn thickets that exclude other plants and make taming daunting. The tree is also susceptible to a number of disfiguring diseases and insects.

REPRODUCTION
Seeds and root suckers.

ORIGIN
North America.

NOTES
Beekeepers prize the sweet honey their bees make from the scented flowers. The wood is very rot-resistant, making it valuable for furniture, construction, and fencing. Bark and leaves are toxic to people as well as animals.

LESS-TOXIC CONTROLS
Cut back and dig out seedlings. Cut down larger trees and remove the stump, if possible. Watch for and cut back new seedlings and sprouts.

CHEMICAL CONTROLS
Paint glyphosate or triclopyr on cut stumps.

NONINVASIVE ALTERNATIVES
Linden or basswood (*Tilia*) is a good, well-behaved flowering shade tree that also attracts honeybees for a delicious honey.

Salix species

Willows

This is a big group, some native, some nonnative, with species cross-hybridizing, and yet it is possible to generalize. They are deciduous trees or large shrubs and, while adaptable, they thrive in moist soil and wet sites. They tend to be fast-growing and weak-wooded. Leaves are generally slender, often darker green above and lighter underneath, and alternate on flexible stems. Spring flowers are produced on separate male and female plants, appearing as catkins or "pussies." Bark on mature trees is textured, often furrowed or ridged. Root systems become extensive, and suckering is common. Among the most aggressive are two nonnatives, crack willow (*Salix fragilis*) and weeping willow (*S.* ×*sepulcralis*). Mature size varies with the species and cultivar.

PROBLEM
Given ample sun and moisture, willows take over, growing densely, monopolizing not only water but also nutrients, and shading out competitors.

REPRODUCTION
Seeds and suckers.

ORIGIN
Some native, some imported from Europe, Asia, and Africa.

NOTES
All willows contain salicylates, chemically similar to the active ingredient in aspirin and long used as a painkiller.

NONINVASIVE ALTERNATIVES
It is possible to manage and enjoy an attractive willow without it becoming invasive, by raising it in a large container, not overwatering, and pruning to control suckers and maintain an attractive shape.

LESS-TOXIC CONTROLS
Cut back and dig out seedlings. Cut down larger trees and remove the stump, if possible. Watch for and cut back new seedlings and sprouts.

CHEMICAL CONTROLS
Only use herbicides expressly labeled for use in wet ground. Certain formulations of glyphosate, imazapyr, and triclopyr will kill willows when correctly applied to foliage, cut stems, and stumps.

Schinus species

Pepper trees

These species can make a fine single-trunked, high-limbed, umbrella-profile shade tree in mild climates. Heavy branches are adorned with light, graceful pinnately compound leaves. In the California pepper tree (*Schinus molle*) these are around 10 inches long with 14 to 40 leaflets; in the Brazilian pepper tree (*S. terebinthifolius*), they are shorter, with 5 to 13 leaflets. Female trees bear drooping clusters of tiny yellow flowers in summer, which are followed by clustered pepper berries in fall. California pepper tree's berries are rosy; the Brazilian ones are bright red. Both species are tough, drought-tolerant plants. California pepper tree attains 40 feet, with equal spread; the Brazilian is shorter, about 30 feet high and wide.

PROBLEM
Unchecked, these medium- to fast-growing trees become multistemmed and thickety, colonizing open areas and excluding native and desirable plants. Surface roots are greedy. There is a lot of messy litter. The trees are subject to rot and pest problems that make them unhealthy and unsightly.

REPRODUCTION
Seeds, which are dispersed by birds, and suckering roots.

ORIGIN
South America for both.

NOTES
The dried berries of either are sometimes used in dried arrangements and wreaths; those of the Brazilian one are sold as pink peppercorns. Some people get a rash from contact with the sap or foliage.

NONINVASIVE ALTERNATIVES
Red-fruited ornamental trees that are better-behaved include flowering crabapples (*Malus floribunda*) and hackberry (*Celtis occidentalis*).

LESS-TOXIC CONTROLS
Cut back and dig out seedlings. Cut down larger trees and remove the stump, if possible. Watch for and cut back new seedlings and sprouts.

CHEMICAL
Use glyphosate or triclopyr on foliage or cut stumps during the growing season.

Sorbus aucuparia

European mountain ash, Rowan

This import was meant for gardens but has escaped and now romps through sunny spots in cooler regions. Never a big tree, it develops a round or ovate, lollipoplike profile. The smooth bark is grayish brown. Pinnately compound leaves, up to 9 inches long and consisting of 9 to 19 leaflets, cloak the tree and often provide nice wine-red fall color in its preferred colder climates. In late spring, white flowerheads appear and unfortunately waft a foul scent. They are followed in late summer by the plant's most recognizable feature, terminal clusters of small ⅜-inch orange-red berries. Birds love them and they do not last long. Mature trees are generally 20 to 40 feet tall, sometimes taller.

PROBLEM

Birds help sow the seeds and thus seedlings proliferate, invading open and waste areas, roadsides, and forest margins, eventually crowding out native and desirable plants. Often escaped plants, without the attention of a gardener, fall prey to insect pests and fireblight disease, until the plant is a ragged mess.

REPRODUCTION

Seeds, which are dispersed by birds.

ORIGIN

Europe, Siberia, and western Asia.

NOTES

Though rather bitter, the berries have been used to make jams and jellies and to flavor game dishes and beverages. The dense wood is used for carving, tool handles, and walking sticks. Was once touted as a potent antiwitchcraft agent.

NONINVASIVE ALTERNATIVES

The native American mountain ash (*Sorbus americana*) is more compact and considered more resistant to pest and disease problems.

LESS-TOXIC CONTROLS

Cut back and dig out seedlings. Cut down larger trees and remove the stump, if possible. Watch for and cut back new seedlings.

CHEMICAL CONTROLS

Use glyphosate or triclopyr on foliage or cut stumps during the growing season.

Tamarix chinensis

Tamarisk, Salt cedar

Synonym *Tamarix ramosissima*
A deciduous tree or big shrub with a full, weeping profile that obscures multiple stems or the trunk from view. It forms a deep taproot. Needlelike foliage is scaly, light blue-green, and resinous; there is a lot of leaf litter. Flowers occur in feathery terminal clusters and vary from creamy white to pink or even purple. The fruit that follows is insignificant. Tamarisk is remarkably tolerant of alkaline and salty soils. Full-grown trees are 6 to 20 feet tall and 4 to 10 feet wide.

PROBLEM
It is extremely fast-growing at up to 10 feet a season. The roots are notoriously greedy and will suck dry already arid settings and alter habitats, particularly streambanks. The fallen foliage is allelopathic. The tree self-sows heavily and where it proliferates, native and desirable plants falter or die out, and fire danger is raised due to the leaves' high resin content. It has become a real menace in the Southwest.

REPRODUCTION
Seeds, which are wind-dispersed.

ORIGIN
Asia.

NOTES
As its common name suggests, it exudes salt from glands in its leaves. Cattle will not eat it, so grazing is not a good control. Goats may be an option. Honeybees like the flowers.

NONINVASIVE ALTERNATIVES
A tough but nonaggressive plant worth considering is the native Apache plume (*Fallugia paradoxa*).

LESS-TOXIC CONTROLS
Cut back and dig out seedlings before they can develop big taproots.

CHEMICAL CONTROLS
Cut down bigger plants with taproots and paint stumps with glyphosate or another herbicide. If a thicket has formed, spraying the leaves is an option, but if the setting is near or adjacent to water, use a product approved for such situations.

Triadica sebifera

Chinese tallow tree, Popcorn tree

Synonym *Sapium sebiferum*

This deciduous tree has furrowed gray bark and an airy, pyramidal to rounded profile. The 2- to 3-inch-wide medium-green leaves look like those of poplars and flutter in the slightest breeze. Fall color is vivid, yellow to orange-red to a deep wine-red hue. Yellow-green catkin flowers occur in spring. "Popcorn" dark brown seed capsules with white, waxy seeds inside, about ½ inch across, develop and then hang on the tree for winter. Adapts to all sorts of soils and settings, but is not very cold-tolerant. Mature size is 30 to 40 feet tall, sometimes up to 60 feet.

PROBLEM

Its speedy growth—up to 3 feet a year—and rampant self-sowing make it a force to be reckoned with. Its leaves contain toxins that alter soil chemistry and discourage native plants from growing or returning. The species has spread widely in the South, Florida, and the Gulf Coast, particularly along waterways.

LESS-TOXIC CONTROLS

Cut back and dig out seedlings. Cut down larger trees and remove the stump, if possible. Watch for and cut back new seedlings and sprouts.

CHEMICAL CONTROLS

Apply triclopyr to cut stumps in late summer.

REPRODUCTION

Seeds, which are dispersed by birds and water. Also spreads by suckers.

ORIGIN

East Asia. Introduced to South Carolina in the late 1700s.

NOTES

The wax on the seeds has long been extracted by the Chinese for use in candles and soap, hence the "tallow" common name. The tree has also been cultivated for centuries as an oilseed crop. The milky sap, fruit, and even the leaves are poisonous.

NONINVASIVE ALTERNATIVES

Get good fall color without stress from sassafras (*Sassafras albidum*).

Ulmus parvifolia

Chinese elm, Lacebark elm

This import has been a popular street tree, thanks to its resistance to Dutch elm disease and its pollution tolerance. Mature bark has a "lacebark" look, that is, it is textured, mottled, flaking, and attractively multicolored. The glossy leaves are small for an elm, no more than 2½ inches long, and dark green for most of the growing season; fall's cooler weather inspires a multicolored foliage show. The inconspicuous flowers develop quite late, in late summer or fall. The light green fruits that follow eventually turn dark red. It adapts to a wide range of soils and settings. Mature size is 50 to 60 feet tall and wide.

PROBLEM

When it escapes cultivation, its fast growth rate, natural toughness, and aggressive roots make it a pest. It out-competes native and desirable plants.

REPRODUCTION

Seeds, dispersed by wind.

ORIGIN

Northern China, Japan, and Korea.

NOTES

There are a number of handsome cultivars of this tree, including aptly named 'Emerald Vase' and the nearly evergreen, weeping 'Drake', best suited to California and other mild-climate areas. This species is a popular choice for beginner bonsai projects because it tolerates pruning very well.

NONINVASIVE ALTERNATIVES

The graceful hop hornbeam (*Ostrya virginiana*) is a nice alternative, growing much more slowly, also tolerating streetside and other challenging conditions, and sporting comparable dark-green foliage.

LESS-TOXIC CONTROLS

Cut back and dig out seedlings. Cut down larger trees and remove the stump, if possible; root systems are close to the surface.

CHEMICAL CONTROLS

Apply triclopyr or imazapyr to cut stumps in late summer.

Ulmus pumila

Siberian elm

A fast-growing tree, it has brittle wood, weak crotches, and both trunk and root suckers. Storms or high winds leave a mess. Leaves are dark green, on the small side for an elm at about 2 inches long, with serrated margins. The spring flowers, appearing before the tree is fully leafed out, are brown or rusty green, and segue to brownish, round-winged seed clusters. The tree is often pest-ridden, primarily with elm leaf beetles. Extremely cold-hardy, but also drought-tolerant and able to prosper in all settings except soggy ground and shade. It is resistant to Dutch elm disease. Mature plant size is 50 to 70 feet tall and wide.

PROBLEM
Siberian elm sows widely, grows fast, and thus opportunistically asserts its messy, suckering, aggressive habits into lots, pastures, roadsides, and forest margins, forming broad thickets. It shades out native and desirable plants.

REPRODUCTION
Seeds, wind-dispersed.

ORIGIN
Northern China, Manchuria, eastern Siberia, and Korea. Imported for erosion control.

NOTES
Its natural resistance to Dutch elm disease has inspired plant breeders to use it in their quest for a healthy, quality elm.

NONINVASIVE ALTERNATIVES
The native winged elm (*Ulmus alata*) is also tough and adaptable but not as burdened with liabilities.

LESS-TOXIC CONTROLS
Cut back and dig out seedlings, then watch for and remove new seedlings. Cut down larger trees. Remove the stump, if possible (root systems are close to the surface); if you do not, there will be suckering. Girdling in late spring, if done correctly, has also proven effective.

CHEMICAL CONTROLS
Use glyphosate on foliage or cut stumps during the growing season.

Problem Areas for Problem Plants

Concern over the spread of invasive plants continues to expand, not only at the international and national levels, but also within individual states, counties, and municipalities. American conservation organizations such as the Nature Conservancy, the Sierra Club, and the Audubon Society are also monitoring invasives on both public and private land.

There is a Federal Noxious Weeds list, but as you might guess, it is not extensive, because to qualify a pest plant has to be very widespread. Individual states, however, have flagged certain plants as "severe threats," "troublesome," or "watch-list" candidates. Furthermore, some states have enacted legislation that bans some or all of the following: importing, moving, selling, purchasing, possessing, cultivating, and distributing such plants. These restrictions are aimed at home gardeners and landscapers as well as plant nurseries that supply them, wholesale and retail. Fines and confiscation are on the books in some places, albeit with spotty enforcement.

While awareness, inventorying, and regulation of invasives certainly varies and is a work-in-progress, there is no denying that people who need to be concerned are taking notice. Gardeners should be among the concerned and do their part to stop or limit the spread of problem plants—whether or not it is already the law where they live.

Thus, the following listings are provisional. If a state is listed after a plant here, it means that state is either monitoring the plant or has already restricted or banned its use. Perhaps also, control measures have been attempted, such as, for example, when volunteers gather to help rid a wetland of purple loosestrife under the supervision of botanists or state officials. More plants and more states are continuing to be added to various lists and

Please note:

Plant groups in the lists follow the order of chapters in this book. Within each group/chapter, plants are arranged alphabetically by botanical name.

States are mentioned in alphabetical order, for easier reference.

If a plant in the lists has no or few states noted next to it, do not assume it is not a potential problem or not invasive. It is. It just has not been formally inventoried, added to the databases, or banned yet.

databases (slim chance that a plant, once listed, is deleted later). When in doubt about any given plant's current status, please check locally or at your state level.

Two databases were used in compiling these lists. The first is the Center for Invasive Species and Ecosystem Health, invasive. org/. This national database is a joint project with the USDA Animal and Plant Health Inspection Service–Plant Protection and Quarantine program (APHIS–PPQ), with additional support from USDA National Institute of Food and Agriculture (NIFA), and U.S. Forest Service. Also helping is the University of Georgia Warnell School of Forestry and Natural Resources and College of Agricultural and Environmental Sciences.

The second source is the U.S. Forest Service, na.fs.fed.us/fhp/invasive_plants/weeds/. This database, under the Forest Health Protection banner, catalogs invasive plants nationwide and issues profile bulletins.

Water and Bog Plants

Butomus umbellatus, CT, MT, NH, VT, WA, WI
Cabomba caroliniana, CT
Caltha palustris
Colocasia esculenta, FL
Egeria densa, CA, CT, DE, ID, ME, NH, NY, OR, TN, VA, VT, WA
Eichhornia crassipes, AL, AR, AZ, CA, CT, DE, FL, GA, ID, LA, SC, TX
Houttuynia cordata 'Chameleon'
Iris pseudacorus CT, DE, MA, MD, MT, NC, NH, OR, TN, VA, VT, WA, WI, WV
Lysimachia nummularia
Myriophyllum aquaticum, AL, CT, DE, GA, ID, MA, MD, ME, NH, OR, TN, VA, VT, WA
Pistia stratiotes, AL, CA, CT, DE, FL, SC, TX

Annuals, Biennials, and Tropical Perennials

Ambrosia artemisiifolia

Anagallis arvensis, AZ, CA, HI, NV

Anthemis cotula, CO, HI, NV, TN

Arctium lappa, CT, MA, ME, NH, NV, NY, SD, VT

Artemisia annua

Centaurea calcitrapa, AZ, CA, NM, NV, OR, UT, WA

Centaurea cyanus, KY, MD, NC, TN

Centaurea diffusa, AZ, CA, CO, ID, MT, ND, NE, NM, NV, OR, SD, UT, WA, WY

Euphorbia maculata

Impatiens glandulifera, CT, ID, OR, WA

Lamium amplexicaule, AL, AZ, FL, GA, KY, LA, MD, MO, NC, OK, SC, TN, TX, VA, WV

Lantana camara, AZ, FL, HI, SC, TX

Melilotus albus

Mirabilis jalapa

Onopordum acanthium, AZ, CA, CO, CT, ID, MT, NM, NV, OK, OR, SD, UT, WA, WY

Stellaria media, HI, KY, MD, NC, NJ, PA, TN, VA, WV

Tradescantia fluminensis, FL

Herbaceous Perennials

Achillea spp.

Aegopodium podagraria, CT, MA

Alliaria petiolata, AL, CT, MA, MN, NH, OR, VT, WA

Allium vineale, CA, MI

Buddleia davidii, OR, WA

Carduus nutans, CA, CO, ID, IL, KS, MI, MN, MO, NC, ND, NE, NM, NV, OH, OK, OR, PA, SD, UT, WA, WV, WY

Carpobrotus edulis, CA

Centaurea solstitialis, AZ, CA, CO, ID, MT, ND, NM, NV, OR, SD, UT, WA

Centaurea stoebe subsp. *micranthos*, AZ, CA, CO, ID, MA, MI, MT, ND, NE, NH, NM, NV, OR, SD, UT, WA, WY

Cerastium tomentosum

Cichorium intybus, CO, SD

Cirsium arvense, AL, CT, FL, GA, KY, MO

Convallaria majalis, IN, WI

Cynoglossum officinale, CO, ID, MT, NV, OR, SD, WA, WY

Daucus carota, MI, OH, WA

Digitalis purpurea, CA, OR, WA

Dipsacus fullonum, CO, MO, NM

Epilobium angustifolium

Euphorbia cyparissias, CO, CT, MA

Euphorbia esula, AZ, CA, CT, IA, ID, KS, MA, MI, MN, MT, ND, NE, NM, NV, OR, SD, UT, WA, WI, WY

Fallopia japonica, AL, CA, CT, DE, ID, MA, MT, NH, OR, VT, WA, WV

Foeniculum vulgare, CA, WA

Glechoma hederacea, CT

Gypsophila paniculata, CA, WA

Heracleum lanatum

Heracleum mantegazzianum, CA, CT, FL, ID, MA, MN, NC, NH, NY, OH, OR, PA, SC, VT, WA

Hesperis matronalis, CO, CT, MA, NH

Hypericum perforatum, CA, CO, MT, NV, OR, SD, WA, WY

Lepidium draba, AZ, CA, CO, CT, IA, ID, KS, MI, MN, MT, NM, NV, OR, SD, UT, WA, WY

Lespedeza spp., AL, KY, IL, NH, SC, TN

Leucanthemum vulgare, CO, ID, MT, OH, WA, WY

Linaria vulgaris, AK, CO, ID, MT, NM, NV, OR, SD, WA, WY

Lotus corniculatus

Lysimachia clethroides

Lythrum salicaria, AL, AR, AZ, CA, CT, IA, ID, IN, MA, MI, MN, MO, MT, ND, NE, NH, NM, NV, OH, OR, PA, SC, SD, TN, UT, VT, WA, WI, WY
Macleaya cordata
Mentha spp.
Monarda spp.
Muscari botryoides
Ornithogalum arabicum
Oxalis corniculata
Oxalis stricta
Pastinaca sativa, OH
Physalis alkekengi
Pinellia ternata
Plantago major, AL, KY, VA
Potentilla recta, CA, CO, MT, NV, OR, WA
Ranunculus ficaria, CT
Ranunculus repens, MA
Rhaponticum repens, AK, AZ, CA, CO, IA, ID, KS, MI, MN, MT, ND, NM, NV, OR, SD, UT, WA, WY
Rumex crispus, IA, MI
Stachys byzantina
Tanacetum vulgare, CO, MT, SD, WA, WY
Taraxacum officinale, AL, GA, KY, LA, NC, OK, SC, TX, VA
Verbascum blattaria, CO, SD
Verbascum olympicum, CO, SD
Verbascum phlomoides, CO, SD
Verbascum thapsus, CO, SD
Vinca minor, KY, MD, SC, TN, WI
Viola spp.

Grasses and Bamboos

Agropyron cristatum, AZ, CA, CO, ID, MT, ND, NM, NV, OR, SD, UT, WA, WI
Arundinaria gigantea
Arundo donax, CA, NV
Bromus inermis, KY, WI
Bromus madritensis subsp. *rubens*, CA
Bromus tectorum, AZ, CA, CO, CT, GA, IL, TN
Cenchrus ciliaris
Cortaderia selloana, AZ, CA, NM, TX
Cynodon dactylon, AR, CA, UT
Cyperus rotundus, AR, CA, OR, WA
Digitaria ischaemum, AL, FL, GA, KY, LA, MO, NC, OK, SC, TN, TX, VA
Eleusine indica, GA, LA, MO, MS, NC, OK, SC, TN, TX, VA
Elymus repens, AK, AZ, CA, CO, IA, KS, MI, OR, UT, WY
Eragrostis curvula, AZ, CA, NM
Festuca arundinacea, CA, IL, KY, SC, TN
Imperata cylindrica, AR, CA, FL, MN, MS, NC, OR, SC, TN, VT
Microstegium vimineum, AL, CT, DE, MA, NH, WV
Miscanthus sinensis, KY
Paspalum notatum, AL, GA, LA, NC, SC, TX
Pennisetum setaceum, NV
Phalaris arundinacea, CT, MA, WA
Phragmites australis, AL, CT, DE, MA, NE, SC, SD, VT, WA
Phyllostachys spp., AL, FL, GA, MD, SC
Sorghum halepense, FL, GA, KY, LA, MO, MS, NC, OK, SC, TN, TX
Taeniatherum caput-medusae, CA, CO, OR, NV, UT
Trifolium pratense
Trifolium repens, GA, KY, LA, NC, SC, TN, VA

Vines

Akebia quinata, DC, KY, MD, NJ, PA, VA

Ampelopsis brevipedunculata, CT, DC, DE, MA, MD, NJ, NY, OR, PA, RI, VA, WI, WV

Calystegia sepium

Campsis radicans

Cayratia japonica

Celastrus orbiculatus, CT, DC, DE, IL, IN, KY, MA, MD, ME, MI, MO, NC, NH, NJ, NY, PA, RI, TN, VA, VT, WI, WV

Clematis terniflora, DC, DE, IL, MD, NJ, TN, VA

Coccinea grandis, FL, HI

Convolvulus arvensis, AK, AR, AZ, CA, CO, CT, DE, IA, ID, KS, MI, MN, MO, MT, ND, NE, NM, NV, OH, OR, PA, SD, UT, VA, WA, WI, WY

Coronilla varia, CT, IN, KY, MD, MI, MO, NC, NJ, OR, TN, VA, WI

Cuscuta japonica

Cynanchum louiseae, CT, MA, NH, NY, VT, WI

Dioscorea bulbifera, AL, FL, HI

Euonymus fortunei, AL, CT, DC, GA, IL, IN, KY, MD, MO, OH, TN, VA, WI

Hedera helix, OR, WA

Humulus japonicus, CT, MA

Jasminum fluminense, FL, HI

Lonicera japonica, CT, DE, MA, NH, VT

Lygodium japonicum, AL, FL

Merremia tuberosa, FL, HI

Parthenocissus quinquefolia

Persicaria perfoliata, AL, CT, DE, MA, NC, OH, PA, SC, WV

Pueraria montana var. *lobata*, CT, FL, IL, KS, KY, MA, MO, MS, OR, PA, TX, WA, WV

Smilax rotundifolia

Toxicodendron radicans and *T. pubescens*

Wisteria floribunda, IL, SC

Shrubs

Alhagi maurorum, AZ, CA, CO, NM, NV, OR, TX, WA
Alnus glutinosa, TN, WI
Aralia elata, PA
Ardisia crenata, AL, FL
Ardisia elliptica, FL
Berberis thunbergii, CT, MA, NH
Caragana arborescens, AK, MI, ND, WI, WY
Cistus ladanifer
Cotoneaster buxifolius, CA
Cotoneaster lacteus, CA
Cotoneaster microphyllus, CA
Cotoneaster pannosus, CA
Cytisus scoparius, CA, ID, MT, OR, WA
Elaeagnus umbellata, CT, DE, MA, NH, TN, WV
Euonymus alatus, CT, MA, NH
Frangula alnus, CT, MA, MN, NH, VT
Hibiscus syriacus, GA, IN, TN
Ilex aquifolium, CA, OR, WA
Ligustrum spp., AL, CT, FL, GA, MA, NH, SC, TN
Lonicera maackii, CT, MA, TN, VT
Lonicera morrowii, CT, DE, MA, NH, TN, VT, WV
Lonicera tatarica, CT, DE, MA, NH, TN, VT, WV
Lonicera xylosteum, CT, DE, MA, NH, TN, VT, WV
Myoporum laetum, CA
Nandina domestica, AL, FL, GA, SC, TN
Rhamnus cathartica, CT, MA, MN, NH, VT
Rhodotypos scandens, DE, IL, TN, WI
Rhus typhina
Rosa multiflora, AL, CT, DE, KY, IA, IN, MA, MO, NH, PA, SD, TN, WI, WV
Rosa rugosa, CT
Scaevola sericea var. *taccada,* FL, HI
Solanum viarum, AZ, CA, FL, MA, MN, MS, NC, OR, SC, TN, TX, VT
Spiraea japonica, GA, KY, MD, SC, TN, VA
Taxus cuspidata, CT, NJ
Viburnum dilatatum, NJ, NY
Viburnum lantana, NY, WA, WI
Viburnum opulus var. *opulus,* MA, ME, WI
Vitex agnus-castus, AZ, CA, LA, TX
Vitex rotundifolia, NC

Trees

Acacia auriculiformis, FL
Acer ginnala, CT
Acer negundo
Acer platanoides, CT, DE, MA, NH
Ailanthus altissima, CA, CT, MA, NH, VT, WV
Albizia julibrissin, TN
Bischofia javanica, FL
Broussonetia papyrifera, FL, GA, SC
Casaurina equisitifolia, FL
Crataegus monogyna, CA, MA, ME, OR, WA
Cupaniopsis anacardioides, FL
Elaeagnus angustifolia, CO, CT, NM, WY
Eucalyptus globulus, CA, HI
Ficus microcarpa, FL, HI
Melia azedarach, AL, FL, GA, HI, SC
Morus alba, CT, IL, KY, MO, SC, WI
Paulownia tomentosa, CT
Populus alba, CT
Pyrus calleryana, AL, GA, IL, MD, SC, TN
Quercus acutissima, GA, MD, SC
Robinia pseudoacacia, CT, MA
Salix spp.
Schinus spp., CA, FL, TX
Sorbus aucuparia, ME, WI
Tamarix chinensis, AZ, CA, CO, ND, NE, NM, OR, SD, WA
Triadica sebifera, FL, LA, MS, TX
Ulmus parvifolia, CA, NV, WI
Ulmus pumila, NM

Metric Conversions

Inch / Millimeter

⅛ in. = 3 mm

¼ in. = 6 mm

⅓ in. = 8 mm

⅜ in. = 10 mm

½ in. = 13 mm

¾ in. = 19 mm

Inch / Centimeter

1 in. = 2.5 cm

1¼ in. = 3 cm

1½ in. = 4 cm

1¾ in. = 4.5 cm

2 in. = 5 cm

3 in. = 8 cm

4 in. = 10 cm

5 in. = 13 cm

6 in. = 15 cm

7 in. = 18 cm

8 in. = 20 cm

9 in. = 23 cm

10 in. = 25 cm

Feet / Meter

1 ft. = 0.3 m

2 ft. = 0.6 m

3 ft. = 0.9 m

4 ft. = 1.2 m

5 ft. = 1.5 m

6 ft. = 1.8 m

7 ft. = 2.1 m

8 ft. = 2.4 m

9 ft. = 2.7 m

10 ft. = 3.0 m

500 ft.^{2} = 46 m^2

1000 ft.^{2} = 93 m^2

Pound / Kilo

1 lb. = 0.4 kg

20 lb. = 9 kg

50 lb. = 23 kg

°Fahrenheit / °Celsius

25°F = −4°C

−10°F = −23°C

−20°F = −29°C

Suggested Reading

Barash, Cathy Wilkinson. 1997. *Vines & Climbers*. New York: Crescent Books.

Brickell, Christopher, and H. Marc Cathey, eds. 2004. *The American Horticultural Society A–Z Encyclopedia of Garden Plants*. Rev. U.S. ed. New York: DK Publishing.

Burrell, C. Colston. 2011. *Native Alternatives to Invasive Plants*. Brooklyn, New York: Brooklyn Botanic Garden.

Cohen, Russ. 2001. *Wild Plants I Have Known . . . and Eaten*. Essex, Massachusetts: Essex County Greenbelt Association.

Dillard, Annie. 1975. *Pilgrim at Tinker Creek*. New York: Bantam Books. Reprinted 2007, Harper Perennial Modern Classics.

Dirr, Michael A. 2009. *Manual of Woody Landscape Plants*. 6th ed. Champaign, Illinois: Stipes Publishing Company.

Dubkin, Leonard. 1955. *The Natural History of a Yard*. Chicago: Henry Regnery Company.

Dunn, Teri. 2005. Can't Miss Water Gardening. *Can't Miss Water Gardening*. Nashville, Tennessee: Cool Springs Press.

Fenyvesi, Charles. 1992. *Trees: For Shelter and Shade, for Memory and Magic*. New York: St. Martin's Press.

Gorman, James. 1986. "Light Elements: Why I No Longer Regard Plants as Salad That's Not Dead," *Discover Magazine* (March): 18–20.

Hinkley, Daniel J. 2009. *The Explorer's Garden: Shrubs and Vines*. Portland, Oregon: Timber Press.

Hopkins, Hilary. 2001. *Never Say It's Just a Dandelion: 125 Wonderful Common Plants for Walkers and Walk Leaders*. Cambridge, Massachusetts: Jewelweed Books.

Jones, Pamela. 1991. *Just Weeds: History, Myths, and Uses*. New York: Prentice Hall Press.

Kaufman, Sylvan Ramsey, and Wallace Kaufman. 2007. *Invasive Plants: Guide to Identification and the Impacts and Control of Common North American Species*. Mechanicsburg, Pennsylvania: Stackpole Books.

Kowalchik, Claire, and William H. Hylton, eds. 1987. *Rodale's Illustrated Encyclopedia of Herbs*. Emmaus, Pennsylvania: Rodale Press. Reprinted 1998.

Lamp'l, Joe. 2007. *The Green Gardener's Guide*. Franklin, Tennessee: Cool Springs Press.

Maxcy, Larry. 2001. *Old-Fashioned Garden Wisdom: Tips, Lore, and Good Advice for Creating a Healthy Garden*. New York: Friedman-Fairfax Publishers.

Muenscher, Walter Conrad. 1980. *Weeds*. 2d ed. New York: Cornell University.

Peterson, Roger Tory, and Margaret McKenny. 1968. *A Field Guide to Wildflowers of Northeastern and North-Central North America*. Peterson Field Guide Series, no. 17. Boston: Houghton Mifflin Company.

Reich, Lee. 2001. *Weedless Gardening*. New York: Workman Publishing.

Scott, Timothy Lee. 2010. *Invasive Plant Medicine: The Ecological Benefits and Healing Abilities of Invasives*. Rochester, Vermont: Healing Arts Press.

Spellenberg, Richard. 2001. *The Audubon Society Field Guide to North American Wildflowers—Western Region*. Rev. ed. New York: Alfred A. Knopf.

Stokes, Donald, and Lillian Stokes. 1985. *A Guide to Enjoying Wildflowers*. Boston: Little, Brown and Company.

Thieret, John W., and William A. Niering. 2001. *The Audubon Society Field Guide to North American Wildflowers—Eastern Region*. Rev ed. New York: Alfred A. Knopf.

Online Resources

Center for Invasive Species and Ecosystem Health. Images, maps, and information on invasive plants, including the archives of the Nature Conservancy's Global Invasive Species Team. *www.invasive.org, www.bugwood.org/.*

Smithsonian National Museum of Natural History, Botany Department. Various searchable databases. *http://botany.si.edu/index.htm/.*

United States Department of Agriculture, Natural Resources Conservation Service (NRCS). Invasive and Noxious Weeds database. *http://plants.usda.gov/java/noxious?rptType=Federal/.*

United States Forest Service, Northeastern Area. Invasive plants fact sheets/Weed of the Week profiles. *http://na.fs.fed.us/fhp/invasive_plants/weeds/index.shtm/.*

Acknowledgments

Heartfelt thanks to Tom Fischer, Linda Willms, Marci LeBrun, and Michael Dempsey at Timber Press, Portland, Oregon; Catherine Herms of Ohio State University, Wooster, Ohio; Joe LaForest of the Center for Invasive Species and Ecosystem Health at the University of Georgia; Rusty Russell and Genna Fleming of the U.S. National Herbarium, Smithsonian Institution; Robert Buchsbaum and John Hanson Mitchell of the Massachusetts Audubon Society; Everett Holt King; Kathleen Pyle; Nina Sandlin; Trish Wesley Umbrell; Christine Shahin; Ann Tomei; Mary Gressler; Sonny Osborne.

Also thanks to Fran and John Soulé, Jude and MaryJane Blau, Wes and Tristan Dunn, Alan Chace, and Phyllis and Paul Chace.

Photo Credits

Tim Abramowitz, iStockphoto.com: page 218.
P. Acevedo, courtesy of Smithsonian Institution: pages 220 and 223.
Adrian198cm, Wikimedia: page 173.
AMB, Shutterstock.com: page 151.
Amorikuma, Wikimedia: page 55.
aubrey1, CanStockPhoto.com: page 126.
Chuck Bargeron, University of Georgia, Bugwood.org: pages 252 and 297.
Franklin Bonner, USDA Forest Service (ret.), Bugwood.org: page 228.
Allan Brown, iStockphoto.com: page 286.
Charles T. Bryson, USDA Agricultural Research Service, Bugwood.org: pages 185 and 264.
John D. Byrd, Mississippi State University, Bugwood.org: pages 92 and 140.
canoniroff, Shutterstock.com: page 205.
David Cappaert, Bugwood.org: pages 69 and 205.
Teri Dunn Chace: pages 10 and 180.
Chas, Shutterstock.com: page 259.
Suphatthra China, iStockphoto.com: page 72.
chris2766, Shutterstock.com: page 81.
Eric Coombs, Oregon Department of Agriculture, Bugwood.org: pages 88 and 112.
G. A. Cooper, courtesy of Smithsonian Institution: pages 75, 134, 221, and 304.
Shelly Dennis, iStockphoto.com: page 113.
Bobby Deal/RealDealPhoto, Shutterstock.com: page 190.
Steve Dewey, Utah State University, Bugwood.org: pages 96,127, 132, 133, 174, 182, 196, and 307.
dirkr, iStockphoto.com: page 102.
L. J. Dorr, courtesy of Smithsonian Institution: page 129.
Dow Gardens Archive, Dow Gardens, Bugwood.org: page 270.
Chris Evans, River to River Cooperative Weed Management Area, Bugwood.org: pages 124, 202, 219, 237, 256, 294, and 305.

Amy Ferriter, State of Idaho, Bugwood.org: page 285.
fotoret, Shutterstock.com: page 116.
Martin Fowler, Shutterstock.com: page 108.
Tatiana Gerus, Wikimedia: page 42.
Ulrike Haberkorn, Shutterstock.com: page 130.
Bonnie Harper-Lore, Federal Highway Administration, Bugwood.org: page 162.
Mary Ellen (Mel) Harte, Bugwood.org: page 117.
E. Haug, courtesy of Smithsonian Institution: page 211.
Tom Heutte, USDA Forest Service, Bugwood.org: page 197.
holbox, Shutterstock.com: pages 118 and 176.
R. A. Howard, courtesy of Smithsonian Institution: pages 70, 73, 103, 135, 139, 141, 142, 147, 155, 165, 203, 207, 240, 244, 268, 271, 273, 276, and 282.
hsvrs, iStockphoto.com: page 66.
W. S. Justice, courtesy of Smithsonian Institution: pages 94, 122, and 158.
Laitr Keiows, Shutterstock.com: page 199.
Jasminka Keres, Shutterstock.com: page 284.
Berit Kessler, Shutterstock.com: page 302.
Christopher Kline: page 234.
Tamara Kulikova, Shutterstock.com: page 210.
Joseph LaForest, University of Georgia, Bugwood.org: page 229.
Marci LeBrun: pages 19, 31, and 35.
LianeM, Shutterstock.com: page 159.
Lidara, Shutterstock.com: page 269.
Marcus Lindström, iStockphoto.com: page 303.
Richard Loader, iStockphoto.com: page 119.
Brian Lockhart, USDA Forest Service, Bugwood.org: page 298.
Nancy Loewenstein, Auburn University, Bugwood.org: page 74.
Ruud de Man, iStockphoto.com: pages 114 and 120.

Magdalena Markiewicz, iStockphoto.com: page 77.

Beverly Martin, iStockphoto.com: page 115.

Brian Maudsley, Shutterstock.com: page 146.

Joe McDaniel, iStockphoto.com: page 224.

Leslie J. Mehrhoff, University of Connecticut, Bugwood.org: pages 67, 131, 149, 154, 156, 214, 239, 245, 246, 258, and 265.

Vladimir Melnik, Shutterstock.com: page 121.

James H. Miller, USDA Forest Service, Bugwood.org: pages 184, 193, 215, 217, 247, 255, 261, and 281.

James H. Miller and Ted Bodner, Southern Weed Science Society, Bugwood.org: pages 148, 187, 189, 222, 251, and 293.

Sean Moffitt, Shutterstock.com: page 248.

David J. Moorhead, University of Georgia, Bugwood.org: page 177.

motorolka, Shutterstock.com: page 83.

T. F. Niehaus, courtesy of Smithsonian Institution: page 138.

Ohio State University Weed Lab Archive, The Ohio State University, Bugwood.org: pages 106, 153, and 204.

oksana2010, Shutterstock.com: page 164.

Jerry A. Payne, USDA Agricultural Research Service, Bugwood.org: page 143.

J. Scott Peterson, USDA NRCS Plants Database, Bugwood.org: page 292.

Pgiam, iStockphoto.com: page 20.

Joe Potato, iStockphoto.com: page 227.

Derek Ramsey: page 266.

Karan A. Rawlins, University of Georgia, Bugwood.org: pages 208 and 306.

Norman E. Rees, USDA Agricultural Research Service (ret.), Bugwood.org: page 157.

Júlio Reis: page 25.

Barry A. Rice, sarracenia.com: pages 71, 86, 111, 123, 188, 192, 194, 213, 291, and 295.

Robert J. Richardson, North Carolina State University, Bugwood.org: page 206.

Rodrigo Riestra, Shutterstock.com: page 109.

Amy Riley, Cape Cod Photo, iStockphoto.com: page 262.

Sue Robinson, Shutterstock.com: page 90.

David Schwaegler: page 163.

R. A. Seelig, courtesy of Smithsonian Institution: pages 235 and 277.

Michael Shephard, USDA Forest Service, Bugwood.org: pages 82, 137, and 161.

Steve Shoup, Shutterstock.com: page 169.

Krzysztof Slusarczyk, Shutterstock.com: page 243.

T. R. Soderstrom, courtesy of Smithsonian Institution: page 170.

R. J. Soreng, courtesy of Smithsonian Institution: page 172.

Lynn Sosnoskie, University of Georgia, Bugwood.org: page 89

Forest and Kim Starr, hear.org: pages 76, 99, and 175.

Forest and Kim Starr, Starr Environmental, Bugwood.org: pages 95, 125, 178, 183, 209, 238, 263, 283, and 288.

stockcam, iStockphoto.com: page 93.

Striver, Bigstock.com: page 97.

sulaco229, Shutterstock.com: page 249.

Dennis Teague, U.S. Air Force, Bugwood.org: page 27.

Terraxplorer, iStockphoto.com: page 231.

Mark Tooker, iStockphoto.com: page 80.

Txanbelin, Shutterstock.com: page 241.

USDA APHIS PPQ Archive, Bugwood.org: page 226.

Sandra van der Steen, Shutterstock.com: page 144.

W. L. Wagner, courtesy of Smithsonian Institution: page 289.

Rebekah D. Wallace, University of Georgia, Bugwood.org: pages 87, 171, and 181.

Roger Whiteway, iStockphoto.com: pages 107, 299, and 300.

Anna Wielgosz, panoramio.com: page 236.

Wirepec, CanStockPhoto.com: page 191.

Paul Wray, Iowa State University, Bugwood.org: pages 278 and 279.

WVU Herbarium, courtesy of Smithsonian Institution: pages 85, 152, and 296.

ZanozaRu, CanStockPhoto.com: page 253.

Index   Boldface indicates an invasive plant.

About the Author

WES DUNN

Teri Dunn Chace is a writer and editor with over 30 titles in publication, including *The Anxious Gardener's Book of Answers* (Timber Press, 2012). She has also written and edited extensively for *Horticulture*, *North American Gardener*, *Backyard Living*, and *Birds & Blooms*. Raised in California and educated at Bard College in New York, Teri has gardened in a variety of climate zones and soil types, from inner city Portland, Oregon, to coastal Massachusetts. She now lives in a small upstate New York village with snowy winters and glorious summers.